S0-ABC-459

TEXAS

ON-THE-ROAD HISTORIES

TEXAS

Mary Jo Powell

Interlink Books

An imprint of Interlink Publishing Group, Inc.
Northampton, Massachusetts

First published in 2005 by

INTERLINK BOOKS
An imprint of Interlink Publishing Group, Inc.
46 Crosby Street
Northampton, Massachusetts 01060
www.interlinkbooks.com

Printed in China

Library of Congress Cataloging-in-Publication Data

Powell, Mary Jo, 1953–
    Texas / by Mary Jo Powell.
    p. cm. — (On-the-road histories)
  Includes bibliographical references.
    ISBN 1-56656-564-2 (pbk.)
1. Texas—History. 2. Texas—Description and travel.
3. Texas—History, Local. I. Title. II. Series.
    F386.P78 2004
    917.6404'64—dc22

                                    2004013083

Front cover images
Top: Emancipation Day Band;
Bottom: Branding; Courtesy Austin
History Center, Austin Public Library
Back cover images
Top: 1950s drought; courtesy the Institute
of Texan Cultures at UTSA;
Middle: the Alamo, courtesy Center for
American History, UT–Austin

Title page photo of Texas canyons
© Elisabeth Miskell

To request our complete
40-page full-color catalog,
please call us toll free at
1-800-238-LINK, visit our
website at **www.interlinkbooks.com**
or write to:
Interlink Publishing
46 Crosby Street, Northampton, MA 01060
e-mail: info@interlinkbooks.com

Contents

The Lay of the Land

There's a little bit of everything in Texas.

—Ernest Tubb

Think Texas is all cowboy desert, tumbling tumble-weeds, and frontier mountains? Actually, Texas has just about every kind of North American land form except glaciers; it has mountains, deserts, high plains, lowlands, rolling prairies, swamps, and savannas—just for starters.

If you get in your car at the southeast corner of the state and drive west, you will be leaving swampy bayou lands that receive an average of 58 inches of rain a year. Provided you make it all the way to El Paso (that's 773 miles), you will end up in desert that gets about 8 inches a year. If instead you were to drive from Amarillo to the south, you would ride down an incline that goes straight into the Gulf of Mexico. If an armadillo were to roll into a ball in the Panhandle, it could speed all the way to Houston—if it did not get run over on a central Texas highway first.

No matter where you start as you cross the state, you will see variety that divides Texas itself and ties Texas to the rest of North America. The Atlantic Coastal Plain begins in Cape Cod and continues to the Rio Grande and inland into the eastern Piney Woods of Texas. As you drive into far west Texas, you will see mountains, which some regard as the southernmost part of the Rockies, that go all the way to Canada. In between you will pass through part of the northern extension of the Chihuahuan Desert that extends into Mexico, the central prairies that continue into the bread basket midwestern United States, and the high plains that roll up into the interior of the continent.

Geographical variety has shaped the history of the state. The deep, rich soils of the rolling Blackland prairies are perfect for growing cotton, and that is the part of the state where slavery in the 19th century laid its deepest roots. Until modern irrigation methods moved west of the 100th Meridian (the traditional dividing line between west and east, arid and non-arid, just east of Sweetwater and San Angelo), cotton couldn't grow in far west Texas—in fact, not much except grass could grow there. Those who kept on moving west in the 19th century raised stock. Not only cows, but sheep and goats covered the rocky hills of the Edward Plateau. On the high plains, enormous ranches grew up out of cheap land and miles of free grass for cattle. Hard-scrabble farms were the only possible agricultural answer in the deep forests of east Texas and the Cross Timbers of the north central regions.

Texas is a state made up of borders—borders both physical and abstract, objective and emotional. The physical borders make for some spectacular scenery as they divide the state into discrete regions, but they have also nurtured discrete cultures. Half of Texas has historically considered itself Southern; the other half or so thinks of itself as Western. This geographically split personality has done much to shape Texas and its legends.

You can start to get your bearings in Texas if you have some idea of the major parts of the state. The Texas Department of Transportation (familiarly known as TxDOT) divides the state into seven major regions. Even in the most built-up and urban parts, you can still find preserved areas that retain a feel for how the land once was.

THE PINEY WOODS

In the east, where the coastal plains receive plenty of water, the gently rolling hills are home to most of the forests in Texas. These Piney Woods grow both pines and hardwoods. Lumbering and logging have long been the economic backbones of the area, but the primeval forest, seeming one with the timberlands of Georgia and other southern states, exists only in isolated patches.

You can roam into the Big Thicket National Preserve, which is still big but not as big as it used to be. At one time the thicket spread over 3 million acres, but today it is about 86,000. What remains of the thicket is much as it was when Native Americans first began exploring it—partly the result of its assignment as a UNESCO International Biosphere

Reserve. You can still get lost in the thicket and maybe run into an alligator or two. The thicket has sheltered outlaws from the law, Union sympathizers from Confederate draft enforcers, and plenty of bootleggers and moonshine makers. If you wander deep into the interior, listen for the ivory-billed woodpecker, now considered extinct but still sought after in the most remote areas of the southeast.

If that level of adventure does not attract you, plenty of well-marked trails can easily guide you through the thicket or a train can carry you at least a little way into the preserve.

GULF COAST

The plains flatten out as you drive south along the coast from the Louisiana border to the Rio Grande. When the European conquerors arrived, grass covered this eastern prairie and it continues to support thriving cattle ranches among the cities that have grown up along the sea. Today cities lord it over the Gulf Coast—Houston, Galveston, Corpus Christi, Port Arthur, Beaumont, all of them having brought industrial development and city ways to the plains.

Still, in a few places you can get some feel for the way this land used to be. You can

FM and RM Roads

FM roads are Farm-to-Market Roads designed to help farmers bring their produce to market and to connect rural Texans with the rest of the state. The first FM road began construction in 1936 and was completed in January 1937 at a cost of $48,015.12.

The farther west you go the more likely your FM road will be called a Ranch Road—ranch-to-market. Ranchers do not like to be confused with farmers in any way. US 281, which runs from the Red River to the Rio Grande, is the dividing line between RM and FM roads. In theory, and according to Texas Department of Transportation (TxDOT) policy, all the market roads to the east are FMs and all those to the west are RMs, but some exceptions do exist.

In 1949, the legislature permanently funded an FM program using gasoline taxes and other funds. This funding may have skewed the Texas highway system toward these smaller roads, but Texans love their FM roads and you will too.

Making up more than half of Texas highways, FM roads are numbered in order of construction, from 1 to 3440. Sometimes, two roads merge or for some other reason a number goes out of circulation. For example, no FM 7, 12, 29, or 42 exists—but there is an FM 13. The longest is FM 168 in Terry County west of Lubbock; it goes on straight as a rifle shot for 140 miles. As cities have changed and grown, FM roads began to run through more than simple countryside. FM 1093, for example, now has eight lanes where it runs past the Galleria shopping center in downtown Houston. These spectacular back roads are an excellent way to get to know the state. RM 170 leaves the vicinity of Big Bend National Park and cuts across Big Bend Ranch State Park going to Presidio with incredible views of the Rio Grande and rugged west Texas topography. RM 337 between Vanderpool and Leakey is an outstanding Hill Country drive of hills and turns and scenery. Don't pass these rural roads up.

experience native tall grass prairie at the Atwater Prairie Chicken National Wildlife Refuge on the San Bernard River and tour the 8,300 acres in your car if you wish. Bird watching is always good here and at other points along the coast. Sea Rim State Park, Anahuac National Wildlife Refuge (NWR), and Aransas NWR all have marshlands that feel primeval and coastal grasslands that attract migratory birds. Even in Houston, where the Houston Arboretum and Nature Center includes 155 acres of walking trails and more than 60 species of native plants and animals, you can manage to experience the land as it was before Europeans came.

SOUTH TEXAS PLAINS

The farther south the coastal prairies go, the more arid they become. By the time you reach the Lower Rio Grande Valley—or the Valley, as Texans call it—cattle have given way to winter vegetables and citrus fruit. A freeze is a rare occurrence in the Valley. North of the Valley and on into the interior of the state is the Rio Grande Plain—chaparral

Texas bluebonnet, the state flower, blankets fields and roadsides during the spring. © Carol M. Sander

brush country. This land was made for running wild cattle and for hiding wild men. In its time it has done both. The dense shrubs, prickly pear cactus, and mesquite usually get about 25 inches of rain a year, much of which is evaporated by the intense summer heat.

Several wildlife refuges preserve some of the original Valley habitats. The Lower Rio Grande NWR will have 132,500 acres in four counties when acquisition is completed. You can explore 11 habitats within its limits, including Chihuahuan thorn forest and sabal palm forest. In the Santa Ana NWR, on the north bank of the Rio Grande near the town of Hidalgo, the subtropical forest, coast, plains, and desert habitats all come together in one place. Choke Canyon State Park near Corpus Christi preserves dense thorny thickets of mesquite and acacia and offers the possibility of seeing javelinas, alligators, or the crested caracara, also known as the Mexican eagle.

Roadside Parks

Off the interstate highways, you will frequently come upon signs that say "Roadside Park, 1 mile." In 1929 what was then called the Texas Highway Department started planning these parks. The department wanted to encourage people to take frequent stops as they plowed across Texas, to show off the beauties of the state, and to promote tourism. The first parks were built in the early 1930s, although the program was officially launched in 1936 at the Texas Centennial Fair in Dallas.

During the Depression, the park program gave young men jobs. Most of the parks of this period were built by the National Youth Administration in the "rustic" style. The work was hand labor: quarrying, preparing, and moving stones to make picnic tables and other outdoor furniture, laying pathways, and constructing barbecue pits. With federally supported labor and land usually donated by local governments, private owners, or civic clubs, the state could afford to build many parks. By the end of the 1930s, Texas had 674 of these miniature parks at minimal cost—the first 200 parks cost $230,000, of which the highway department paid a third.

Highway expansion dealt a death blow to this first generation of roadside parks and today only 41 of the Depression parks exist. Most are in east Texas, the Big Bend, and the Hill Country. The nine in Big Bend were built in the 1940s, but TxDOT lumps them with the Depression parks because the same materials and construction techniques were used.

The department has a guide with a map to these Depression parks. You can get one at the travel centers run by the department or by writing to TxDOT: Communications Section, 125 E. 11th St. Austin, TX 78701-2483. Alternatively, you can find the map at www.dot.state.tx.us/insdtdot/orgchart/env/comun.htm.

THE PRAIRIES

The Blackland Prairie was a magnet for early European settlers where the rich soil could grow almost anything. Early settlers claimed they didn't even need to plow. The eastern fork of the Cross Timbers, a dense forested finger of scrub oaks, cuts throught the western part of this region. Settlers moving west found these thick stands almost impassable. Stories about the name differ, the forest being seen as something that had to be "crossed" to reach better lands or as itself "crossing" the more tractable prairies.

Probably the best place left to get some idea of the original prairies and the Cross Timbers is at the Fort Worth Nature Center and Refuge, a 3,500-acre urban refuge northwest of the city. Just ten miles from the skyscrapers of downtown

Fort Worth, the center's limestone ledges and overgrown vegetation give you some idea of the difficulties the primeval Cross Timbers presented to anyone traversing them.

In the northeastern county of Fannin, the 261-acre Bonham State Park and the Caddo National Grasslands also offer glimpses of the original prairie lands. Cedar Hill State Park, southeast of Dallas, preserves a stand of tallgrass prairie, and Lake Tawakoni State Park, southeast of Greenville, holds more tallgrass prairie interspersed with post oak forests.

Another untouched area within the prairies is the "lost pines" of Bastrop County, east of Austin. Bastrop State Park preserves an isolated area of loblolly pines and hardwoods stuck in the middle of the prairie separated from the other pines of east Texas.

Hill Country

As you head west from the southern prairies, the Balcones Escarpment rises above the flat lands, dividing east Texas from west and marking the beginning of the Hill Country. The Spanish explorer Bernardo de Miranda named this geological feature because he thought the rocky cliff resembled a balcony jutting over the plains below.

Native Americans and Europeans alike found this region congenial for settling. The uplifted rocks harbor many springs and creeks that offer water in an area that can be quite arid. One example is Barton Springs in Austin, even though the swimming area within the city no longer resembles anything Native Americans or pioneers found. You can, however, hike the green belt above the popular site and perhaps get more of a feel for the original countryside.

The geological forces of this area also created many caves and overhangs that sheltered roaming Native Americans and later visitors. Longhorn Cavern State Park, near the town of Burnet, has been a shelter since prehistoric times. McKinney Fall State Park, just east of Austin, has an overhanging ledge that sheltered Comanches and a gringo bandit or two.

Pedernales Falls State Park between Austin and Johnson City preserves typical country. Stony cliffs intercut by the river and covered with live oaks give a good idea of the countryside's original appearance.

Panhandle Plains

Sitting right on top of Texas, high and lonesome, is the arid and sparsely settled Panhandle, made up mostly of plains broken by occasional deep canyons. When Francisco Vázquez de Coronado, the first European to explore the area, first crossed this land it was covered by grasses and little else. Today, it is almost impossible to find some place where you can recapture the fright the conquistadors felt as they realized that these plains were unbroken and apparently limitless. Coronado wrote that it was as if "we had been swallowed up by the sea....there was not a stone, nor a bit of rising ground, nor a tree, nor a shrub, not anything to go by."

Perhaps the best place to try to recapture some of that terror would be in one of the national grasslands in the northernmost part of the Panhandle, such as Rita Blanca National Grassland north of Dalhart or Blue Kettle National Grassland on the Oklahoma border east of Canadian. Some woodlands break up these grasslands but you can try to imagine the original experience of the Spanish conquistadors.

The Caprock Escarpment is another jutting cliff that, like the Balcones, forms a physical boundary. In this case the border lies between the high and lower plains of west Texas. It reaches its highest elevations in Borden, Briscoe, Crosby, Dickens, Floyd, Garza, and Motley counties. A trailway made up of railroad and hiking trails runs through the Caprock Can-yons State Park, southeast of Amar-illo, for 64 miles.

South of the Canadian River and west of the Caprock Escarp-ment is the Llano Estacado or the "staked plains." The Llano Estacado appears isolated from the rest of the world. To its north the Canadian River cuts it off from the high plains, to the west the Mescalero Escarpment separates it from the plains of New Mexico, and to the east lies the Caprock. Only to the south does it have easy access to another region—the Edwards Plateau.

Part of Texas mythology is that the Llano Estacado got its name from stakes that Coronado, Native Americans, or westward-moving pioneers hammered into the soil so they could find their way over the featureless plain. But apparently the escarpments gave the plain its name. When you approach from the south or the west, the cliffs of the Mescalero and the Caprock appear to rise like stockades from the plain below. Coronado described the "palisades, ramparts, or stockades." In 1844 Thomas Falconer, who wrote about the ill-fated Texan-Santa Fe Expedition, described the Mescalero Escarpment as "elevated or palisaded much as palisaded sides of a fort."

Another feature of the Panhandle Plains is thousands of small (anywhere from an acre to 250 acres or so) ephemeral lakes called *playas*, which is the Spanish word for beach. These shallow, round depressions are probably best viewed from an airplane. It is hard to believe that they are natural, so neatly their circles dot the plains below. In theory, wind forms the disc-like depressions in the impermeable clay soil—and this is indeed the windiest region in the United States. Collapsing soil may cause some *playas*. One story, obviously a myth, has it that they were formed by buffaloes rolling in the dirt. In any case, when rain falls, water collects in these depressions and stays until it is used by animals or evaporates. In the past, ranchers used *playas* as a water source, although an undependable one. Today, the temporary nature of these little lakes makes it hard to predict when they will appear. Muleshoe NWR, south of Muleshoe, usually has three *playas* but they are episodically dry. Still, the basins remain stopovers for migrating waterfowl.

BIG BEND COUNTRY

The Chihuahuan desert and three mountain ranges overwhelm the topography of the Big Bend Country. The region, where the population density is the lowest in the state, probably resembles the early landscape of the Texas more closely than any other part. You can lose yourself for a day or a lifetime here and never have to see a single person. In fact, one county—Loving—has a population of only 67 in an area of 677 square miles, with 15 people living in the county seat and only town, Mentone. Loving is the least populated county in the United States.

According to Ross A. Maxwell, the first superintendent of Big Bend National Park, the original inhabitants of the region had an explanation for its complex geology. They claimed that their "Great Creator" fashioned the earth, placed the stars in the sky, and created fish, birds, and other creatures to inhabit the world. When the Creator was finished, however, a pile of rubble remained. Not knowing what to do with it, he heaved the leftovers just north of the Rio Grande and formed the Big Bend.

The traditional name for this region is the Trans-Pecos, because most of it is on the far side of the Pecos River from the rest of the state. The name Big Bend, however, is more recognizable. But the real Big Bend—Big Bend National Park—is only a portion of the region. The typography of the Trans-Pecos isolates it from the rest of the state. Most of the region is desert, known as the Chihuahuan Desert, and it spreads as far as Mexico and New Mexico.

Only at the highest elevations is there enough rain to make the area semi-arid. Fortunately, this region has the highest elevations in the state. All seven of the Texas peaks above 8,000 feet high are west of the Pecos, the highest being Guadalupe Peak, part of Guadalupe Mountains National Park, in Culberson County at 8,749 feet. Other notable mountain

ranges here include the Davis, Chinati, Franklin, and Chisos, each of which is included, at least partly, in a park of some kind. All 24,248 acres of the unusual Franklin Mountain State Park, the largest urban park in the United States, are within the city limits of El Paso. The park is a good way to see typical desert flora and fauna, even an occasional cougar.

The Rio Grande cuts this region off from Mexico to the south. Below Big Bend National Park, the Rio Grande is an officially designated wild and scenic river for 196 miles until it reaches the Val Verde County line. If you have experience with riding wild waters, a trip down this portion of the river can transport you into its unexplored and dangerous past. The Rio Grande is also the longest of Texas's many rivers, and like all of Texas's rivers, it has shaped the culture and economy of the state.

The Guadaloupe Mountains of the Trans-Pecos region during a storm. John Suhrstedt, courtesy TxDOT

Humans have altered the rivers of Texas but these major streams continue to affect Texas culture and history. Map courtesy Texas Water Development Board.

RIVERS AND LAKES

In a state with arid regions, water sources assume great importance. Texas has 11,247 named streams, but only 13 can be considered major. Even the largest of them was too sluggish most of the year to be dependable transportation for early European settlers. All of these streams, however, offered water for man and beast at some time, and many have names that reflect the history and legends of the state.

The Rio Grande is the southernmost river in Texas and the boundary between Texas and Mexico. The Spanish explorer Juan de Oñate was the first to call it the Rio Grande, or "big river." Before Oñate, Antonio de Espejo had called it Rio del Norte. Other names have included Rio Grande del Norte, Rio San Buenaventura, Rio Ganapetuan, Rio Bravo, and Rio Turbio.

In 1689 Alonso de León named the spring-fed Nueces for the pecan trees along its banks (*nueces* is Spanish for "nuts"). Alonso de León also named the Guadalupe River, which commemorates Mexico's patron saint, Our Lady of Guadalupe. Other Spanish explorers found buffalo grazing near a river they named *Lavaca,* Spanish for "cow," which is what they first thought the bison were.

The Colorado and Red rivers were both named for the red dirt each carries most of the year, *colorado*. The Colorado is the largest river wholly within the state. For a while, early settlers navigated the Colorado as far north as Austin, but a natural logjam called a "raft" eventually cut off access to the Gulf.

The Brazos River was originally called the Brazos de Dios, "arms of God," but the origin of the name is obscure.

Caddo Lake, the largest natural lake in Texas. Courtesy TxDOT

Pronunciation Problems

The rich cultural mix of Texas has resulted in place names with some strange pronunciations. Some words are Anglicized from Spanish or other languages and others are pronounced as if they were still in their original language. Take the word *Llano* for example. The central Texas county, city, and river that go by that name are all Anglicized: LA-no. Most Texans, however, pronounce the first word in Llano Estacado in the Spanish way: YAH-no.

A favorite trick word that Texans love to spring on newcomers is *Bexar*, the original name for San Antonio and now the name of the county that city inhabits. The "x" is silent. The official pronunciation is something like BA-ar, but if you say "Bear" everyone will be impressed. But if Texans insist on pronouncing that county correctly, they insist on Anglicizing the river that runs nearby, the Guadalupe.

It's not just Spanish words that are a problem. Austin has a street named Koenig, and natives still approximate the German pronunciation by saying KAY-nig. Newcomers say CO-nig, however, and the pronunciation may be changing. Other confusing German pronunciations that linger include the Hill Country towns of Boerne (BER ne) and Gruene (green, both the translation and Texan pronunciation).

In central Texas, the towns of Burnet, Manor, and Manchaca all have idiosyncratic pronunciations: BER-nay, MAY-ner, MAYN-shek. Texans consistently pronounce Pedernales as PER-da-na-lays.

Sometimes the same sound comes from different spellings. The naming of the town of Waco and of Hueco Tanks State Park come from the same Native American group and are pronounced the same: WAY-ko.

The *Texas Almanac,* published every other year by *The Dallas Morning News*, always devotes several pages to a "Texas Pronunciation Guide." It covers only cities and towns—no rivers, lakes, and other purely geographical features—but it is a start.

Many tales involve someone—Coronado or other explorers or sailors who had run out of water—naming the river out of simple gratitude. Two stories are given for the naming of the San Jacinto River (*jacinto* is Spanish for "hyacinth"). The first claims that the river was choked with water hyacinth when it was discovered, and the second that the river was discovered on August 17, St. Hyacinth's Day.

The river with the most industrial development, largest population, and most urban concentration along its banks is the Trinity. That champion river namer, Alonso de León, originally called it La Santisima Trinidad (the Most Holy Trinity), which was shortened to Trinidad and later anglicized to Trinity.

The strangest river name may well be that of the most northern river in Texas—the Canadian, which crosses the Panhandle in a deep gorge. Some say that early explorers thought the river fed into Canada; others that the first to discover the stream were French Canadians who named it in honor of their home. Nonetheless, the Canadian is bedeviled by quicksand, and the deep gorge that surrounds it made it one for cattle drivers to avoid.

The largest natural lake in Texas was the Caddo, but it was dammed in 1914 in an attempt at flood control. Other lakes and reservoirs of any size were also the result of damming. Many of these projects were carried out during and after the 1930s in order to supply electricity, especially to rural areas, and to control floods, ensure water supplies, and offer employment and recreation.

One of the most dramatic projects came about in the Lower Rio Grande Valley. An international agreement between Mexico and the United States called for a lake and dam on the border in the Texas counties of Starr and Zapata. The new reservoir was to be named Falcon after one of the area's oldest families and the village of Old Falcon, which would be covered with water when the dam was completed. The government offered to move the village to Zapata, the nearby county seat with schools, sewage, and other amenities, but the citizens of Falcon insisted on their own community. Nonetheless, Presidents Dwight Eisenhower and Adolfo Ruíz Cortines forged ahead, dedicating the dam and closing the gates. Texas was in the grip of a severe multi-year drought and everyone thought that even after the dam gates shut, the people of Falcon would have plenty of time to move to higher ground.

Then a big rain came. The villagers had to flee, leaving their possessions behind. A local landowner marked off lots on her land nearby and sold them to the refugees for $100 each. The people of Falcon were never reimbursed for their homes and belongings.

If you go to this area at a time when the lake level is low, take a trip across the border to Viejo Guerrero in Mexico. The town was built by master stonemasons and even today, after 50 years of water damage, the old church and other buildings emerge almost intact from the surrounding lake.

Throughout the area, inhabitants had to endure the physical difficulties of what is now Texas: unpredictable water sources, difficult land transportation, and a predilection toward sudden storms. These attributes have shaped the lives of everyone who has tried to live here. Let's now turn to their stories.

EARLY TEXANS

For more than 13,000 years, humans have lived in Texas. The earliest evidence of human habitation comes from the Clovis Complex—people who are also called Paleo-Indians. The Clovis people are known mostly for their distinctive spearheads (called "points" by archeaologists). Clovis points have been found along the Canadian River, in central Texas, and with an extensive massacre of mammoths in Roberts County (in the Panhandle). In Denton County, archeaologists unearthed a buried campsite full of Clovis points, blades, and the stone "flakes" left over from making the sharp instruments. Other Clovis sites dot the state. Since most of what we know about these people comes from such remains, all we can really say about them is that they were skillful tool makers who hunted buffalo and other game.

About 1,000 years after the Clovis people flourished, another group that archeologists call the Folsom Complex made distinctive artifacts. In Val Verde County, a kill site littered with Folsom points has thousands of butchered bones from an extinct type of bison as well as from other animals. Toward the end of the Folsom culture, the climate of Texas changed, becoming warmer and drier, until it began to resemble the climate of today.

Early Texans changed their ways along with the weather. In the Archaic period, they experimented with new plants and hunting techniques. They made some attempts at settled agriculture and added grinding implements to their collections of points and tools. They also developed an amazing new weapon, the spearthrower (also called an *atlatl*), which increased the distance a point could be hurled and greatly improved hunting accuracy. This new weapon must have increased food supplies and made them more predictable. Even though the hunters and gatherers in this period moved from place to place, archeologists interpret the appearance of cemeteries with extensive burials as an indication that some intended to return regularly to particular territories.

The Archaic Texans also traded with people from other regions and developed a sophisticated artistic sensibility. Roving Texas bands especially enjoyed trading stone items from what is now Arkansas. In west Texas and throughout the lower Pecos region, rock art and multi-colored pictographs decorated cliff overhangs and other protected spots. This vast area, where the Edwards Plateau, the Trans-Pecos west, the plains, and the south Texas brush country merge, harbors one of the greatest concentrations of pre-European rock art in the United States.

Gradually, many groups of early Texans adopted the bow and arrow and developed techniques for making pottery. Other new tools, such as beveled knives, appeared as the Archaic gave way to the Prehistoric period. Agriculture also became increasingly important. In east Texas the precursors of the Caddoan culture, another group that greeted the advancing Europeans, settled villages with ceremonial centers that incorporated ceremonial buildings and cemeteries. In the Panhandle and along the Llano Estacado, people built simpler villages. Even the arid Trans-Pecos was settled by people who farmed and constructed shelters.

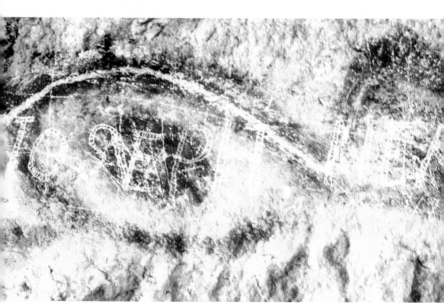

Pictographs near the Concho County town of Paint Rock.
O.C. Garza, courtesy TxDOT.

Trade took off during this Prehistoric period as early Texans made contact with others throughout the continent. Obsidian items (the hard rocks used to fashion tools and weapons) can be found at many prehistoric Texas sites, and since scientists can trace the geologic origin of obsidian using X-rays and other methods, we can get a good idea of where the items came from. Most Panhandle obsidian items can be traced to the Jemez Mountains in New Mexico and northern Mexico. Obsidian items found in south and central Texas originated as far away as southern Idaho, Wyoming, and central Mexico. For their bison skins, salt, and bows made from the wood of the bois d'arc tree, the Caddo swapped copper from the Great Lakes area and shells from the Gulf Coast. From the Trans-Pecos to the Piney Woods, early Texans grew corn, beans, and squash, all originally cultivated by inhabitants of central Mexico.

Many prehistoric Texas cultures changed almost constantly, but the arrival of the Europeans cut this development short. We will never know what kinds of cultures the early Texans would have created had they been left to thrive, because the invaders fundamentally altered their lives by introducing not only new languages and political and religious structures, but also guns, horses, and lethal diseases.

Texas: Where Did the Name Originate?

The Native Americans of east Texas used a word, variously spelled as *Texas, Tejas, Techan, Teysas*, and other forms, as a greeting and to describe other groups. The word apparently meant "allies" or "friends." In 1689 Father Damián Massanet described meeting Native Americans who, he thought, called themselves Techas. Later he met their leader and described him as the "governor" of the land of the Techas. When he left the area, Massanet left behind a missionary named Francsico de Jesús Maria who tried to clear up the meaning of the word. According to Jesús Maria, the word did not apply to any one native group but was used to indicate those who had joined together to fight the Apaches.

Later erroneous definitions of the word include "tiled roofs" or "land of flowers." None of these explanations have any corroboration from materials of the time. The Spanish appeared to use words related to Texas to describe the Neches-Angelina Indians and not the place. Exactly when the word became attached to the physical place is not known. In any case, the state motto "Friendship" harks back to the original meaning of the name.

Cabeza de Vaca and Esteban: A Couple of Firsts

What can you say about someone who chooses to call himself Mr. Cowhead? Alvar Nuñez Cabeza de Vaca preferred to use his mother's family name because of its aristocratic flavor. (In the 13th century an ancestor had cinched a Christian victory against the Moors by marking an unguarded pass with a cow skull. In gratitude, King Sancho of Navarra gave the family the new surname.) Maybe if he had chosen to call himself Alvar Nuñez, we would not remember his name so vividly today.

Cabeza de Vaca wrote the first tourist memoir of Texas. He had no intention of going to Texas, and he stayed a little too long—seven years. Still, he and three companions, including Esteban, the first known black person in Texas, were the only survivors out of the 300 who landed with Pánfilo de Narváez in the vicinity of present-day Tampa Bay.

Narváez had permission from the king of Spain to start a colony in Florida, which in those days was everything along the Gulf Coast from today's Florida to Mexico. The expedition stumbled around in the Florida peninsula for a while and then killed all their horses for meat and set out on the Gulf in five homemade rafts. In November of 1528, two of these rafts landed on Galveston Island with 80 survivors.

Cabeza de Vaca was separated from the other survivors for many of the seven years. In that time he became the first European trader in Texas; he would exchange sea shells and mesquite beans from the coast for skins and dyes from the interior. He also developed a reputation as a medicine man, although his treatment mainly consisted of blowing smoke on injuries. In 1532 Cabeza de Vaca and another survivor left the island that would be Galveston and headed south. When his companion disappeared, Cabeza de Vaca continued on and eventually ran into three other survivors on the banks of what they called the "river of nuts."

They waited two more years before they headed west in search of Spanish outposts. Cabeza de Vaca removed an arrowhead from an Indian to add to his list of firsts: the first European to perform surgery in Texas. In March 1536, they came upon the village of Culiacan in the Spanish province of Nueva Galicia.

Here the little band went in separate directions. Esteban's owner sold him and the slave ended up the property of a Franciscan friar who took him back to Texas as a guide. Some place, probably in New Mexico or the Panhandle of Texas, Native Americans killed Esteban. Many legends have grown up about his death; some say he had seduced women of the tribe, others that he carried an item that had been stolen from the tribe.

Like many of his countrymen, Cabeza de Vaca had been primarily motivated by visions of easy wealth in the New World. He instead founded Texas literature with his traveler's tales of life in Texas: *Relacion de Cabeza de Vaca*. His book fed many an adventurer's dreams of gold and wealth in the New World.

When the Europeans arrived in Texas they found four distinct cultural areas: along the Gulf Coast, in the eastern Piney Woods, throughout the plains, and in the Trans-Pecos region. Each invader described the original inhabitants as he saw them; a single group could earn many names. Consequently, we can not be sure how many groups existed in Texas before the Europeans arrived. Furthermore, while priests, merchants, and others tried to portray the languages and customs of the people they met, their linguistic and conceptual systems often tainted their descriptions.

Gulf Coast

After almost a decade of roaming the area, Cabeza de Vaca was the first European to write about the original inhabitants of Texas. For most of that time he lived with the people of the Gulf Coast, including the Coahuiltecan and the Karankawa.

The Coahuiltecan lived in the southern coastal plain; the center of their territory appears to have been near San Pedro Springs in modern San Antonio. They existed on mesquite beans, fruits, nuts, acorns, and the occasional deer. According to Cabeza de Vaca, they controlled game by setting grass fires or driving prey into the bay until the creatures drowned, but prickly pears and pecans were their primary foods. Every summer they would move from their primary camp to gather prickly pears. Pressed by their meager resources, these Native Americans practiced female infanticide to such an extent that men had to obtain wives from other native groups. They seem to have been a people on the edge of disaster and when the Spanish became a prominent force in the region, the Coahuiltecan were absorbed into the nameless masses of mission natives.

The Karankawa lived a little farther north along the coast, but their lives seem less desperate than that of the Coahuiltecans. Moving from barrier island to mainland in a constant search for food, the Karankawa used hollowed-out logs as dugout canoes. They also fashioned baskets from local vegetation and made waterproof pottery from a tarlike substance found on the beach—oil—a substance that would someday profoundly affect the history of Texas. The

Karankawa also seem to have understood fermentation since they brewed an intoxicating drink from the yaupon bush and drank it as part of their ceremonies. Cabeza de Vaca was probably lucky to have survived his brush with them, since the Karankawa were said to practice ceremonial cannibalism. And if cannibalism stories did not keep people far enough away, the Karankawa had another weapon to hold off strangers: They rubbed themselves with alligator or fish fat to repel mosquitoes, a smell that certainly worked on European invaders, even if it didn't on the insects.

After Cabeza de Vaca left them, the Karankawa entered European history again when they attacked the struggling French colony of the explorer Rene Robert Cavalier Sieur de LaSalle and killed all the settlers except six children. The Karankawa themselves were attacked by colonists from the Austin colony, the Spanish and Mexican military, Texas militia, and other Native American groups until they were eventually extinct, and they took the secret of their mosquito repellent with them.

EASTERN FORESTS

The confederacy of the Caddo lived in very different circumstances from those of the coastal Native Americans Cabeza de Vaca had known. In 1542 the survivors of the expedition of the eastward-moving explorer Hernando De Soto stumbled on the Hasinai, a Caddo group, and described people with healthy food reserves who lived in settled but widely scattered villages. Probably related to the mound-building Native Americans of the Mississippi basin, the Caddoan culture had clearly worked out religious and political hierarchies and traced their family descent along maternal lines.

Of all Texas Native Americans, the Caddo seem the most technologically sophisticated, using clay, stone, wood, bone, and other materials to make tools, pots, and ornaments. When the Spanish and French came to the region, the Caddo enthusiastically entered into the fur, horse, and gun trade, exposing them to the epidemics and land greed that would severely reduce their populations. Remaining Caddo moved to the north central reaches of the Brazos River and finally to the Indian Territory that became Oklahoma. Today you can get a glimpse of what

No Escape from the Island of Doom

Cabeza de Vaca and 79 other survivors were stranded on Galveston Island, which they named Malhado, or Island of Doom. Here is Cabeza de Vaca's description of an attempt to escape:

As the sun rose the next morning, the Indians appeared as they had promised, bringing abundance of fish and certain roots which taste like nuts, some bigger than walnuts, some smaller, mostly grubbed from the water with great labor.

That evening they came again with more fish and roots and brought their women and children to look at us. They thought themselves rich with the little bells and beads we gave them, and they repeated their visits on other days.

Being provided with what we needed, we thought to embark again. It was a struggle to dig our barge out of the sand it had sunk in, and another struggle to launch her. For the work in the water while launching, we stripped and stowed our clothes in the craft.

Quickly clambering in and grabbing our oars, we had rowed two crossbow shots from shore when a wave inundated us. Being naked and the cold intense, we let our oars go. The next big wave capsized the barge. The Inspector and two others held fast, but that only carried them more certainly underneath, where they drowned.

A single roll of the sea tossed the rest of the men into the rushing surf and back onto shore half-drowned.

We lost not only those the barge took down; but the survivors escaped as naked as they were born, with the loss of everything we had. That was not much, but valuable to us in that bitter November cold, our bodies so emaciated we could easily count every bone and looked the very picture of death. I can say for myself that from the month of May I had eaten nothing but corn, and that sometimes raw. I never could bring myself to eat any of the horse-meat at the time our beasts were slaughtered; and fish I did not taste ten times. On top of everything else, a cruel north wind commenced to complete our killing.

The Lord willed that we should find embers while searching the remnants of our former fire. We found more wood and soon had big fires raging. Before them, with flowing tears, we prayed for mercy and pardon, each filled with pity not only for himself but for all his wretched fellows.

—Alvar Nuñez Cabeza de Vaca, *Cabeza de Vaca's Adventures in the Unknown Interior of America*
Trans. Cyclone Covey

Buried Gold, Lost Mines, & Other Get-Rich-Quick Schemes

Since Cabeza de Vaca crossed the plains of south Texas, tales of lost treasure have lured people to follow secret trails looking for untold riches. Native Americans, pirates, lost priests, and wandering animals have all played a part in the legends of lost lucre, buried treasure, and missing mines.

San Saba Mines

Probably no treasure trove has gone missing more often than the lost San Saba mines. San Saba silver first came to European attention in 1756 when Lieutenant-General Bernardo de Miranda reported finding a cave with thick veins of the metal along the banks of the San Saba River. Miranda requested permission to mine the deposit, but before he received authorization, he was sent on a military expedition to the Sabine River area and was never heard from again. Legend has it that the priests at the short-lived San Saba Mission spent more time looking for the silver than converting the heathen. The Comanches eventually destroyed the mission, and the Spanish never again ventured into the area.

In the early 1830s, Harp Perry and some friends worked silver in the vicinity of the San Saba and Llano rivers. Every three weeks they would bring 10 to 12 burro loads of silver to San Antonio, but in 1834 Comanches attacked the mine and killed everyone except Perry and two companions. Perry hid for three days and then escaped to Mexico, where he lived off his silver findings for many years. In the hope of rediscovering the mines, he returned to the San Saba in 1865 but could not pick out any familiar landmarks.

Legend also holds that Jim Bowie befriended an Apache chief in order to get the secret of the lost mines. He was supposed to have made several deposits in San Antonio banks, but the secret location of the mines died with him at the Alamo. In 1852 a young Mexican woman who had been captured by the Comanches and ransomed by a white trader told San Antonio newspapers that she had been with the band when they camped on the banks of the San Saba. The Comanches would go up Los Moros Creek and be gone for about an hour. They would return carrying bags of silver ore. The last person to claim to know where the mines were was Adam Beasley, who had been part of a posse of Lampasas-area ranchers pursuing Comanches. His horse wondered off, and in his search for his mount he stumbled onto an ore-filled cave. He did not immediately return to the cave because of the Comanche threat, and then moved to Tennessee for three years. By the time he returned, he could no longer find the cave. Treasure hunters still search for the lost San Saba mines, but if anyone has found them, the discovery has been kept secret.

Lafitte's Treasure

The pirate Jean Lafitte dug up every square inch of Galveston Island if he buried all the treasure attributed to him. Most of the tales involve the pirate burying fabulous amounts of loot just before being chased off the island by the U.S. Navy. One story has a very old man named Robinson roaming the streets of New York City begging in the 1920s. A wealthy businessman named Selkirk helped the old man, and when Robinson was dying, he gave his benefactor a parchment map and related a tale involving being a cabin boy for pirates who worked with Lafitte. Pursued by Spanish warships, the pirate captain had run his ship aground on silt deposits in the Colorado River. While the other pirates fought off the Spanish, the pirate captain, Robinson, and two others buried the ship's treasure. The next morning everyone on the ship, except Robinson, was killed. He escaped with the map and eventually made his way to California where he lived most of his life.

The stories do not explain how Robinson made it to New York (or why he didn't return to Texas instead), but Selkirk is supposed to have bought 6,000 acres on Matagorda Bay and become a cattle rancher. He appointed a man named Ellis his foreman. One day some treasure hunters appeared at the ranch and asked Ellis to take them to a spot on a map they had found. Ellis helped them dig and on his own found a chest. He did not share his discovery with the adventurers but when he returned the next day the chest was gone. The story goes that the treasure hunters returned in the night and hauled it away.

Lost Padre Mine

In 1659 Spanish priests established a church in today's Ciudad Juárez, across the river from modern El Paso. In addition to building their church and preaching to the locals, the priests also worked a gold mine in the Franklin Mountains. The finished church had a 35-foot bell tower, and each morning the priest who rang the bell could look out toward the mountains and see the mouth of the mine. Each month the priests sent several mule-loads of ore back to the capital. But then came the Pueblo Revolt.

When word came of the uprising in New Mexico, the Juárez priests loaded golden chalices, candlesticks, and other valuable items into wagons and carried them across the river to the mine—supposedly up to 250 mule loads. The priests hid the valuables and covered the mouth of the mine with river silt. When the Spanish regained control of the region, none of the priests who had been at the mission was still living in the province nor could anyone find the mine.

But over time several people have tried. In 1901 L. C. Criss did find a shaft. He cleaned out 125 feet of the tunnel and found several artifacts from the Spanish period including a spur and an anvil. The items were displayed in El Paso for a while. The shaft Criss had found branched at the bottom. When the work crew had removed the fill, Criss saw that the walls of the tunnel had to be reinforced. He went into town to get lumber and left word that no one was to dig any further. But one man did, the shaft collapsed, and the man was killed. With the shaft filled with rocks and himself out of funds, Criss abandoned the project. Others have shown up in El Paso with old maps and documents and claimed they could find the mine, but so far the treasure has remained hidden.

Many other tales of lost treasure abound in Texas. Get yourself a copy of W.C. Jameson's *Buried Treasures of Texas* or the granddaddy of them all, J. Frank Dobie's *Coronado's Children*, and keep them handy as you ride the back roads.

Modern inhabitants find the Texas coast more enjoyable than the Karankawes did. © Craig Shelley

Caddo life may have been like at Caddoan Mounds State Historical Park. The park preserves temple mounds, a burial mound, and a typical village.

To the west of the Caddo was the Wichita confederacy, a loose grouping of related bands. The French were the first Europeans to mention the Wichita when traders ran into them near the Arkansas River in Oklahoma. Europeans were always impressed by the Wichita's extensive tattoos. In fact, the name the Wichita called themselves translates as "raccoon eyes" and came from the men's habit of pricking the skin around their eyes with sharp objects and rubbing charcoal dust into the designs. The Wichita, who spoke a language related to Caddo, were outstanding middlemen. With the arrival of the French, and later the Spanish, the Wichita brokered trade between Native American and European groups. Even before the Europeans entered the picture, the Wichita had been the buffer group between the Caddo and fierce newcomers on the open plains, the Apache and Comanches.

THE PLAINS

The population of the Texas plains was in flux when the Europeans arrived. Between 1000 and 1400 CE, various Apache bands moved from the north into the area and displaced several nomadic groups. While the Apaches were also nomads who depended on the buffalo for sustenance, they tried to control their food supplies by planting corn, beans, and other crops in temporary settlements the Spanish later called *rancherías*.

The Apaches organized themselves in bands, and the dominant band in Texas was the Lipan. Their basic social unit was the extended family and several families would stay together as a hunting unit. These units could come together if one was attacked or wished to attack another group, but even then, their organization was loose and leaders were not necessarily permanent.

When the Apaches first reached Texas, they used large dogs to move their tents and other possessions. When Spanish horses came to the region, however, the Apaches were among the first Native Americans to incorporate these fantastic animals into their culture. Their time as rulers of the plains was cut short, however, when a new tribe, the powerful Comanches, moved in from the north at about the same time as the Europeans moved in from the south and east.

Must-See Historical Parks

Hueco Tanks State Historical Park near El Paso and Seminole Canyon State Historical Park in Val Verde County have sites for viewing rock art. When the lake in the Amistad National Recreation Area, also in Val Verde County northwest of Del Rio, was impounded along the U.S.–Mexico border, a spectacular amount of rock art was affected. Some sites were made inaccessible or destroyed, but Panther and Parida caves, with 4,000-year-old pictographs, can be visited by boat. Call (806) 775-7591 for information.

Several varieties of liatris, also called gay feather or blazing star, grow throughout Texas from mid-July to October. © Carol M. Sander

The story of the Comanches really belongs to a later period of Texas. They swooped into the state behind the Apaches and soon became the most feared riders of the plains. The horses that they caught wild on the plains, bought from the Wichita middlemen, or stole from anyone careless with his mounts, gave the Comanches exactly the tool they needed to perfect their raiding style and follow the buffalo herds. The Spanish, Mexican, and Texan governments all had to worry about their relations with the Comanches and often had to allocate resources to dealing with the band to the neglect of other issues.

TRANS-PECOS

In the far west of the Trans-Pecos, Europeans found Native Americans settled along the river basins and trying to supplement their bison kills with regularly grown crops. Usually called the Jumano, these people were probably part of the Mogollón culture that reached into Arizona and northern Mexico. They built pithouses that were partially under-ground so that they stayed cool in the summer and warm in the winter. Some of the houses even had adobe extensions and resembled pueblo villages. To cope with the aridity of their environment, the Jumano developed many dry farming techniques, including runoff diversion and some forms of river irrigation. A few drought years, however, could bring a village to the brink of disaster. By the time the Spanish claimed the area, most of the Jumano had moved north.

Eventually, European descendants pushed the remnants of all these cultures into smaller and smaller areas. The Europeans not only had more people and better firepower, they also had invisible allies: disease. The original inhabitants of Texas had no natural immunity to the illnesses Europeans had lived with for centuries, such as measles, smallpox, and chicken pox. By the time the surviving Native Americans had developed a pool of immunity, European settlers were advancing across Texas with new kinds of weapons, communication, transportation, and agriculture. The first of these settlers came from Spain and pushed back the original inhabitants of the coast and eastern forests, while they found the Native Americans of the plains and those in the Trans-Pecos more difficult to deal with.

While the Alabama-Coushatta are two tribes, they left Alabama together and settled in the Big Thicket of Texas as one group. Today they occupy the oldest reservation in the state on 4,600 acres near Livingston in east Texas. Cultural dances are often open to the public. Courtesy TxDOT

Who Invented Chili?

In 1977 the Texas State Legislature named chili the state dish but did nothing to clear up the question of who invented the bowl of red. There are many contradictory ideas about its origins, and no one is prepared to give up the argument. While chili might have its ultimate ancestors in Mexico, no Mexican cook will acknowledge the dish as part of her culinary heritage. Mexicans think of chili as a purely Tex-Mex invention.

The dim past of chili, however, probably lies in some pemmican-like concoction ground up by pre-European natives to season the food of their wanderings. Chiles, animal fat, and corn merged into one greasy portable mush that could be boiled on its own or, on lucky days, mixed with the meat of whatever game had been killed.

Skip ahead now to the shadowy beginnings of recorded Texas history: When Canary Islanders settled in San Antonio in the late 17th and early 18th centuries, they brought their ancestral cooking methods with them but added ingredients closer at hand, including chiles. Lore says that in the evenings the Canarian women would bring their stew pots out to the plazas so families could eat dinner while chatting with neighbors.

Move on now to stories that have a bit more documentation: In the 1950s a Dallas chili lover named Everrette DeGolyer found records that he believed showed that Texas cowboys and adventurers on their way to the California gold fields had made something called chili bricks. These bricks were made of pounded dried beef, fat, and chiles, with other seasonings added to individual tastes. They would be tossed into boiling water along with some beef or venison for trail eating. Some trail cooks were rumored to have planted chiles and herbs, such as oregano, along the major cattle trails so they could have fresh ingredients when needed.

Another legend of 19th-century chili making involves the *lavanderas* who followed the many armies that visited the state in its early history. These washerwomen took care of the various needs of the soldiers, including dietary, and made a stew of chiles with goat meat or venison.

Or, chili could be an invention of Texas prisons. The cheapest food available for feeding the incarcerated from the middle of the 19th century and on was stew made from the economical, but tough, beef of range cattle. Chiles and other flavorings were mixed in and the whole mess was cooked in water until the meat could at least be chewed. Many freed inmates were said to miss their bowls of prison chili.

After the Civil War ended, San Antonio's Hispanic women would sell stew from open-air stalls around the Military Plaza in the evenings. These purveyors of stew made from chiles and beef were called Chili Queens. Eventually, they added to their repertory other staple foods of Tex-Mex cooking: tamales, tortillas, enchiladas. The Chili Queens remained a fixture of downtown San Antonio until 1943 when Mayor Maury Maverick closed down their stalls as unhygienic.

Sometime in the 1890s standardization came to chili. Chili lovers from north Texas say that DeWitt Clinton Pendry, an immigrant to Fort

In the fourth weekend of October, chiliheads flock to Flatonia for Czhilispiel. Michael Amador, courtesy TxDOT

Worth, was the first to sell what we call chili powder. Pendry opened a grocery store and, when it burned down in 1890, he sold his powdered blend under the name Mexican Chili Supply Company. (No evidence indicates that the store burned down because the chili powder was too hot.)

San Antonians, however, hold that the first chili powder was ground out by William Gebhardt, one of the many German immigrants who settled in New Braunfels, north of San Antonio. His blend continues to be packaged today by Gebhardt Mexican Food Company, although it is now owned by Beatrice Foods.

Another 19th-century chili that is still sold today was concocted by Lyman T. Davis of Corsicana. He made chili and sold it at saloons for five cents a bowl (and all the free crackers you wanted). Eventually, Davis opened his own meat market where he sold chili bricks called Lyman's Famous Home Made Chili. In the 1920s he canned his chili and named it Wolf Brand in honor of his pet wolf, Kaiser Bill, whose picture still appears on the can.

Some folks attribute chili powder to an unidentified visiting British explorer. This legend holds that the unknown Brit saw the possibilities of adopting the curry powder model to chili making and made and marketed the first chili powder. Unfortunately, not a hint of evidence supports this tale.

By the beginning of the 20th century the chili joint was a familiar fixture throughout the state. Usually, it was a one-room affair with some stools around a counter and, if the owner had some pretensions of gentility, a curtain to separate the diners from the kitchen. Chili at this stage of its evolution was considered cheap, and usually poor quality, food. In the 1960s, however, chili began a renaissance with the first chili cookoff. In 1967 Wick Fowler and H. Allen Smith, two humorists, each claimed to cook the best chili in the world. To settle the issue, they faced off in the ghost town of Terlingua, on the western border of Big Bend National Park. This first cookoff ended in a tie, but competitions are still held every year in Terlingua and throughout the state. A reasonably up-to-date listing of cookoffs can be found at www.vvm.com/ctba-bbq/texas%20cookoffs.html.

Spain in Texas

The Spanish claimed Texas but could not control it. The mightiest European country in the 15th and 16th centuries, Spain extended its reach across the Atlantic but often that reach exceeded its grasp. Texas was on the fringe of Spanish territory and the motherland would often neglect her far-off colony only to be jolted back into action by threats, perceived or real, from other Europeans or indigenous Americans.

The first Spaniards to reach Texas were commanded by Alonso Alvarez de Pineda, who landed four ships at the mouth of what is now the Rio Grande in the fall of 1519. They stayed for 40 days repairing their ships and exploring, warmly greeted by Native Americans. A year later, Diego de Camargo heaved into view with three ships full of provisions and manned by not only sailors but masons as well. The locals apparently figured out that Camargo was planning on a long stay and turned on the Spaniards, forcing Camargo and his men to retreat. When they returned to Veracruz, the main port of Mexico, their one and only ship sank in the harbor.

In 1523 the governor of Jamaica, Francisco Garay, set sail for Texas with 16 ships and 750 soldiers. His plan was to establish a colony to rival that of Hernan Cortéz in Mexico, but he could find no site to support his planned city of Garay. He later ended up in the prisons of Cortéz where he befriended Pánfilo de Narváez.

The Search for the Golden Cities of Cibolo

The governor of Cuba had sent Narváez to Mexico to arrest Cortéz (that part of the story need not concern us here), who then turned around and arrested the would-be arrestor. When Narváez finally returned to Spain, he used the information he had gained from Garay to obtain royal permission to explore the Texas coast and gain potential control of that coast from the Atlantic to the Rio Grande. The crown also appointed a treasurer for the anticipated colony—Alvar Nuñez Cabeza de Vaca. Cabeza de Vaca's recount of his adventures fueled the gold hunger of the Spanish government.

Four years after Cabeza de Vaca and his companions entered the Mexican capital, Francisco Vázquez de Coronado, the younger son of a family of lesser nobles, set out to make his fortune in western gold. Many of Coronado's companions had found themselves in situations similar to his: young men raised in families of relative wealth who had been cut off from that life by the rules of inheritance. Others were simple thrill seekers, though even more were rapscallions and criminals looking for a second chance or just trying to get away from their first. All expected to make their fortunes. Few did.

Coronado's expedition included not only Spanish soldiers and priests but also five Portuguese, two Italians, a Frenchman, a German, and a Scotsman. This small army ventured through Arizona and New Mexico, and somewhere along the trail picked up a guide the Spanish named "the Turk." The Turk claimed to know how to reach the seven cities of Cibola with their streets of gold and multi-storied buildings. Instead of leading the conquerors directly to these riches, however, the Turk wound them through the high plains of Texas and Oklahoma and most likely even into present-day Kansas. The Turk may have been deliberately drawing the Spanish away from the pueblos of what is now New Mexico.

Whatever his plan, the Turk introduced Europeans to the frighteningly empty spaces of the Llano Estacado. One of Coronado's men wrote, "Traveling in these plains is like voyaging at sea for there are no roads other than cattle [buffalo] trails. Since the land is so level, without a mountain or a hill, it was dangerous to travel alone or become separated from the army, for losing sight of it one disappeared." Things could have been worse for Coronado's men. They entered the plains during a time when the grass was high, water available, and buffalo plentiful. In another season, they might have found bone-dry dirt with no water and no game. They apparently stumbled onto Palo Duro Canyon, but they did not discover the golden streets of Cibolo—or any gold at all for that matter.

Eventually, the Spanish realized that the Turk was deceiving them and they garroted him and left his body someplace in the desolate plains. Certainly, on the way back with different guides they made much better time over more direct routes. But both going and returning, the men of the expedition needlessly alienated the native peoples by burning, raping, and pillaging. The Native Americans rejoiced at their leaving, but did not prepare themselves for the conquistadors' return. The expedition's most lasting results were whetting the Spanish appetite for gold and introducing the horse into the local cultures. Rumors of gold kept bringing the Spanish back, and the horse finally gave the people of the plains and Trans-Pecos an effective means for fighting the would-be conquerors.

While Coronado and his men had been approaching Texas from the west, Hernando De Soto led a party into Texas from the east. Before Coronado had even left Mexico City, De Soto had been named governor of Cuba and given control of Florida. De Soto now had the right to explore and claim anything to the west of that peninsula. His potential lands could reach as far west as the cities of Cibola and their gold. If he hurried, he could be the one to claim their riches. Some people think that Coronado and De Soto came very close to bumping into each other. The Native Americans, according to this theory, worked hard to keep the two expeditions from doing so, although the two Spaniards would probably not have been happy to see each other.

On April 6, 1538, De Soto left Spain with 10 ships, more than 600 soldiers, many priests, and a few family members of officers. In Cuba he added more provisions and passengers and set out for Florida. He and his men plundered their way across the peninsula. With archers and shooting specialists, smiths, carpenters, and other skilled workers, De Soto's entourage was much better equipped than Coronado's. But the eastern Native Americans extracted a heavy toll on the conquerors, killing and wounding men and horses as the Spanish marched by. De Soto himself was wounded in a battle outside the site of today's Mobile, Alabama. The expedition crossed the Mississippi River and traveled north through present-day Arkansas before turning back toward the Gulf Coast. Somewhere in Louisiana, De Soto died and his body was shoved into the Mississippi River he had claimed for Spain. But before he died, De Soto named Luis de Moscoso de Alvarado his successor.

Moscoso decided that the best way out of their predicament was to march by land to Mexico rather than trust the vagaries of the Gulf waters. Following this plan, the survivors of De Soto's party pushed into Texas from the east and contacted the Caddo nation. They possibly reached the Brazos River before lack of translators and provisions forced them back to the Mississippi. There they built seven crude ships and took two months to reach Tampico on the eastern Mexican coast.

After the remnants of Coronado's and De Soto's expeditions returned home, the Spanish left Texas alone for 40 years, although in 1568 a bizarre twist of fate sent some Englishmen through. When the privateer Jack Hawkins was ignominiously defeated by Spanish ships in Veracruz harbor, several dozen of his shipmates went ashore and three began walking north. Of these, we only know David Ingram, but apparently they walked from Veracruz to Nova Scotia, a truly incredible journey.

Expectations of trade, gold, and missionary work kept alive Spanish hopes of settling Texas. In the 1580s, exploratory expeditions passed through, and then in 1598, Juan de Oñate gained the right to develop parts of what was to become New Mexico. In April of 1598, on the way to his grant, Oñate's party stopped at the area the Spaniards called El Paso del Norte and were believed to have celebrated the first European Thanksgiving in what is now the United States—23 years before the pilgrims set foot on Plymouth Rock.

When the Pueblo Indians revolted against Spanish rule in 1681-1682, survivors of the revolt returned to this part of the Rio Grande to settle down, naming their communities after places they had left in New Mexico. Today, Ysleta, Socorro, and San Elizario, now all part of El Paso, are considered the oldest continuous European settlements in Texas. Missions were eventually established on these sites and predate all other missions in the Southwest.

THREATS FROM THE FRENCH

In 1682 the Spanish received strong warnings for their colonial plans. Not only did the Pueblo Indians revolt against their conquerors, but the French were threatening Spanish control of the Southwest. In that year, Rene Robert Cavalier Sieur de La Salle explored the Mississippi River and claimed all territory drained by it—about half of the modern lower 48 states—for France. In 1684 he returned with four shiploads of colonists to begin French settlement of the lower Mississippi.

But mistakes were made. One was a navigational error: The French overshot their intended target by 400 miles and ended up establishing Fort Saint Louis not on the Mississippi but just above Lavaca Bay. During a two-month layover in the Caribbean, many of the crew deserted. Of those who stayed, many picked up smallpox, syphilis, and other diseases that would decrease manpower available to the colony. Two ships were also lost, one to pirates on the voyage over and the other to shipwreck as they landed on the barrier island off the Texas coast, and along with those ships went a significant amount of their supplies.

Perhaps the most important mistake, however, was the choice of La Salle himself as colony leader. La Salle was secretive, distrustful, bad tempered, and frequently depressed. He seems to have been paranoid for good reason, however, since his own men had previously tried to poison him—three times. He never shared his plans with anyone else, so his subordinates and the colonists were often in the dark. Whether La Salle initially knew they had overreached their target or thought they were on the Mississippi is unclear.

Less than a month after the landing, one of the remaining two ships returned to France. Apparently, this return had been part of La Salle's plan from the beginning, but more than 100 of the would-be colonists decided to go back with the ship. The captain carried a message from La Salle to the king asking for more supplies, but the king ignored the message. Of course the colonists never knew this since their only source of contact with the rest of the world was the one remaining ship, *La Belle*, which one historian has described as being "the size of a boxcar."

Upon their landing in Texas, La Salle stayed true to his personality and alienated the local Karankawa by confiscating their canoes. Using these canoes and *La Belle*,

La Belle

The sinking of La Belle must have seemed like the final blow to the people of La Salle's wretched colony. The little ship, which might have gotten them to Florida or Mexico or someplace beside the Karankawa-filled coast where they were, was irretrievably gone. It stayed gone for more than 300 years. In 1995 J. Barto Arnold, a marine archeologist with the Texas Historical Commission, found the sunken ship's site in Matagorda Bay. He and his crew salvaged an inscribed cannon, but they could not bring up the ship itself.

In 1996, however, archeologists from the commission constructed a double-walled cofferdam to keep water away from the wooden ship and methodically excavated.

Since the ship had become encased in mud almost the moment it sank, its contents, from ropes to dishes, had been largely preserved from the sea water. Even the wooden hull, while water-logged, was in workable pieces. The original builders had numbered timbers to guide them as they assembled the ship, and these helped scientists reassemble the craft.

The ship yielded many objects: a wooden crucifix, a ruby ring, bronze candlesticks, leather shoes, three cannon, and hundreds of thousands of glass beads intended for trade. The remains of bodies were also found: one human skeleton and the bones of deer and dogs. A reconstruction of the human skeleton showed him to have been a stocky man with a broken nose and bad teeth.

In 1997 the excavation of La Belle was complete. Now, the Conservation Research Laboratory at Texas A&M University studies and analyzes the artifacts. In an abandoned aircraft hanger, the hull lies in a giant vat full of water and stabilizer, replacing the water in the wood and hardening it until the boat can be moved to the Bob Bullock Museum in Austin. Other artifacts from La Belle are already on display at this museum, part of the Capital complex that offers permanent and visiting exhibits and an IMAX theater. Call (512) 936-8746 or (866) 369-7108.

the colonists moved themselves, their remaining supplies, and timbers off the sunken ship from the barrier islands to the mainland where they began to build Fort Saint Louis. Within six months of their arrival, more than half of the colonists who had survived the voyage and chosen to stay with the colony died of disease, overwork, and, no doubt, hopelessness.

Despite the desperation of Fort Saint Louis, La Salle took around 80 of the most robust men and set out in La Belle and the canoes to "explore the Mississippi." Of course, he was nowhere near the Mississippi, but they sailed south and did stop to explore. Marching west after they landed, La Salle's men ended up on the Pecos River near today's town of Langtry. Many believe La Salle knew exactly where he was and was searching for Spanish silver mines. During this time, LaSalle would return to the ship and canoes, sail a little farther, and go ashore and explore again. With each repetition, he lost a few more men; some died, others deserted and wandered lost or joined the Native Americans.

Meanwhile, back at the colony site, the settlers had managed to build only a few miserable huts of grass and mud. They planted their French seeds at the wrong time of the year, and the few that grew were destroyed by hogs. An alligator killed one colonist, a rattlesnake another. Some just became "lost in the woods" and were never seen again. Several died from eating the fruit of the prickly pear, which they had seen the Karankawa eat, but had neglected to observe how the natives removed the skin with its almost-invisible thorns.

In January 1686, *La Belle* sunk in Matagorda Bay, leaving La Salle to continue his explorations on foot. When he returned to the wretched settlement only about 40 colonists remained alive. For seven months, he considered whether to go for help. Finally in January 1687, he took 17 of the strongest men and most of the supplies and headed out, telling the colonists to wait there for his return, as if they had another choice. About two months later somewhere in east Texas, La Salle's men turned on him, murdered him, and left his body to the elements. Apparently, more efficient means than poison were used this time. The survivors eventually made their way to Canada and home to France.

For almost two years, the 20 or so remaining colonists managed to hang on. They thought they had made peace with the Karankawa and so relaxed their guard, but in the winter of 1688-1689, the Karankawa made a final assault on the settlement and killed all adults. Six children, five from the Talon family, were spared and taken to live with them. About five months after the massacre, Alonso de León, governor of Spanish Coahuila, found the remains of the settlement. He and his men buried three bodies and eight cannon. A year later, de León returned and rescued the

Talon children and several French deserters who were still roaming the coast. In Mexico City, the Talons, their faces tattooed in Karankawa style, told the Spanish authorities that La Salle had been a miserable leader who had treated both colonists and Native Americans harshly and unfairly. Later, the male Talons made their livings as guides and translators for both Spanish and French in east Texas.

ATTEMPTS AT PERMANENT SETTLEMENT

La Salle's expedition did not benefit the French, but it did concentrate Spanish attention on Texas. De León had reported that the land seemed attractive. The French were establishing a hold in Louisiana and posed a threat to Spanish control of whatever was in east Texas. One of the priests who had accompanied de León's search party, Father Damián Massanet, volunteered to establish missions in the territory. The government agreed to his plan, at least in part so they could secure the area against the French.

In May 1690 Massanet founded the first mission in east Texas, San Francisco de los Tejas, probably in modern Houston County near the present-day town of Augusta, but the mission was short-lived. After a little less than three years, with only three soldiers stationed to protect them from the Native Americans, the priests buried the cannon and bells, torched the buildings, and fled. While floods and the enmity of the local Native Americans had driven them back to Mexico, the Spanish had gained more knowledge of the land and its people.

Tired of the lukewarm or nonexistent support of the Spanish government and military, Massanet decided to stop cooperating with either institution. As the 17th century neared its close, however, one of his fellow missionaries, Father Francisco Hidalgo, stationed in the Spanish province of Coahuila, wrote to the governor of French Louisiana suggesting that the French governor and the Spanish priest could work together to establish missions among the Native Americans of east Texas. The governor was Antoine de la Mothe Sieur de Cadillac, who had long believed that only trade with the Spanish colonies would make the French colony profitable. Spanish law, however, prohibited such trade. Father Hidalgo was offering the French the opportunity to do good and to make a profit at the same time. Cadillac knew just the fellow to establish contact with the Native Americans and, maybe, with isolated Spanish settlements yearning for French trade goods—his near relative, the charming and dashing Louis Juchereau de St. Denis.

St. Denis's charge was to go into Texas, establish contact with Father Hidalgo, and set up a trading program in New Spain. He crossed into disputed territory in 1713 and built a storehouse in what became Natchitoches, Louisiana. He did some trading, got to know the local Native Americans, and set out once more to "look for Father Hidalgo." By the end of 1716, St. Denis had married a Spanish woman, led a Spanish expedition of about 70 people into east Texas, and helped the Spanish establish six missions there. The Spanish wanted these missions to establish their claims to the territory, and St. Denis wanted them located close enough to Louisiana to make for easy trade.

The Franciscan fathers were responsible for all of these missions. A fort was built at the western edge of the string of missions—proof that the government and military were now taking east Texas seriously. A new viceroy in Mexico City, the Marques de Valero, strongly supported them and soon gave his permission for another mission and fort to be built as a resting place between the eastern missions and the Rio Grande. On May 1, 1718, near a river with steady water supply, the mission San Antonio de Valero (its chapel was soon to be called the Alamo) was established and four days later the fort, San Antonio de Béxar, was set up about a mile to the north. Ten families settled around the fort. With the establishment of the future city of San Antonio, the Spanish commitment to Texas was sealed.

But building the missions did not secure Spanish east Texas. By 1719 France and Spain were at war in Europe. Communications being what they were, the New World French found out about the conflict before the Spanish, and seven soldiers from Natchitoches captured a mission and its two inhabitants. One of the two Spaniards used the squawking of chickens to cover his escape and subsequent dash to both the nearby settlement and the fort set up to protect it. Soldiers and civilians retreated from the area. The appropriately named Chicken War showed how tenuous Spain's control of east Texas still was and ended

St. Denis

While La Salle had been dour, introspective, and aloof, the other major French figure in colonial Texas, Louis St. Denis, was gregarious, dashing, and charming, using his charms to the benefit of himself and France.

Born near Quebec City, St. Denis was educated in France. In 1699 he left for Louisiana with an expedition led by his relative Pierre Lemoyne d'Iberville and soon was commanding forts in Biloxi Bay and on the Mississippi, using these sites as stepping off points for western explorations. Here he met the Caddo and learned to survive in the wilderness. His guide and translator on his excursions was Pierre Talon, the survivor of the LaSalle expedition and of Native American captivity.

In 1713 St. Denis led a company of men to the site of Natchitoches (in present-day Louisiana). With his natural charm opening paths for him in the forest, St. Denis came to believe that French trade could include Spanish soldiers and civilians isolated in frontier presidios and missions. The fact that Spanish law forbid such trade was of little concern to him.

St. Denis's first trip across Texas ended up in the Rio Grande settlement San Juan Bautista where the military commander, Diego Ramon, put him under house arrest and contacted Mexico City for further orders. Nine months later the government's response reached Ramon, but by that time St Denis was already set to marry Don Ramon's granddaughter, Manuela.

Sent to Mexico City on charges of being a Frenchman illegally in New Spain, he convinced the government to allow him to join an expedition led by his father-in-law to reestablish Spanish settlements on the west side of the Sabine River. This was a goal shared by the government of New Spain and St. Denis, although the former may not have realized exactly what St. Denis had in mind. In 1716 St. Denis, his wife, his father-in-law, and the usual accompaniment of priests and soldiers marched through east Texas establishing missions, including the village of Nacogdoches across the river from Natchitoches (a double naming that has confused generations of schoolchildren).

But St. Denis's charm could not extend across the Atlantic. Changes in the Spanish government led to a new viceroy in Mexico City and a new governor of Coahuila, and neither man was as amused by the Frenchman as his predecessor had been. On an excursion into Texas, St. Denis was arrested and sent to Mexico City where the government decided to exile him to Guatemala. St. Denis, however, stole a horse and rode for Louisiana where he spent the rest of his life as commander of the fort at Natchitoches. In 1744 St. Denis died in Natchitoches, a contented family man with four, maybe five, children, and his property is now part of the campus of Northwestern Louisiana State University.

Because of St. Denis's influence with the Caddo, the Spanish government needed many more soldiers along the border than did the French. In the end, St. Denis had a more lasting effect on Texas than did the more famous La Salle. His presence forced the Spanish to maintain settlements in east Texas, and his twin cities of Natchitoches and Nacogdoches helped to establish the Sabine River as the real border with Louisiana.

Spain's second attempt to settle the area. The refugees moved into the new community on the banks of the San Antonio River.

In 1721 a new governor of Coahuila and Texas tried to start the east Texas missions up again. This time he sent in not only people, both military and civilian, but also herds of sheep, goats, cattle, and horses. These animals are the real beginning of ranching in Texas. Two new forts were added to those that had been built before, one of which was called La Bahía, a name shared with a nearby mission, and was built on the site of La Salle's failed settlement. In just six years, however, military strength in east Texas fell away and San Antonio was again vulnerable to attack.

Part of the Spanish plan to shore up east Texas involved attracting new settlers to San Antonio. In March 1731, 55 Canary Islanders arrived in the settlement. These people are often called the first civilian settlers of San Antonio, but civilian families had been part of the settlement from its beginning. The growing civilian population did not help fend off Apache attacks, which only seemed to increase. Relations with the French, however, relaxed somewhat. Between 1747 and 1755, the Spanish government started 24 towns, including Laredo, and 15 missions. Many old Hispanic families of Texas trace their land holdings to grants issued during this period.

In 1757 the government seriously overreached. Increasing Comanche raids led the Lipan Apache to ask the Spanish to establish a fort and mission on the San Saba River, far from the growing centers of population. Near the present town of Menard, San Luis de las Amarillas Presidio (*presidio* being Spanish for fort), and Santa Cruz de San Sabá Mission rose up to stave off the Comanches. This alliance between Spaniard and Apache only infuriated the Comanches and their allied tribes. In March 1758 they attacked and destroyed San Sabá Mission. The next year they attacked the Spanish settlers that remained and destroyed their herds of horses and cattle. The military made several sorties into Comanche lands, and the priests tried to convert the Apaches, but San Sabá lay too far from the main Spanish settlements. In the end, both fort and mission had to be abandoned. The Spanish fell back to San Antonio and points south of that city, and no Europeans attempted to settle in the San Sabá area again until the 1840s.

France, meanwhile, was feeling the economic pinch of colonial wars. In 1762 the French ceded all of their territory west of the Mississippi River to Spain. Spain was having enough trouble trying to develop Texas; now the added burden of Louisiana was too much. Even worse, rather than having the easy-going French as neighbors, Spanish territory now found itself right up against westward-moving English-speaking colonies of what would become the United States. The addition of Louisiana also pointed out some flaws in Spanish administration. In general, Spanish colonies could not choose their trading partners. By law, Texas had to send all of its exports and receive all of its imports through Mexico City. The French, however, had insisted that Louisiana retain its ability to trade as it pleased. Now Texas and Louisiana, though right next to each other and controlled by the same government, could not legally trade with each other.

Faced with these problems, King Charles III of Spain ordered the Marques de Rubí to inspect the settlements in Texas and make reform recommendations. Rubí recommended consolidation. All settlers and missions in east Texas should be moved to San Antonio and the government should focus on developing better relations with Comanches and allied tribes. But Rubí made the mistake of assuming that the Native Americans were a bigger threat than anyone to the east.

The settlers did not see the consolidation of the east Texas missions and San Antonio as a success. The people who had been displaced from the eastern villages complained that the established San Antonians denied them good land and irrigation water. Under the leadership of Antonio Gil Ibarvo (sometimes spelled Ibarbo, Ybarvo, Ybarbo, or Y'Barbo), the displaced easterners petitioned for the right to return to their homes. Probably tired of listening to their complaints, the government allowed them to move back but forbade them to live within 100 leagues of Natchitoches. In the August of 1774, they established the town of Bucareli within the area the government had prescribed. The Bucareli site frequently flooded, however, since it was on the banks of the Trinity River. Without governmental knowledge or consent, Ibarvo moved them to the abandoned mission at Nacogdoches, which now joined La Bahiá, San Antonio, and Laredo as permanent Texas settlements. Ideas about Ibarvo's motives for this move differ; many historians think he was mainly interested in smuggling and other illicit activities, an interpretation bolstered by the citadel-like house Ibarvo built.

SPANISH CONTACTS WITH THE UNITED STATES

With the death of Charles III, the quality of administrators on the frontier declined. In addition, Spain sided with England and the French royalty against Napoleon Bonaparte. In 1800 Louisiana reverted to France, and in 1803 Napoleon sold the land to the new United States of America.

This deal was just as well, for the Spanish were having a hard time populating Texas. Try as they did to encourage Spanish speakers to move north of the Rio Grande, the government could not make it a viable territory. In 1777, the

The "house" built by Gil Ibarvo as it appeared in the 1880s or 1890s. Called the Original Stone Fort, this structure was demolished, but a replica built of the original stones now stands on the campus of Stephen F. Austin University in Nacogdoches. Courtesy Center for American History, UT-Austin.

La Bahiá Presidio in Goliad is a reconstruction of the original fort and mission. The name Bahiá means "the bay" and traveled with the institution when it moved from its original site on the Gulf.
J. Griffis Smith, courtesy TxDOT

census counted 3,103 inhabitants, in 1785, 2,919, and in 1790, 2,417. Obviously the province was not growing. Without Louisiana to worry about, the government could focus its efforts on bringing people in to Texas.

But losing Louisiana had its drawbacks. The boundary between Louisiana and Texas had never been clear and the new treaty between France and the United States failed to define the exact border between Spanish Texas and the Louisiana Purchase. The French and Spanish had dealt with border ambiguities by ignoring them. President Thomas Jefferson wanted something more definite and held that the purchase extended to the Rio Grande, while the Spanish government held out for the Red River as the border. The Spanish sent troops to fortify their borders and the U.S. government sent soldiers to Louisiana. Into this stand-off came the fugitive vice-president of the United States, Aaron Burr, fleeing from a murder charge after killing Secretary of the Treasury Alexander Hamilton in a duel. Reports held that Burr was massing an expedition to take over Texas.

But the governor of Louisiana and de facto U.S. army commander in the west, General James Wilkinson, on the verge of being removed from office, was himself one of the more slippery characters of American history. Wilkinson may have been part of Burr's plot, may have made up the whole idea of a Burr plot, or may have been actively working against Burr by pretending to take part in the plot. In any event, he turned Burr in, and in 1806 negotiated the Neutral Ground Agreement with the Spanish military commander Lieutenant Colonel Simón de Herrara.

This agreement created a neutral area between Texas and Louisiana and forced the Spanish to remain to the west of the Sabine River. The Sabine eventually became the border between Texas and Louisiana, but for a while this agreement created a no-man's land neither Spain nor the United States could control. Bandits, filibusters (those plotting to overthrow Mexican, Central American, or other governments), and other outcasts tended to congregate here and plot their forays into wealthier, more civilized areas. This sinkhole was not cleaned up until the signing of the Adams-Onís Treaty in the 1820s.

Wilkinson created other uproars as well. In 1806 U.S.

The Pirate of the Gulf

Jean LaFitte in uniform. Drawing courtesy Center for American History, UT-Austin.

Jean Lafitte was the younger of the Lafitte pirates, but he was the one about whom legends were made. The family came from Bayonne, France, to the New World. Jean was probably in his early 20s when he and his older brother Pierre began their pirate life in New Orleans. Around 1808—few dates are clear in the life of the Lafittes—the brothers set up smuggling headquarters in Barataria Bayou, west of the mouth of the Mississippi.

The governor of Louisiana made some half-hearted attempts to clean up the pirate nest, but he had no success until the War of 1812. While the British fleet was attacking New Orleans, the governor took the opportunity to destroy the Barataria site. Even so, Jean Lafitte turned down a British request for his help, and instead supplied General Andrew Jackson with men, supplies, and, most importantly, his knowledge of the area. After Jackson's success in New Orleans, the Lafittes hoped to have their confiscated booty returned. Jean went to Washington, D.C., to put their case before President James Madison, but—while they were pardoned—the brothers never got their Barataria plunder back.

Instead of using their pardon as an opportunity to go straight, the Lafittes now transferred their operations from the United States to what was still Mexico. They moved to Galveston Island where another shady character, Louis Michel Aury, had already set up an establishment and had made contact with some of the Mexicans plotting to declare independence from Spain. During their time on Galveston, the Lafittes, in addition to being pirates, were secret agents of the Spanish government. They managed to undermine Aury's control over his men until so many deserted that Aury was forced to abandon the island in July of 1817.

Jean Lafitte then became the master of Galveston, where he shipped captured loot overland in mule trains to New Orleans for resale and set up a scam dealing in slaves. In 1819 Lafitte was approached by James Long to take part in his revolution against Mexico. Some say that Lafitte rebuffed Long and refused to have anything to do with revolutionaries, others that Lafitte accepted Long's commission to be an admiral and the governor of Galveston Island. Since nothing came of Long's rebellion, it is hard to say which side Lafitte was on, though he probably intended to be with the winner, whoever that might be.

Despite being a Spanish secret agent, Jean Lafitte claimed that he attacked only Spanish ships and that he hanged any pirate captains who set upon U.S. ships. But the U. S. Navy was still determined to rid the Gulf of his influence. By 1821 Jean Lafitte had boarded his ship *Pride* and sailed to the coast of Yucatán. He set up another headquarters on Mugeres Island and continued his smuggling and pirating until he died. The circumstances of his death are not clear, but he is thought to have contracted yellow fever and died around 1835.

Legend has it that Lafitte was a handsome man of courtesy and charm, and many tales of buried treasure cling to him. One holds that, as they were preparing to abandon Galveston, a buccaneer heard him mutter that he had "left his treasure under the three trees." The man returned to Galveston to dig and struck a chest, but when he opened it, he found the body of Lafitte's dead wife.

President Thomas Jefferson decided to send a scientific expedition up the Red River. The president had heard reports that the Red might connect to Santa Fe and he also wanted to find out exactly where the southwestern borders of the Louisiana Purchase might be. To lead this southern equivalent of the Lewis and Clark Expedition, Jefferson picked Thomas Freeman, an astronomer and surveyor, and Peter Custis, a medical student and naturalist. They set out in April 1806 with $11,000 from the Congress—about three times the money Lewis and Clark received.

Wilkinson of course knew about this expedition and told Spanish officials that Jefferson was using the pretext of a scientific study to establish claims to Spanish lands. Some people think Wilkinson hoped to provoke a war between the United States and Spain so that he could profit from the battle, either monetarily or by military glory. Others believe that Wilkinson had always been a Spanish spy. In either case, the Spanish immediately sent out two separate military excursions to find the expedition and turn them back.

On July 28, 1806, Freeman and Custis ran into a band of Spanish soldiers and turned back without a confrontation. If provoking battle had been Wilkinson's motivation, he failed. Instead, Spain decided to be more conciliatory toward the United States and this attitude, in essence, opened the back door for Americans to sneak into and settle the Red River watershed.

Perhaps one reason that Spain let this confrontation

sputter out was that it had other, more pressing problems than possible U.S. infiltration of Texas. Three men claimed the throne of Spain, leaving the colonial administration without centralized edicts of the king. On September 16, 1810, Miguel Hidalgo y Costilla issued the Grito de Dolores, a call for Mexican independence from Spain (the Mexican fiesta of Diez y Ses celebrates this event), but another decade passed before that dream was fulfilled. To control the threat of white immigration from the United States, Spain issued an 1813 colonization law that allowed them to settle within 52 miles of the international border, but only if they obtained special permission. Without realizing it, the Spanish had sealed their fate in Texas.

THREATS FROM THE EAST

In 1812 Augustus W. Magee, a graduate of West Point, and Jose Bernardo Gutiérrez de Lara, a Mexican revolutionary, met in the area of Natchitoches-Nacogdoches and marched a combined army into Texas. Magee, who had been a rising star in the U.S. military, died in November 1812 during a siege of La Bahía. His mysterious death is believed to be the first of many suicides that haunted early Texas history. In the spring of 1813, the invaders marched into San Antonio where they proclaimed the first Republic of Texas. Almost immediately, the victorious forces were riven by dissension between those advocating a centralized government and those opposing it. Weakened by disagreements, the revolutionaries were beaten back in the Battle of Medina River during the summer. (A young officer named Antonio López de Santa Anna was recognized for bravery in that battle.) Soldiers from the royalist forces went on a rampage that severely depleted the population of the province, and the last Spanish governor of Texas claimed these forces had "drained the resources of the country, and laid their hands on everything that could sustain life." Texas east of San Antonio was still seriously depopulated and a different kind of settler took over this vacuum.

In 1818 soldiers cleared out a settlement of Napoleonic sympathizers, but in the next year a greater threat appeared. James Long was a trader and doctor from Mississippi who thought that the Adams-Onís Treaty had given Spain too much land. In June 1819 he led a party of like-minded men

Austin's Colonists

In 1827, when he was 19, Noah Smithwick left Kentucky for Texas where he worked odd jobs as a blacksmith, tobacco smuggler, and miller, and was an eyewitness to much of early Texas history. The Civil War sent Smithwick, a Unionist, to California where he lived the rest of his life. In his 92nd year, he dictated his memoirs to his daughter:

Many hard things have been said and written of the early settlers in Texas, much of which is unfortunately only too true. Historians, however, fail to discriminate between the true colonists—those who went there to make homes, locate land, and, so far as the unfriendly attitude of the Indians permitted, resided on and improved it—and the outlaws and adventurers who flocked into the towns.

To the lasting honor of Stephen F. Austin, be it said, that he conscientiously endeavored to comply with this contract with Mexico to settle none but respectable families on the land allotted to his colony. It being also stipulated that they should be Catholic in religion, Austin probably placed a liberal construction on the word "Catholic," which Webster defines as "universal," his colonists as a rule being of no particular opinion on religious matters. They were honest and kindhearted, never refusing to lend a helping hand to those in distress, and if that isn't universal religion it is near enough for all practical purposes….though Austin was temporarily invested with discretionary power for the government of his colony…his function ceased with the establishment of a general system of government; after which the local conduct of affairs was vested in the ayuntamiento, the members of which were elected from the different sections of the colony. So that, at the period at which we have arrived, Austin had been divested of every semblance of authority; his colony being under the domination of the ring, the leader of which had skipped his bonds in Alabama to avoid prosecution on a criminal charge, bringing with him all of his personal property and leaving his friends to mourn his departure to the tune of several thousand dollars.

Faulty statutes in the United States sent many a man to Texas. Dueling was still practiced in many of the states, a trivial matter often ending in the death of one party, the other fleeing the country.

Another fruitful source of emigration was debt; and, while some absconding debtors took their property along, others gave all up and went to Texas to take a fresh start and grow up with the country…. It was a regular thing to ask a stranger what he had done, and if he disclaimed having been guilty of any offense he was regarded with suspicion.

—Noah Smithwick, *The Evolution of a State or Recollections of Old Texas Days*

out of Natchez, Mississippi. By the time they reached Nacogdoches, their ranks had reached 300 and they declared themselves the new government of the town.

To shore up his position, Long left Nacogdoches for Galveston to seek the support of the pirate Jean Lafitte. While he was gone, the Spanish swept down on Nacogdoches and captured, or sent running, Long's army. Long was not deterred. He returned to New Orleans where he gathered another army and left for Point Bolivar on Galveston Bay. Accompanying him was his wife Jane, who was the niece of General James Wilkinson and a formidable force in her own right. From their small mud fort at Point Bolivar, Long and a group of about 50 men marched to La Bahía where they were received cordially. By this time, unknown to Long, Mexico had won its independence from Spain. Forces in La Bahía who were loyal to the new government in Mexico City sent Long to the capital where he stayed for six months until he was shot, possibly by accident, by a soldier.

Back at Point Bolivar the very pregnant Jane Long was left behind with her three-year-old daughter, Ann, her slave, Kiamatia or Kian, and her dog, Galveston. Her determination

Among the many legacies of Spanish and Mexican control of Texas is cuisine. Today, Hispanic families continue the traditions of early Texas. These Manor residents are preparing tamales. J. Griffis Smith, courtesy TxDOT

to be with her husband and remain in Texas had always been strong. When James Long had started on his first Texas expedition, Jane stayed in Natchez long enough to give birth. Then without telling her family, she set out with a two-and-a-half-week-old child, her older child, and her slave for her sister's house in Alexandria, Louisiana. The trip took 20 days (today you can drive it in about an hour) and she arrived sick. It took a month for her to recover enough to leave the children with her sister and make her way to Nacogdoches. She was in the town when the Spanish scattered her husband's forces. When she made it back to Alexandria, she found that the baby had died and the sheriff was holding the family's property against debt.

Somehow the Longs satisfied the sheriff and at the close of 1820, Jane and her small entourage were ensconced in the fort at Bolivar. James was gone and soon the remaining soldiers lost what discipline they had and left for the mainland, each taking enough supplies that eventually Jane and her family had little left but some muskets and ammunition, several fish hooks, and one fishing line. Across the bay was an encampment of Karankawa and when the Native Americans gathered on the beach, the women fired off the cannon the way they had seen soldiers do. The Karankawa disappeared.

Legend has it that winter was unbelievably cold that year, freezing Galveston Bay a quarter mile from the shore. On a bitterly cold night, December 21, 1821, Jane Long gave birth to another daughter; the next day she was picking up frozen fish that had washed ashore and pickling them. Eventually, a ship carrying 15 settlers bound for Stephen F. Austin's colony picked up the little band of women and their dog.

Today, you can get some feeling for the Long family's predicament by taking the free ferry across Galveston Bay to Point Bolivar. The area is now built up with summer cottages and other trappings of modern life but a little imagination can people the shore opposite with terrifying Karankawas. All trace of the little mud fort is gone, however.

Jane Long has been called the "Mother of Texas" because many people thought her child was the "first white child" born in Texas. While her story is inspiring, such a title for Jane Long ignores a lot of women. Census records indicate that she was not the first English-speaking woman to give birth in Texas—although perhaps her story is the most dramatic.

Jane was tough and brave but she was also headstrong, willful, and impetuous. She probably shared many of those characteristics with other Texas settlers. Her rescue, however, is almost emblematic of Texas at this turning point. The next band of more or less successful colonizers swept in and picked up the survivors of the last failed filibuster's family. One page in the history book touches the next.

Must-See Missions

Ysleta, Socorro, and San Elizario
Although the original structures have fallen to flood, fire, and restoration, you can visit reconstructions of the three oldest European settlements, some with features from the original 17th century buildings. Ysleta Mission is also called Nuestra Señora de Monte Carmell, San Elizario Presidio Chapel has a special section on military history, and Socorro Mission, Nuestra Señora de la Concepción del Socorro, uses some original handcarved beams in the 19th century church. Check out all of these missions at www.missiontrails.com.

St. Denis's Missions
Among the six missions that St. Denis helped to establish were the reestablished San Francisco de los Tejas and the Mission Nuestra Señora de los Dolores de los Ais (Mission of Our Lady of the Sorrows of the Ais, the Ais being a local Native American group). A reconstruction of Mission Dolores is south of San Augustine. Visitors may try on friars' robes, lie down on a replica of a missionary's bed, and walk along Ayish Bayou. Call (936) 275-2815.

San Antonio Missions National Historical Park
Today, four missions make up the San Antonio Missions National Historical Park: Mission Concepión, Mission San Francisco de la Espada, Mission San José, and Mission San Juan Capistrano. (The Alamo is separate from the missions park.) All of these missions are still functioning Roman Catholic churches and are administered by the local archdiocese, the National Park Service, and the State of Texas. The dam and aqueduct at Mission Espada are some of the best preserved remains of the colonial irrigation system in the United States. Contact the park at (210)534-8833.

La Bahía Mission
You can see a reconstruction of La Bahía Mission in the Goliad State Historical Park. The reconstruction occupies the spot to which the mission moved in 1749. Other mission replicas and ruins are also in the park, which is south of the town of Goliad. Call (361) 645-3752.

REVOLUTIONS AND REPUBLICS

Spanish authorities must have felt swamped by problems. The Native Americans within the missions constantly reverted to ancestral ways or simply deserted. Without anyone to convert, the missions failed. Out of fear of Native American attacks, the sparse European population was concentrated in a few settlements, such as La Bahía and San Antonio, rather than spread over the province. Filibusters, bandits, and other outcasts harassed the government and the few settled inhabitants—when those inhabitants were not the bandits themselves. And last, the Spanish felt pressure from migrants streaming in from the burgeoning republic to the east.

EL GRITO

Suddenly events were moving quickly. A new, more liberal constitution in Spain alienated the upper classes of Mexico who, improbably enough, joined forces with the other classes that had kept Father Hidalgo's cry for freedom going after his death. Agustin de Iturbide, an officer in the king's army, marched out to fight the forces controlled by Vicente Guerrero, a rebel leader. Instead of fighting, however, the two men proclaimed the Plan de Iguala, the Mexican equivalent of the Declaration of Independence. This Mexican statement, however, was fundamentally conservative, for it set up Mexico as an independent constitutional monarchy with an official religion, Roman Catholicism. It did, however, offer equal rights to both the *peninsulars* (those born in Spain) and the *criollos* (people of European heritage born in Mexico). On May 18, 1822, Iturbide was proclaimed Agustin I, the emperor of Mexico. Most of his support came from the military, but he was unable to sustain his power and abdicated on March 19, 1823.

Agustin I had been unable to reconcile the various forces in the country. The odd coalition that brought about Mexico's independence contained the conflicts that would later make it difficult to govern. *Criollos* could never get over the belief that the *peninsulars* considered themselves better in every way. And both *criollos* and *peninsulars* believed themselves superior to *mestizos* (those of mixed European and Native American or African parentage), Native Americans, and Africans. The army had ended Spanish control but did not trust civilian government. Some Mexicans wanted a constitutional monarchy, some a republic. Anti-clerical forces wanted to end the power of the Church, which, of course, wanted to continue its privileged position as the official state religion. Mexican federalists wanted to distribute power to the states; centralists wanted power to be concentrated in the capital. As these antagonistic groups tried to create a working government, white settlers from the United States continued to push on Mexico's borders.

These settlers were not the first large group to move west into Texas from the United States. The U.S. government, especially during the administration of Andrew Jackson, pushed Native Americans off valuable lands in the southeast. As early as 1807, the Alabamas and Coushattas set up a village on the banks of the Trinity River. Eleven years later, Cherokees who had left their lands back east settled north of Nacogdoches between the Trinity and Sabine rivers. Soon Shawnee, Delaware, and Kickapoo followed. The government did not interfere with this migration, perhaps because the Spanish saw the civilized Cherokees as a moderating influence for the existing Texas tribes, as more desirable settlers than the whites, or as a convenient buffer between Spanish lands and the United States.

EMPRESARIO GRANTS

In tinkering with its immigration policy, the Spanish government had set up a position called *empresario*, a person who would recruit settlers, see to their transportation to Texas and to the division of lands among them, and build settlements for them. Even before Mexican independence, Moses Austin had applied for an empresario grant from the Spanish. Born in Connecticut, Moses Austin moved to Virginia and eventually to Missouri, where for a while he was a Spanish citizen. In March 1821, Moses Austin and the governor in charge of Texas agreed that he would settle 300 families between the Colorado and Brazos rivers and from the Gulf to El Camino Real (the road connecting San Antonio and the east). Before he could begin, however, Moses Austin died. His college-educated son, Stephen F., had just taken the oath of office as a circuit judge in Arkansas. He changed his career goals and set out for San Antonio.

In the summer of 1821, the governor recognized Stephen F. as the heir to Moses Austin's grant. In Natchitoches, Stephen F. Austin found about a hundred letters from people applying to join his colony, but before families could start out for Texas, the Mexican Revolution succeeded and the younger Austin's Spanish contract became invalid. Austin had to journey again to San Antonio and, from there, to Mexico City. He lobbied with Iturbide's government, and in January 1823 a colonization law favoring him was passed. But before Austin could return to Texas, Iturbide abdicated and Austin was back at the beginning. Austin stayed in Mexico City longer to secure his grant. When he finally returned, many of the original families, beset by drought and violence and worried about Austin's long absence, had left. Austin and his land commissioner Baron de Bastrop immediately handed out land titles to those who remained.

By the summer of 1824, they had issued 272 titles and 297 families had received land (some of these families were made up of single men, who set up housekeeping together in order to be considered a family and, thus, be eligible to receive a larger grant). This original group of Austin colonists was called the "Old Three Hundred." The seat of government was located near the Brazos River and named San Felipe de Austin.

Before Austin's colony began, however, other colonizers had hoped to settle families in the region. In fact, some held that Austin double-crossed them. General Arthur Goodall Wavell held that he and Austin had agreed in July of 1822 to divide the granted land between them. As part of that agreement, Wavell claimed, he sailed for Europe to seek capital. He landed in Liverpool in November and wrote Austin several times asking for proof of their grant's existence to show to interested investors. For whatever reason, Austin held off sending proof to Wavell until the latter was finally forced to return to Mexico. Wavell, who

San Antonio was a major focus of the Texas Revolution. Today the city is a major industrial, educational, and medical center, and a magnet for visitors to the state. Here the River Walk is readied for Christmas.
Jack Lewis, courtesy TxDOT

may have been too interested in searching for silver and other minerals to fit in with Austin's goals for the colony, ended up getting an empresario grant for 400 families but was never able to attract the necessary numbers.

Another rival empresario also accused Austin of deception—Sterling Clack Robertson, who was connected with the Texas Association of Nashville. In 1822 representatives of the association had petitioned for a contract and some had even inspected land for settlement. Several things went wrong for them, however. They failed to meet certain stipulations of the Mexican colonization laws, and one of the association's representatives, in dire financial straits in Texas, had given Austin power of attorney for the Nashville group, apparently without asking anyone back in Tennessee. Eventually, Robertson went to court to retain the title to land he felt was his by right of the grant. For decades, Robertson took Austin and his partner Samuel May Williams to court. In turn, Austin or Williams sued Robertson, accusing him of bribery, while Robertson accused Austin and Williams of similar crimes. In 1847, long after the principles were dead, a Texas court found for Robertson, or rather for his heirs.

Other empresarios settled families in Texas. The Mexican authorities encouraged the settlement of Roman Catholic Europeans to ensure that co-religionists were well-represented in Mexico's northern province. John McMullen and James McGloin brought the first Irish families to south Texas. In 1829, they received permission to settle 84 families at Refugio. In 1831 they made San Patricio (St. Patrick) the main town of the grant. Another group of Irish, under the leadership of James Power and James Hewetson, also settled in the same area. Power and Hewetson had about 200 titles to give out. While the government believed that religion would tie the Irish to Mexican culture and that they would act as a buffer to the United States, the south Texas Irish were no more likely to remain loyal to the central government than any other national group.

In 1826 David Burnet, Lorenzo de Zavala, and Joseph Velein gained the right to settle families between the 29th and 33rd parallels, and they transferred these rights to the Galveston Bay and Texas Land Company, based in New York City. The company did not have the right to sell land

Driving the Revolution

Whatever the cause of the revolution, you can retrace its steps on your own. You might start in San Antonio, scene of the best remembered battle, or in Houston at the site of the final battle or at any of the small coastal towns that played a part in starting the war. If you start at Gonzales, you will be at the scene of the first real battle. From there a drive down Interstate 40 would take you near many sites important to the revolution.

La Grange, just north of Highway 77, is proud of its Muster Oak where men gathered to join up for the war. From there, drive northeast over the prairie on Highway 159 to Highway 105 almost to the Brazos River.

Washington-on-the-Brazos is where the Texas Declaration of Independence was written and the constitution drafted. Many restorations convey a feeling for the period. The Barrington Living History Farm and the Star of the Republic Museum focus on Texas's period of independence. A drive down Highway 36 will take you over the Brazos and its fertile bottom land, through the village of Chappell Hill with its historic homes, to the main settlement of Stephen F. Austin's colony.

In San Felipe, meetings of enraged Texans helped fuel the fire of revolution. Since Santa Anna burned the city, little remains from the pre-republic years. Stephen F. Austin State Historical Park includes the site of the original township where the Consultation of 1836 was held. In nearby Richmond, the Fort Bend Museum has extensive background on the colonial and revolutionary periods. The drive will also take you over lands of the Austin grant.

From Richmond take Highway 59 to Houston and to the pre-eminent site connected with the revolution, the San Jacinto Battlefield, built originally on the site of the Texans' camp. (Be sure to say a little thank you to Peggy McCormick as you walk her former holdings.) A museum on the battlefield offers exhibits and regular screenings of the 35-minute *Texas Forever!* In 1939 citizens erected the 570-foot San Jacinto Monument; you can ride an elevator to the top for a view of the entire battlefield.

Negotiate Houston's freeway system to reach Galveston next. Perhaps Highway 45, which parallels the larger highways, might be the more restful drive. In Galveston, you are in the city where the retreating government of the burgeoning republic stayed during the Runaway Scrape.

A drive south along the Gulf on Highway 3005 will eventually hook you up with Highway 36 and take you to West Columbia, the first capital of the new republic. At 14th and Hamilton, you can see a replica of the cabin where the delegates met. Before they met indoors, the delegates often gathered under the Independence Oak, which, unfortunately, is now dead. The Brazoria County Historical Museum has many exhibits including a diorama of 1820s East Columbia.

Out on the road again take Highway 35 to Victoria. The trip passes over coastal plains and skirts the Gulf. Victoria was the main town of the de León grant. The Evergreen Cemetery has graves from pioneers of this period. West of the town on Highway 59 is the Fannin Battleground State Historic Site where Fannin and his men were surrounded and captured by the Mexican Army.

Driving west on Highway 59, you come to the town where Fannin's men were imprisoned, Goliad, a town with many historical sites. You can explore a restored Spanish fort, two missions, and many memorials of the revolution. Goliad State Historic Site encompasses Mission Espiritu Santo and Mission Nuestra Senora del Rosario. Across the San Antonio River is the Presedio La Bahía. Goliad deserves at least a whole day for exploring. If you drive south on 183 you will come to Refugio, the site of Irish colonies and of the revolutionary Battle of Refugio.

From Goliad take Highway 181 to San Antonio where you can spend several days on colonial, revolutionary, and republic period sites along the San Antonio Missions Trail. Within the downtown area is Military Plaza flanked by the Spanish Governor's Plaza. But the destination of every visitor to the city is the Alamo, the "cradle of Texas liberty." In 1905 the Daughters of the Republic of Texas obtained the building and they maintain it today.

in Texas, but it advertised extensively and extravagantly, hired subcontractors, and sold scrip for about 7.5 million acres at one to ten cents an acre.

At this time the average acre of land in the United States went for $1.25, and a depression was taking an economic toll. Buying cheap land in Texas seemed like an excellent investment. Speculators gobbled up the scrip, often without realizing they were buying scrip not land. When two groups of settlers sponsored by the Galveston Bay and Texas Company finally landed in the province, the authorities would not honor their titles. Publicly, the company acted surprised at the government's reaction, but private papers indicate that the Galveston Bay and Texas officers knew all along they were selling worthless paper and believed the Mexican government would be under such pressure to acknowledge the settlers' claims that it would give in. They were right. Eventually the government removed legal impediments to the settlers' land ownership and recognized at least some of their claims. Between September 1834 and December 1835, Galveston Bay and Texas settlers received 936 land titles.

Others received grants but their holdings were usually much smaller than those of the primary empresarios and they settled far fewer families. The most successful period for colonization of Texas would come later after Texas left Mexico.

GRIEVANCES ON ALL SIDES

Settlers continued to hold grievances against the Mexican government. They wanted Texas to be its own state, but Mexico included Texas in the larger and stronger state of Coahuila. Each settler also had to swear that he or she was a Roman Catholic in order to migrate there. Although they had known of this requirement before they moved, many now complained about their loss of religious freedom. In addition, the settlers wanted freer trade with more ports allowing foreign ships to trade along the coast.

Another source of contention was slavery. Most of the migrants into Texas came from the southern parts of the United States, and even those who did not have slaves tended to accept slavery as part of the cultural and economic landscape. But the Mexican government had never been comfortable with the North American model of slavery and in 1824 prohibited slave trading. White Americans could still keep the slaves they had brought with them, and Stephen F. Austin was able to convince the state legislature to provide for a labor contract in which slaves were technically free but bound to an owner for life.

Many of those who had come to Texas were escaping from something in their past, usually debt. To protect these absconders, Stephen F. Austin saw to it that the legislature of Coahuila y Texas passed a law in which plaintiffs could not seek debt collection in the province for 12 years. Austin also convinced the central government that the settlers should not have to pay tariffs for seven years. When those seven years were up and the government began exercising its right to collect these moneys, the settlers had another grievance to add to the pile.

By 1830 the census showed a Texas population of 15,000. For every Hispanic Texan there were four whites. Austin alone had issued 1,540 land titles. Many of these settlers now worried about the stability of the Mexican government. In 1828 Vicente Guerrero, claiming the recent election fraudulent, ousted President Manuel Gomez Pedraza, making many a white Texan wonder if Mexico could ever become a functioning republic.

CENTRALISM VS. FEDERALISM

In July of 1829 Spain tried to reconquer Mexico, but General Antonio Lopez de Santa Anna led an army that beat back the invading forces. Vice President Anastasio Bustamante, a conservative and a centralist, took advantage of the situation to overthrow Guerrero and set up a strongly centralized government. The Bustamante government passed the decree of April 6, 1830, ordering the collection of customs duties in Texas and setting up troop garrisons in the province. But the section of the law that most outraged white Texans was Article XI, which forbade citizens of countries bordering Mexico from settling in the country. Empresario contracts that had not yet been filled were void, and many empresarios did not have enough settled families for their contracts to continue. Still, they continued settling families and giving out land titles in the belief that the law could not stand. The Texas tradition of dubious land dealings continued.

Bustamante set up a military dictatorship and the forces of liberalism and federalism rallied behind the military hero Santa Anna. White Texans also saw the general as a champion against centralization and dictatorship. But all were to be sorely disappointed in their champion.

The first conflicts about paying duties involved two loyal Mexican citizens who had not been born in Mexico. George Fisher, a Serbian who had been a citizen of the United States but a Mexican citizen since 1825, was the customs collector for all ports east of the Colorado River. In Anahuac, Colonel John (sometimes Juan) Davis Bradburn was the military commander on Trinity Bay. By trying to enforce the law, each of these men contributed to Texans' wariness of the Mexico City government.

In 1830 Bradburn arrested Francisco Madero, the general land commissioner of Texas who had been giving out land titles to any settlers who showed up—with or without contracts. Fisher, meanwhile, enforced orders from his commanding officer that all ships leaving certain ports must go through Anahuac. Since this side trip would add new costs to the prices of goods, all Texans resented the order.

When some shippers tried to get around the requirement, shots were fired and a soldier was killed. A deputy commissioner was assigned to Brazoria to keep the peace, but none of this fostered trust on either side.

Bradburn then offered asylum to two runaway slaves from Louisiana. The owner of the slaves employed two lawyers—William Barret Travis (future commander of the Alamo defenders) and Patrick Jack—to obtain the return of his human property. The two dropped hints about armed men coming from Louisiana, and Bradburn threw both attorneys into jail for sedition.

Under Mexican law, Bradburn had acted correctly, but the Texans cared little about the details of Mexican law. To the Texans, Bradburn was a petty despot carrying out the orders of a more powerful despot farther away. Forces led by Patrick Jack's brother and a man who may have been a distant relation of Stephen F. Austin besieged Bradburn in Anahuac on June 10, 1832. The Texans were pushed back to Brazoria, but there they obtained cannon and prepared to attack the fort. The Nacogdoches garrison commander intervened to stop the spread of rebellion and negotiated release of the prisoners and a means for citizens to petition for the redress of grievances. Bradburn resigned and left the region. The Texans dispersed, but the situation remained tense.

Back in Mexico, Santa Anna was leading an army against President Bustamante. Since Bradburn had been a loyal supporter of the president, the Texan forces around Brazoria declared their support for Santa Anna and the Constitution of 1824 in a document called the Turtle Bayou Resolutions. Now possessing cannon, they captured the fort at Velasco on the mouth of the Brazos. Soon every Mexican soldier had been driven out of eastern Texas and the political leaders of San Antonio declared support for Santa Anna and his insurgent army.

Emboldened by their successes and by the lack of response from a distracted central government, the Texans met at San Felipe and petitioned for the repeal of the repugnant laws, especially the one ending immigration from the United States. They also called for separating Texas from Coahuila. Several other petitions were prepared, but none of these requests ever made it to Mexico City. The only concrete results of this meeting were the establishment of a committee of safety and correspondence, and added fuel on the fire of Texan resentment. In a second meeting, these delegates again drew up a list of grievances and selected three Texans to carry the list to Mexico City. Only Stephen F. Austin was able to make the trip.

Austin never made a simple visit to Mexico City; something always complicated his business in the capital. On this trip he had to deal with a cholera epidemic and a personal squabble with the interim president. While Austin was in the capital, however, Santa Anna assumed power, and the Texan found the new president friendly. Santa Anna agreed to all of the Texans' demands except separation from Coahuila: He repealed the ban on immigration, improved mail service, modified the tariffs, and called on the governor to allow trial by jury in Texas. Austin left Mexico City with hope for Texas as a state in Mexico. On January 3, 1834, however, he stopped to see the commandant of Saltillo and was arrested on a trumped-up charge of trying to incite rebellion in Texas. The governor sent Austin back to Mexico City where he languished in the Prison of the Inquisition. It took almost a year and a half for him to obtain release and return to Texas.

Meanwhile, Santa Anna renounced liberalism and dismantled federal forms of government in favor of centralization. States became departments with a governor appointed by the president. Appointed councils replaced state legislatures. The state of Zacatecas rebelled and Santa Anna sent 5,000 troops to repress the uprising and sack the capital, meaning Zacatecas to be an example for other states.

The chaos that followed Santa Anna's assumption of power and his ideological about-face fueled the rapaciousness of the land speculators. In 1825 legislation had allowed a Mexican citizen to obtain as much as 11 *sitios* for almost nothing (a *sitio* is 4,428 acres or a square league). A law passed in April 1834 gave governors the right to sell up to 400 *sitios* with the profit going to supporting militias in the fight against Native Americans. Another law almost a year later gave the governors 400 more *sitios* to sell. A month later, yet another law gave the governor total discretion in "securing the public tranquillity." Selling more land to raise more revenue seemed like one way to reach security.

The Yellow Rose of Texas

Legend has it that a "beautiful slave girl" or a "handsome mulatto woman" spent time with Santa Anna in his tent on the morning of his defeat at San Jacinto. Commonly, southerners called mulattos "yellow" or "high yellow." So, it would not be unusual to call a beautiful mulatto woman a "yellow rose." This name has been attached to the legend of Santa Anna's dalliance.

At one time, the Yellow Rose was identified as Emily Morgan or Emily West Morgan, said to be a slave belonging to James Morgan, a plantation owner. In the list of the slaves Morgan brought with him to Texas in 1831, however, no one is named Emily. Some claim that she was a free mulatto who signed up with Morgan for a year as an indentured servant. An Emily D. West, a free woman, did come to Texas with the second wife of Lorenzo de Zavala. Mrs. de Zavala was also named Emily West. Were they related in some way? During the Runaway Scrape the de Zavala family took shelter at the Morgan home on San Jacinto Bay. Morgan was loading flatboats for Houston's army.

Houston made Morgan a colonel and asked him to go to Galveston to help refugees. The legend says that Emily remained in charge of loading the boats. No one explains why a female slave or servant would be put in charge of the boats. Perhaps Emily was unusually talented or forceful? While loading these boats, Emily and others were captured. Supposedly, a young slave named Turner escaped and warned Houston that Santa Anna had reached the area.

Now the improbabilities begin to pile up. Houston is said to have climbed a tree in order to spy on Santa Anna. On coming back down he is supposed to have expressed the hope that Emily would keep Santa Anna occupied all day. Houston, however, was on the other side of the battlefield from Santa Anna's tent. Even if you accept scrambling up a tree as a likely activity for a general, Houston could not have seen clear across the battlefield into Santa Anna's tent. Further, if you accept for the moment that Emily kept Santa Anna occupied in order for Houston to get his army ready, the question remains—how did she know that Houston planned to attack that day?

The most telling detail against the accuracy of this story, however, is what was not said. After he lost the battle and the war, Santa Anna was viciously criticized in print by officers of the Mexican army. Not one mentioned a tryst on the day of the battle. Certainly, the disgruntled officers would have spread the tale of hanky panky if it had happened.

After the battle, Emily West returned to the de Zavalas. She and Mrs. de Zavala went back to New York in 1837 and she disappears from history. The legend about her surfaced in *William Bollaert's Texas*, first published in 1956 by the University of Oklahoma Press. Bollaert was a British naturalist; he claims in a footnote that he got the Yellow Rose story from an unpublished letter Houston wrote to a friend. No letters in *The Personal Correspondence of Sam Houston*, however, mention any dalliance in Santa Anna's tent.

What about the song? The publication of Bollaert's observations about the republic more or less corresponded with the popularity of Mitch Miller's 1950s version of *The Yellow Rose of Texas*. A few facts about the song can be substantiated.

Some hold the song was written in 1836 and that a manuscript version is in the archives of the University of Texas, but the first copyrighted publication appeared in New York in 1858. The cover says it was "Composed and Arranged Expressly for Charles H. Brown by J.K." Clearly, an African American sings this first version about a love left behind. The opening lines of the first stanza read:

> *There's a yellow rose in Texas, that I am going to see,*
> *No other darky knows her, no darky only me.*

The first line of the chorus is "She's the sweetest rose of color this darky ever knew."

The 1858 song was popular and Confederate soldiers adopted it as a marching song but they replaced "darky" with "soldier." They also changed the first line of the chorus to "She's the sweetest little flower this soldier ever knew." As the war was winding down a new stanza was added:

> *And now I'm going southward, for my heart is full of woe,*
> *I'm going back to Georgia, to see my Uncle Joe.*
> *You may talk about your Beauregard and sing of Bobbie Lee,*
> *But the gallant Hood of Texas played hell in Tennessee.*

Sometimes the third line ends "sing of General Lee."

In the Mitch Miller version the second line of the first stanza reads "Nobody else could miss her, not half as much as me." The first line of the chorus became "She's the sweetest little rosebud that Texas ever knew." The Civil War stanza was dropped. The sheet music describes the song as a "traditional folk song" adapted for Miller by Don George.

So a song originally meant to be sung by African Americans in praise of the beauty of a mixed race woman was appropriated by Confederates and sung as they made their way home from defeat in the war to defend slavery. Eventually, the song returned to the American repertoire in a version claiming to be traditional but shorn of all allusions to race and sectional discord.

Speculators tried to control as much Texas land as possible. Some of these speculators had political motivations, but most were looking solely for the profit of reselling land to new settlers. The phrase "land office business" was coming into its own.

Speculators spread stories that Santa Anna was bent on invading Texas and establishing direct dictatorship. Some Texans came to see war as a looming possibility—and even a necessity. This small war party was balanced by an equally small peace party. Most Texans were somewhere in between and probably would have agreed with George Smyth of Nacogdoches who believed that Texans would never go to war with Mexico. In May 1835 Smyth wrote, "Come what may I am convinced that Texas must prosper. We pay no taxes, work no public roads, get our land at cost, and perform no public duties of any kind." This sweet deal was not enough; the Texas settlers wanted to control the direction of their state.

The settled portions of Texas at this time were mainly in the east and were divided roughly into four parts. The northeast centered on Nacogdoches with its reputation, left over from days as part of the Neutral Ground, for attracting thieves, murderers, and others on the lam from U.S. law. The middle section of Texas focused on San Felipe and the rich Brazos River bottoms. This area was politically active and respectable and heavily weighted toward the interests of slave owners. The southeast was anchored by San Antonio. While whites and their slaves dominated other areas of Texas, San Antonio was predominately Hispanic. The last region was the coast with its excitable ports of Anahuac, Galveston, and Velasco.

Push Comes to Shove

Santa Anna pushed on the Texans and some shoved back. In January 1835 he sent soldiers to Galveston and Anahuac to collect duties Texans owed on imported items. Now, the customs collector at Velasco had been bending the law and collecting duties only on ship tonnage. Galveston and Anahuac collectors took the full legal duties, not only on the ship's weight but also on the materials it carried. An Anahuac merchant, Andrew Briscoe, protested this inequality. Fighting followed and Briscoe ended up in jail.

Members of the war party in San Felipe seized a government courier, opened his messages, and found that reinforcements were on the way to Anahuac. Enraged, those who wanted war overrode the objections of others and ordered Travis, the lawyer in the case of the runaway slaves, to attack the garrison in Anahuac and see that the soldiers left town. With about 30 men under his command, Travis managed to force the surrender of the garrison of about 45 on June 30, 1835. Briscoe was freed.

Seven Texas communities formally condemned the actions of Travis and the San Felipe war party. Even in San Felipe, the peace party gained ascendancy and sent apologetic messages to the military commander of Texas, Martin Perfecto de Cos. Cos accepted the apologies but demanded that Travis and certain other troublemakers be handed over for a military tribunal. Excitement increased and committees of safety and correspondence in several towns called for a consultation of all the towns in a meeting in Washington-on-the-Brazos on October 15, 1835. This decision may have been the turning point that led to revolution.

Until this point most Texans had seen their future as part of Mexico, albeit a Mexico more in keeping with their ideas of a successful government. Few doubted that those ideas could become reality. The war party, however, doubted such a transformation and eagerly spread propaganda against the central government. In their confusion, most settlers looked to Stephen F. Austin for guidance. In July 1835, upon his return from the Mexico City jail, Austin gave his blessing to the Consultation in Washington. In fact while in jail, Austin had moved from believing Texas had a place within Mexico to embracing separation and the war necessary to achieve it. He had also come to believe that Texas had to be "a slave country."

The desire to keep slaves played a part in developing war fever. Fear of a slave revolt gripped the Brazos region—where most slaves lived. On October 17, B. J. White wrote to Austin that "the negroes [sic] on Brazos made an attempt to rise. Major Sutherland came on here for a few men…he told me." Apparently, about 100 slaves had been implicated in a plot to overturn the slave society and make whites into slaves, according to Austin's correspondent. Many of the plotting slaves were whipped and a few executed. Slave owners firmly believed that the Mexican army intended to liberate their property and use freed slaves against them. On October 6 Thomas J. Pilgrim wrote Austin, "Would there not be a great danger from the Negroes should a large Mexican force come so near?"

Events seemed to be tumbling toward one end.

Gonzales, the Alamo, and Goliad

In 1831 the government had given the town of Gonzales a cannon to protect itself against the Native Americans. In September 1835 Colonel Domingo de Ugartechea, who was in charge of troops in San Antonio, decided that the Gonzales cannon was more likely to be used against Mexican troops than against Comanches and sent troops to retrieve it. The alcalde of the town, however, buried it and told the army he had no power to surrender the weapon. He also released messengers into the countryside with calls for aid. On September 29 Mexican troops camped across the Guadalupe River from the town. Three days later, about 160 Texans swarmed across the river and routed the troops. Only one Mexican soldier was killed and no Texans, but war had begun. Texans now had a battle flag: a white banner with a crude drawing of a cannon and the words "Come and Take It."

Conflict in Gonzales and San Antonio (where Mexican forces under General Cos made a humiliating retreat) delayed the Consultation and required that it move from Washington to the safer San Felipe. In the meantime, another attempt at provisional government had failed, and the Consultation became the second attempt to govern Texas without Mexican resources. The Consultation consisted of delegates from the 12 towns in the Brazos and Nacogdoches departments. Even these men could not agree on whether the goal of their struggle was independence or a fight for their rights under the Constitution of 1824. By a vote of 33 to 15 they rejected immediate cessation from Mexico but at the same time issued a document attacking Santa Anna's tyranny, supporting the Constitution of 1824, and offering to aid all Mexicans who would join the Texans' fight.

Unknown to the Texans, however, their fight for the Constitution of 1824 was already lost. On October 3 Santa

Escape from Goliad

J. C. Duval's story reads like an early Texas tall tale, but Duval was at Goliad; some survivors did escape, and Duval did live to write a book. Duval was put into prison with the other captives. One day a Mexican soldier appeared and marched the prisoners in double ranks out to the prairie. About a half a mile outside of town, they stopped, and the army turned and fired on them. Duval was in the second rank and when the man in front of him fell, he was knocked over. He continues the story:

When I rose to my feet, I found that the whole Mexican line had charged over me, and were in hot pursuit of those who had not been shot and who were fleeing towards the river…. I followed on after them, for I knew that escape in any other direction (all open prairie) would be impossible and I had nearly reached the river before it became necessary to make my way through the Mexican line ahead. As I did so, one of the soldiers charged upon me with his bayonet…. As he drew his musket back to make a lunge at me, one of our men coming from another direction, ran between us, and the bayonet was driven into his body. The blow was given with such force, that in falling, the man probably wrenched or twisted the bayonet in such a way as to prevent the Mexican from withdrawing it immediately. I saw him put his foot upon the man, and make an ineffectual attempt to extricate the bayonet from his body, but one look satisfied me, as I was somewhat in a hurry just then, and I hastened to the bank of the river and plunged in. The river at that point was steep and swift, but not wide, and being a good swimmer, I soon gained the opposite bank, untouched by any of the bullets that were pattering in the water around my head. But there I met with an unexpected difficulty. The bank on that side was so steep I found it impossible to climb it, and I continued to swim down the river until I came to where a grape vine hung from the bough of a leaning tree nearly to the surface of the water. This I caught hold of and was climbing up it hand over hand, sailor fashion, when a Mexican on the opposite bank fired at me with his escopeta [sic], and with so true an aim, that he cut the vine in two just above my head, and down I went into the water again. I then swam on about a hundred yards further when I came to a place where the bank was not quite so steep, and with some difficulty I managed to clamber up.

—J.C. Duval, *Early Times in Texas*

Anna forced the Mexican congress to enact the *Siete Leyes*, a series of laws that established an authoritarian central government.

The Consultation also adopted a plan for an army (but, crucially, did not come up with an army or the funds to pay for one), appointed Sam Houston the commander-in-chief, and sent Stephen F. Austin to the United States to solicit support, immediately depriving Texas of the two men best qualified to lead the new provisional government. Instead, Henry Smith, the political chief of the Brazos department and a strong supporter of the war party, was made governor.

In addition, the Consultation came up with a hare-brained scheme to invade Matamoras in the belief that the Mexican people would then rise up against Santa Anna and make common cause with Texas. To his credit, Governor Smith opposed this idea. On January 10, 1836, he sent the council a vitriolic message in which he intemperately outlined the misdeeds of specific members—by name. The council responded in similar language but also declared the governor's office vacant and appointed the lieutenant governor to the position. Smith refused to leave. The provisional government had just about destroyed its own authority, but the council continued its plan to invade the south, and appointed a man named Frank W. Johnson to lead a voluntary expedition. Johnson's army took 400 volunteers, food, medical supplies, and munitions from the garrison in San Antonio. Perhaps these men and supplies would have made a difference in San Antonio later in March. In any event, they did not invade Matamoros; the volunteers wandered the countryside for a while but never made it back to San Antonio.

Santa Anna decided that the Texans were in rebellion and that he should personally lead the army to restore order. In January of 1836 he held a dazzling review of the army in Saltillo, commanding 6,000 men, and then marched to the Rio Grande.

Sam Houston had advised the council against the Matamoros plan and, offended that he had been ignored, took a furlough from the army. He went to eastern Texas and negotiated a treaty with the Cherokees. In February the Cherokees signed an agreement that guaranteed them title to their lands as long as they remained at peace with Texas.

While still in command of the army, Houston had ordered Jim Bowie to go to San Antonio and destroy the fortifications there. Bowie was to take the remaining munitions and supplies to Gonzales. When Bowie arrived at the Alamo mission complex that was used as a fort, he decided to disobey his orders, and he and his 25 men settled in. Meanwhile, Governor Smith, acting on his own, ordered William B. Travis to recruit 100 men and proceed to San Antonio. Travis could not find 100 willing to go to San Antonio but soon showed up with 25. The volunteers under Bowie refused to accept Travis as their commander, so for a while the Alamo had two leaders. Broken by grief over the recent cholera deaths of his wife, their children, and both of his wife's parents, and by the bottle he had turned to for consolation, Bowie gave up any claim to command. Others trickled into the abandoned mission—including James Bonham, an Alabama lawyer and Travis' life-long friend, and David Crockett, a former congressman from Tennessee.

As a siege fortification, the Alamo had thick, high walls, ready water, and plenty of room for storing supplies. Unfortunately, the defenders had very few of these supplies. The building had its drawbacks too: The grounds were so large that many more men would have been required to defend it adequately, and an uncompleted section of wall was a mere pile of rubble and stones. Recent research has also shown that one completed wall was so deep that the defenders could not shoot over it without exposing themselves to return fire.

On February 16 Santa Anna's army crossed the Rio Grande and headed for San Antonio, despite the pleas of other Mexican generals that he relieve San Felipe. The first troops reached San Antonio on February 23; Travis had not expected them for at least another month. Travis sent a request for help to Gonzales and two days later sent Juan Seguin to the same place with another request. On March 1, 32 men (some say 31, others 33) from Gonzales slipped through Mexican lines and into the Alamo.

On March 3 Travis sent out John W. Smith with several messages, including one to the convention he thought would be convening at Washington-on-the-Brazos. That same day, Bonham, Travis' messenger to the forces of James Fannin,

Who Died at the Battle of the Alamo?

Ever since the gun smoke cleared from the cottonwoods on the banks of the San Antonio River, Texans have agreed that the Alamo defenders died heroically. In the 1970s, however, doubt was cast on the deaths of some—especially on that of David Crockett. In 1975 Texas A&M Press published *With Santa Anna in Texas: A Personal Narrative of the Revolution* by José Enrique de la Pena, a Mexican officer who was at the battle. These memoirs, supposedly written in 1836, describe seven survivors being brought before Santa Anna and immediately executed. Crockett was the only one of the seven de la Pena named: "Though tortured before they were killed, these unfortunates died without complaining and without humiliating themselves before their torturers."

Apparently Texans of the republic period always acknowledged that some of the defenders did not die immediately and were executed later, but Crockett was usually not among them. Some observers have declared the memoirs a hoax; others have cast doubt on whether de la Pena would have recognized Crockett's body. Perhaps he just picked a name he thought would be recognized. No evidence indicates that any of the Mexican military would have recognized the men they had just killed. In fact, after the battle, Santa Anna called in the alcalde (mayor) of San Antonio to identify the bodies.

Other Mexican contemporaries, including Ramon Martinez Caro, who had been Santa Anna's personal secretary, mentioned an execution after the battle but did not name Crockett: "Among the 183 killed there were five who were discovered by General Castrillon hiding after the assault. He took them immediately to the presence of His Excellency....When he presented the prisoners he was severely reprimanded for not having killed them on the spot, upon which he [Santa Anna] turned his back upon Castrillon while the soldiers stepped out of their ranks and set upon the prisoners until they were all killed." This account was published a year after the battle.

Several U.S. newspaper stories of the time named one or more of the well-known prisoners as among those executed but offered no evidence. On March 29, 1836, *The New Orleans True American* said that after daylight seven of the defenders, including Crockett and Bonham, were still alive. They "cried for quarter but were told there was no mercy for them. They then continued fighting until the whole were butchered." The accuracy of this account is dubious, however.

The only compelling contemporary evidence that Crockett may have survived the initial assault was found in a July 19, 1836 letter from George M. Dolson, a Texas army officer. On July 18, Dolson said he had been translating for Colonel James Morgan and Colonel Juan Alamonte, Santa Anna's aide and a prisoner of war on Galveston Island. According to Dolson, Alamonte said that Crockett (whom he knew) had been among six battle survivors. He said that when Castrillon presented the prisoners to Santa Anna, the general ordered them shot. This tale would appear to be strong corroboration of the de la Pena story, except that Alamonte's diary did not mention this episode.

In 1904 William P. Zuber, a veteran of the Texas army, said that during interrogations some Texans would repeat rumors to Mexican prisoners and ask them if they had heard whether such things had happened: "Many of them, to seem intelligent, confirmed them, answering in effect, 'Yes, that is true. I saw it.' These yarns spread from mouth to ear, as facts, among the prisoners, and even some of the [Mexican] generals utilized them in modified form." In this way some Alamo legends may have entered general knowledge.

Santa Anna himself sent a dispatch to Mexico City in which he said, "The fortress at last fell into our power with its artillery, ammunition, etc., and buried among the ditches and trenches are more than 600 bodies, all of them foreigners [this figure is a gross exaggeration; there were fewer than 200 defenders].... Among the dead were the first and second in command of the enemy, the so-called colonels Bowie and Travis, Crockett of equal rank and all the other leaders and officers." Santa Anna does not seem like the kind of man who would have shied from telling that he had ordered an execution.

So when exactly did Crockett die? It seems fair to say that the case can not be made for either argument. In the end the exact time of his death probably does not matter. Even if you accept de la Pena's account, Crockett's death is still described as brave: "These unfortunates died without complaining and without humiliating themselves."

"San Antonio De Bexar, with the Alamo, where the lamented Crocket fell." Circa January 1857. Courtesy Center for American History, UT-Austin

crept back through the Mexican lines to rejoin the defenders. He brought the news that Fannin refused to come to their aid. The next day Santa Anna moved his cannon closer to the building and the shelling increased. Just before dawn on March 6, 1836, the Mexican army stormed the building. When the third attack came at daybreak, a Mexican general seized the Texans' big guns and turned them on the interior. Shots flew every which way, felling Mexicans with Mexican bullets, Texans by Texan.

The fighting lasted for almost an hour more. The barbarity and fierceness of the slaughter dismayed even the victors. The next day they gathered wood and built a pyre for the defenders' bodies. The Mexican dead (estimates vary from 600 to 1,600) were buried in the cemetery or thrown into the river. Some defenders did survive: Santa Anna released some Mexican women and children who had been in the chapel along with Mrs. Susanna Dickinson, the widow of a Texas officer, and her fourteen-month-old daughter. A slave also survived, but accounts differ on whether he was Travis's slave or one of Mrs. Dickinson's.

The Alamo today. © Rebecca Conners

The bravery of the defenders—and of the attackers (who after all had to scale the walls in the face of withering fire)—cannot be questioned. What can be debated is the need for this battle in the first place. If Santa Anna had ignored the garrison and headed straight for the eastern settlements, he could have hit before the Texans had even begun to prepare for him. Certainly the band of fewer than 200 behind his lines in San Antonio would have had little effect on his army of thousands. Also, if he had bypassed the Alamo, he would have had many more supplies and living soldiers when the telling battles came. In any case, it seems Santa Anna was acting out of pride and revenge. San Antonio had humiliated Cos's Mexican army in the winter and in the spring Santa Anna destroyed San Antonio.

The Texans also could have ignored San Antonio. If Bowie had followed orders, the building would have been destroyed and its munitions and supplies used in Gonzales or Goliad or other, possibly more defensible, places. What the defenders did accomplish was the creation of a uniting myth and a battle cry.

The battle at Goliad followed the fall of the Alamo. Travis had sent messages to James Fannin, the commander of the forces there, offering, some say, to relinquish his position as leader of the Alamo forces if Fannin would only bring his 400 troops as relief. For whatever reason, Fannin stayed in Goliad. On March 14 Houston ordered Fannin to leave for Victoria, but the indecisive commander waited for the return of two bands of troops, neither of which ever came. On March 18 General José Urrea reached Goliad and the next day Fannin began his belated retreat.

In the mid-afternoon of the first day of retreat, an ammunition wagon broke down and Fannin ordered his forces to camp in the open prairie. Officers under Fannin argued over his decision, since only two or three miles away was a forest with cover and the water of Coleto Creek. But Fannin insisted they could not abandon the wagon and its contents. Urrea's troops soon surrounded them. The next morning more Mexican troops arrived with cannon. Fannin surrendered. His troops, 400 men more or less, were marched back to Goliad and confined to small hot rooms with little food or water. General Urrea protested, but on Palm Sunday the Goliad survivors were taken to the prairie and shot, their bodies stripped of clothes, stacked, and burned. Some doctors, nurses and valued craftsmen were spared and some soldiers managed to escape.

THE RUNAWAY SCRAPE, RETREAT, AND VICTORY

The victors' brutality at the Alamo and Goliad spread panic. Soldiers deserted their comrades, rushed home, and tried to sweep their families and belongings to safety. Civilians and soldiers choked roads and bridges as people fled in terror from Santa Anna's forces in the episode called the Runaway Scrape. Heavy rains had turned the roads to mud and made rivers and streams impassable. Soldiers did not always make it home to help their families load their few belongings on wagons or horses to head east. "Women led donkeys packed with a few household treasures, and her [sic] more precious treasures, her children," wrote Angelina Peyton, a widow who observed her neighbors' rush to leave.

All that stood between the Texans and Santa Anna was Sam Houston, who had rejoined his troops. Houston's original army of 1,400 now numbered 900 after the clutch of desertions. His forces must have seemed a meager defense, especially since Houston continued to retreat. His men muttered darkly of mutiny as he marched them farther east.

But Houston used the retreat to organize his troops and develop his strategy. Finally, the army camped on the banks of the San Jacinto River and waited for Santa Anna. Houston may have made up his strategy as he went along, but the core of it was to move steadily east, closer to possible supply sources and the remote chance of rescue by the U.S. army. Also, the farther east he lead Santa Anna, the farther the Mexican army was from its supply lines. All Houston had to do was wait for Santa Anna to make a mistake. Eventually, he did.

Houston's army was poorly equipped. They had no tents and only two wagons with two teams of oxen, but Houston did have a secret weapon. In contrast to the imported volunteers under Fannin, Travis, and Crockett, Houston's army was made up mostly of settlers who had a stake in protecting the countryside. They also had two cannon, called the twin sisters, a gift from the people of Cincinnati. When

Santa Anna tested Houston's forces on April 20, the cannon repelled his infantry. The Mexican forces fell back to camp and prepared for a final assault the next day.

Inexplicably, the more numerous Mexican forces did not attack first thing on April 21. They may have been waiting for more reinforcements or letting General Cos's newly arrived troops rest for the coming battle. In any case, Santa Anna dawdled in camp and when spies reported to Houston that the enemy had stacked their guns for siesta he knew the time had come. At 3:30 in the afternoon, he ordered his troops to advance quietly. By 4:00 they were in place and soon the 900 Texas troops attacked an estimated 1,300 to 1,500 Mexicans. The battle was over in less than half an hour. Yelling "Remember the Alamo, Remember Goliad," the outnumbered Texans threw themselves on the Mexican army and gave no mercy. According to Houston, eight Texans were killed while 630 Mexicans died and 730 were taken prisoner, among them Santa Anna and General Cos.

Apparently, not everyone was pleased. Peggy McCormick owned the land where the battle took place. She demanded that the bodies be removed immediately and Houston replied, according to legend, "Madam, your land will be famed in history as the classic spot upon which the glorious victory of San Jacinto was gained!" To this Mrs. McCormick replied, "To the devil with your glorious history." She and her two sons buried the bodies themselves.

The captured Santa Anna issued orders to his field generals to withdraw their troops south of the Rio Grande. He signed two treaties with the Texans: a public one to end hostilities and a secret one to grant Texas independence. On April 26 Houston wrote, "To the Troops and the People of the East: Tell our friends all the news, and that we have beaten the enemy…tell them to come on and let the people plant corn."

Corn planting was still not uppermost on Texans' minds. The revolutionary fight might have been ending, but building a functioning state created a lot of questions. Could the revolutionary generation become satisfactory leaders of a state at peace? Could they reconcile the controversies that had torn the province apart? Why had the Texans found it impossible to live peaceably as part of Mexico?

Some questions still remain. Was the Texas Revolution a slaveholder's conspiracy to bring Texas into the Union as a slave state? In the United States, anti-slavery forces certainly had their suspicions. The desire to keep slaves and add to them fired the passions of many Texans, but slavery was not the only cause of the revolution.

Cultural and ethnic differences are frequently offered as an explanation for the Texans' inability to fit in with Mexico. Religion, language, and experience with government certainly differed between white and Hispanic Texans of the period, but the differences can be exaggerated. The two groups intermarried and formed business partnerships and lasting friendships. Moreover, the rebels included many Hispanics. Juan Seguín, Lorenzo de Zavala, and others fought, first, to establish the Constitution of 1824 in Texas and, second, for Texas independence.

One difference crossed ethnic lines but had ethnic shadings. More whites than Hispanics had some investment in opposing a centralized government, but many Hispanics shared this view, especially in Texas. The extreme disappointment when Santa Anna revealed himself to be a dictator fed into the revolutionary fervor of all.

Many contemporaries attributed the revolution to land speculation. To them, people with connections to important office holders corruptly enriched themselves by buying large tracts of land and would stop at nothing—not even war—to hold onto their ill-gotten gains. Desire to hold onto land led to intrigues within the Mexican government and counter-intrigues among the white Texans.

Freemasonry has been labeled as another factor. While 1 to 2 percent of the Texas population were Masons, Masons made up 30 percent or more of those making important decisions. The interim president David G. Burnet, his vice president Zavala, the three presidents of the republic, and their vice presidents, cabinet members, and other officeholders were all Masons. Most likely, however, Freemasonry was only a means for bringing men together, rather than the stuff of conspiracies.

The unpredictability and instability of the Mexican government did its part to lead to a lack of faith in the state and its ability to perform its needed functions. Much of this instability was the result of Santa Anna's pursuit of power. Instability also weakened the Mexican government and made it easier to think about leaving.

Even though the idea of manifest destiny did not form in the United States as a whole until 1845, wisps of this idea were already forming in Texas. The idea of a Texas reaching to the Pacific was intriguing. Many believed the will of God required Protestant English speakers to take over the west from Roman Catholic Spanish speakers.

Probably pieces of all these controversies played a part in the opening days of war. But after the shooting started, the war developed its own momentum.

Must-See Sites

Rattlesnake Races and Early Irish Settlements

Visitors flock to Refugio and San Patricio counties for their beaches, bird watching, fishing, and other recreational opportunities at sites such as the Guadelupe Delta Wildlife Management Area. Frequently they are unaware of the early Irish settlements. Only one house built by an original Irish colonial family, the O'Brien Ranch House, still stands. In 1901 a new church replaced the last mission founded by the Spanish. Every St. Patrick's Day, San Patricio holds the World Championship Rattlesnake Races to honor the saint's driving of all the snakes from Ireland. You can bring your own snake or rent one, but only rattlers are allowed.

The Alamo

Considered the "Cradle of Texas Liberty," the Alamo is a major tourist attraction in Texas. Officially named Mission San Antonio de Valero, the name "Alamo" comes either from the cottonwood trees that grew along the San Antonio River (*alamo* means cottonwood in Spanish) or from the names of a Spanish cavalry company that occupied the building in the early 19th century—the Flying Company of San Carlos de Parras del Alamo. The familiar small building was once the chapel of the mission, which was much larger when the battle occurred. In the immediate area of the battle site are many other attractions: an IMAX theater that shows *Alamo: The Price of Freedom*, the Institute of Texan Cultures and the Instituto Cultural Mexicano, King William Historical District, La Villita Historical District, and the meandering River Walk.

FROM INDEPENDENT NATION
TO PART OF THE UNION

While free of Mexican political control since the early 19th century, Texas has never escaped the effects of Spanish and Mexican culture and mores. From its water law to the names of major cities and landmarks, Texas continues to display its Hispanic heritage.

From the Rio Grande to Amarillo, El Paso to the Sabine River, the land is marked by Spanish place names. Of the 254 counties today, 42 have names derived in some way from Spanish (some are misspellings, like Uvalde which should be Ugalde, and some Anglicizations, like Galveston).

The practices of ranching, the economic bedrock of Texas until the discovery of oil, were borrowed completely from Spanish culture. From keeping brand books to wearing chaps, the cowboy and the rancher took liberally from Spanish custom and law. The Spanish also brought their irrigation methods, European crops, and farming techniques to Texas. Spanish and later Mexican influences undergird much of Texas government and day-to-day laws regarding families, water use, and land ownership.

Many of the Texas rebels were men of Spanish heritage—including the famous Juan Seguín, José Antonio Navarro, and Lorenzo de Zavala. Not long after the revolution, however, whites began to turn on anyone with a Spanish surname. Even family members of the empresario de León were driven from their homes. In 1839 Texas whites forced more than a hundred families from their homes and farms in old Nacogdoches. In his memoirs, Seguín (who had been Travis's messenger to Fannin, a hero of San Jacinto, and, as mayor of San Antonio, the man in charge of seeing that the remains of the Alamo heroes were properly buried) wrote, "At every hour of the day and night, my countrymen ran to me for protection against the assaults or exactions [sic] of these adventurers. Some times by persuasion, I prevailed on them to desist; some times also, force had to be resorted to. How could I have done otherwise?" In 1842 threats of assassination, accusations of betrayal, and arguments with white squatters on city land finally drove Seguin and his family from San Antonio to live in Mexico.

While sheer antagonism and war memories contributed to these hostile feelings, desire to appropriate Hispanic-owned lands also played a part. Those who lusted after these lands frequently had not fought for independence but appeared immediately after. The *Telegraph and Texas Register* reported in 1837 that "crowds of enterprising emigrants are arriving on every vessel." In the summer of 1838, 6,000 were supposed to have crossed the Sabine River at one ferry crossing. In 1836 the white population had reached an estimated 34,470, growing to 102,961 by 1847. Most were attracted by the call of cheap—or even free—land.

SAM HOUSTON'S FIRST ADMINISTRATION

The dominating personality for all white settlers during the republic was Sam Houston. With no established political parties, the people divided themselves into Houstonian and anti-Houstonian factions. Houston believed that the goal of the revolution had been joining Texas to the United States. For ten years, however, the new nation and the slightly older nation could not agree on terms for merger.

One immovable roadblock to statehood was John Quincy Adams, former president and now a member of Congress and an implacable foe of admitting Texas to the Union. While president in the 1820s, Adams argued that the boundary of the Louisiana Purchase extended to the Rio Grande and, so, included Texas. By the time he was a former president sitting in the House of Representatives, however, he believed that the admission of Texas was part of a slaveowners' plot to control the U.S. Senate and, thus, the government. Andrew Jackson, president at the time of Texas independence, did not want to squander his political resources by fighting Adams on the issue. His successor, Martin Van Buren, also passed on statehood. Texas had to shape the institutions and policies of an independent country whether it wanted to or not.

To bring stability to the new nation, interim president David Burnet called an early election—September instead of the December date the convention had set. The first to announce his candidacy was Henry Smith, the bad-tempered former head of the provisional government. Influential citizens convinced Stephen F. Austin to run. Austin, however, had lost favor with the populace (he had initially opposed independence and held other unpopular opinions). Eleven days before the election, the people's choice announced his candidacy: Sam Houston won with 5,119 votes out of the 6,640 cast. In the same election, voters widely favored annexation to the United States.

Houston made Austin secretary of state and Smith secretary of the treasury, though Austin died two months after taking office. Houston faced more pressing problems than bringing his opponents into the government. The army was out of control. Mercenaries and others intent on making quick fortunes flocked to Texas to sign up with the army under the promise of land for service even though the war was over. Since the sale of public land was the main income for Texas, giving away land cut into available funds, leaving Treasury Secretary Smith, for example, with no stationery and no money to buy any, and the army without needed supplies.

To rein in the army and reduce it to a manageable size, Houston appointed as commander-in-chief Albert Sidney Johnston, a West Point graduate and a capable army officer. The soldiers, however, objected and insisted that the temporary commander Felix Huston stay in the post. Huston was a soldier of fortune who, in good Southern tradition, immediately challenged Johnston to a duel to decide who would be commander. Johnston was wounded and Huston retained the post (although he later resigned in favor of Johnston). To Sam Houston the only recourse was disbanding most of the army; he furloughed all but 600 men.

Army reductions, however, left Texans feeling vulnerable to attack by Native Americans. Drawing on his understanding and tolerance of the Cherokees, Houston had negotiated a treaty during the revolution that promised the Cherokees title to land they occupied if they remained neutral. When peace returned, however, the Senate refused to ratify the treaty. In the summer of 1838, Vincente Cordova, a Mexican citizen, led between 400 and 600 Mexicans and Native Americans onto an island in the Angelina River. From there they declared they owed no allegiance to the new nation of Texas. Thomas Rusk, a San Jacinto hero, and his men chased the rebels from the encampment. While Cordova made it to Mexico and most of those arrested went free, this incident increased settler intolerance of Native Americans. Sam Houston observed, "If I could build a wall from the Red River to the Rio Grande, so high that no Indian could scale it, the white people would go crazy trying to devise a means to get beyond it."

Houston considered the vote for annexation a mandate and he worked hard to bring Texas into the Union. He went so far as to send Santa Anna, still a prisoner, to Washington, D.C., to plead the Texas case. President Jackson ignored the messenger and sent him home to Veracruz on a U.S. naval ship. Jackson had hinted to a Texas emissary that he would recognize an independent Texas if the U.S. Senate recommended the step to him. After heavy lobbying, the senate appropriated money for a diplomat to Texas. In his last presidential act, Jackson appointed a Texas charge d'affaires. The Texans pressed for annexation, but the United States again refused. Houston now opened diplomatic relations with England and France. Texas was acting like an independent nation.

Mirabeau B. Lamar's Presidency

The constitution did not allow Houston to succeed himself and the Houston party looked for someone to run against Mirabeau Buonaparte Lamar, the vice-president and certain anti-Houstonian candidate. When approached, Thomas J. Rusk refused and the Houstonians turned next to Peter W. Grayson, the attorney general, who agreed to run. While on official business in Washington, D.C., however, Grayson committed suicide. James Collinsworth, hero of San Jacinto and chief justice of the supreme court, was the next choice. He agreed to run, but in July 1838 he jumped from a boat in Galveston Bay, another in the string of suicides that haunted early Texas. Just a few weeks before the election, the Houston party agreed on Robert Wilson of Harrisburg, but by then Lamar's election was a sure thing.

Lamar's administration is notable for his support of public education and of the Homestead Exemption Law, a law forbidding seizure of some property to repay debt. Lamar also convinced the legislature to move the capital from Houston (legend says that Lamar could not stand living in a town named for his arch-rival) to a site on the Colorado River near the hamlet of Waterloo. The town's name was changed to Austin and the government moved in October 1839. By the turn of the year the population had passed 800.

Lamar is probably best known, however, for his abrupt change in the Texas policy toward Native Americans. While Houston sought to make treaties and set aside areas where the Native Americans could live their lives without contact with European settlers, Lamar insisted Native Americans conform to Texas laws, leave the nation, or die.

The Cherokees felt the first blows even before Lamar took office. When Houston was out of Texas in July 1839, the Cherokees were defeated at the Battle of Neches, near Tyler, and Chief Bowles, a friend of Houston's, was shot, scalped, and skinned by Texan forces. The surviving Cherokees moved across the Red River into Indian Territory. Other Native Americans in east Texas, such as the Shawnee, saw the future and followed the Cherokees into present-day Oklahoma.

Several battles with the Comanches followed until, in March 1840, the Comanches and the Texans met in San Antonio to discuss peace. Terms for this council included release of all Comanche captives, but the Comanches showed up with only one 16-year-old white girl and some Hispanic children. The Texas representatives demanded that more captives be let go. Soldiers entered the Council House to seize the Native Americans and hold them for exchange with the white captives. Some Comanches managed to escape but most of them in the Council House were killed. Of the 27 Comanches captured, one woman was released to carry back the demand that white captives be exchanged for the prisoners. Many Comanche leaders responded by killing their captives. Meanwhile, most of the Comanche captives escaped.

The Council House Fight hardened the Comanche belief that the Texans could not be trusted, stepped up white dislike of Native Americans, and increased Native American raids into settled portions of the republic. Certainly, by increasing distrust on both sides, the episode only fed the violence.

A Red River Plantation

Frederick Law Olmstead was a landscape artist, engineer, and early urban planner (he designed Central Park in New York City) who described Texas from the viewpoint of someone opposed to slavery. He and his companions on his 1857 Texas trip started out from Natchitoches in Louisiana and followed the Old San Antonio Road. Here he describes the first habitation they came to in Texas:

We rode on from ten o'clock until three, without seeing a house, except a deserted cabin, or meeting a human being. We then came upon a ferry across a small stream or "bayou" near which was a collection of cabins. We asked the old negro who tended the ferry if we could get something to eat anywhere in the neighborhood. He replied that his master sometimes took in travelers, and we had better call and try if the mistress wouldn't let us have some dinner.

The house was a small log cabin, with a broad open shed or piazza in front, and a chimney made of sticks and mud leaning against one end. A smaller detached cabin, twenty feet in the rear was used as a kitchen. A cistern under a roof, and collecting water from three roofs, stood between. The water from the bayou was not fit to drink, nor is the water of the Red river, or of any springs in this region. The people depend entirely on cisterns for drinking water. It's very little white folks need, however—milk, claret, and whiskey being the more common beverages.

About the house was a large yard, in which were two or three China trees, and two splendid evergreen Cherokee roses; half a dozen hounds; several negro babies; turkeys and chickens, and a pet sow, teaching a fine litter of pigs how to root and wallow. Three hundred yards from the house was a gin-house and stable, and in the interval between were two rows of comfortable negro cabins. Between the house and the cabins was a large post, on which was a bell to call the negroes. A rack for fastening horses stood near it. On the bell-post and on each of the rack-posts were nailed the antlers of a buck, as well as on a large oak-tree near by. On the logs of the kitchen a fresh deer-skin was drying. On the railing of the piazza lay a Mexican saddle with immense wooden stirrups. The house had but one door and no window, nor was there a pane of glass on the plantation.

Entering the house, we found it to contain but a single room, about twenty feet by sixteen. Of this space one quarter was occupied by a bed—a great four-poster, with the curtains open, made up in the French style, with a strong furniture-calico day-coverlid. A smaller camp bed stood beside it. These two articles of furniture nearly filled the house on one side the door. At the other end was a great log fire-place, with a fine fire. The outer door was left constantly open to admit the light. On one side the fire, next the door, was a table; a kind of dresser, with crockery, and a bureau stood on the other side, and there were two deer-skin seated chairs and one (Connecticut made) rocking-chair...

Several memorable battles between Comanches and Texans followed the Council House Fight. On August 6, 1840, around 1,000 Comanches raided Victoria and captured 1,500 horses but were unable to enter the town. The next day they headed south and on August 8 surprised the residents of Linnville, a port with many stuffed warehouses on Lavaca Bay (near today's Port Lavaca). Most of the townspeople saved themselves by rushing out into the bay in small boats, from which they watched the Comanches destroy their village. Only one building was left standing. The raiders loaded their booty onto pack mules and headed north.

On August 12, the Comanches' trek back to the plains was halted by Texas forces from Victoria, Linnville, and other Gulf settlements. At the Battle of Plum Creek, almost 100 Comanches were killed, but the survivors escaped with most of the plunder. The Comanches tried to kill their captives, but at least one lived. Juliet Watts' life was saved when her corset stays stopped an arrow. She subsequently returned to Lavaca Bay and opened the first hotel in the new town of Port Lavaca.

Lamar's Expansionist Policy

President Lamar believed he needed to quell Native American attacks so Texans could move west. Not as committed to annexation as Houston, Lamar harbored dreams of an imperial Texas reaching to the Pacific Ocean. Declaring independence, the leaders of the republic had not confined themselves to the territory of the old Spanish and Mexican province of Texas. Instead, they insisted that the Rio Grande was both the southern and western boundary and that the new country extended north into what is now Wyoming. This purported boundary put within Texas the town of Santa Fe, still part of Mexico. Lamar saw control of Santa Fe, with its power over the Santa Fe Trail, as a hope for establishing Texas's claims to the west, improving trade, and bringing prosperity to the new nation.

Three times Texas tried to exert its power over Santa Fe and each attempt failed. Congress refused to fund the most famous of these projects. On his own, President Lamar commissioned an expedition to establish a trade route to Santa Fe and to offer the people of that town the opportunity to join Texas.

The band of 321 adventurers set out from Kenney's Fort, north of Austin, on June 19, 1841. The party was made up mostly of traders in 21 oxen-drawn wagons filled with supplies and trade items. Military escort included five infantry companies and one artillery company.

George Wilkins Kendall, editor of the New Orleans *Picayune* and future Texas sheep rancher, was part of the expedition and left a chronicle of the miserable journey. June was the wrong time of year to cross west Texas and heat and hunger plagued the men. Comanches and hostile Mexican forces dogged their trail. They mistook the Wichita River for the Red River and followed it until they realized their mistake. Somewhere in today's Motley County, on Quitaque Creek, the party split up. The more mobile mounted men rode out to find a route to Santa Fe, while the main part of the expedition waited with the supply wagons.

Both the expedition members and President Lamar assumed that the people of Santa Fe were eager to join up with Texas. They were wrong. As the exhausted travelers straggled into Santa Fe and the eastern towns of New Mexico, they were greeted by the Mexican military and immediately arrested. After being marched to Mexico City, they were parceled out among several prisons. Most of the survivors were eventually released in April 1842.

Texas could not control other areas that it claimed. The area between the Nueces River and the Rio Grande, called the Nueces Strip, became a new Neutral Ground that neither the Texan nor the Mexican governments could control. Bandits murdered anyone stupid enough to wander alone out of the populated areas and the Mexicans called it Desierto Muerto—the desert of death.

REGULATOR–MODERATOR WAR

From 1839 to 1844 outright warfare raged between two factions in present-day Henderson and Shelby counties within the original Neutral Ground. The fight began between Sheriff Alfred George and a man named Joseph Goodbread. Some sources say the disagreement was over the sale of a slave. The sheriff called on Charles W. Jackson, a fugitive from Louisiana law, to assist him and Jackson shot Goodbread. Two factions emerged from this murder: The Regulators sided with Sheriff George and Jackson and said they were organizing to put down cattle rustling. The Moderators opposed the Regulators, who they claimed were using a battle against cattle rustling as a cover for their own crimes.

The story of the Moderators and the Regulators is incredibly complicated, involving judges who were members of one group or the other, gangs of gunmen intimidating juries, the burning of homes and barns, accusations of hog theft, and lots of murders and hangings. At one point Sam Houston said that Shelby County and the surrounding area should be declared "free and independent governments…let them fight it out."

The Regulators and Moderators finally disbanded when both sides joined Capt. L. H. Mabbitt's company to fight in the Mexican War. The Texas authorities were delighted with this solution, but General Zachary Taylor was furious at being stuck with such uncontrollable "soldiers."

HOUSTON RECLAIMS THE PRESIDENCY

Lamar's term ended in 1841 and Houston ran for re-election. The Lamar forces chose David Burnet. While the election could have focused on such issues as Native American policy, financing of the government, and land distribution, instead it focused on rumor, name calling, and gossip. Houston won handily with 7,915 votes to Burnet's 3,616.

Lamar's administration was expensive, spending $5 million in three years. Houston's first term had cost about $500,000 and he now set out to restore frugality to government. One failed attempt to save money involved selling the Texas navy—all four ships. Somehow, the citizens of Galveston heard of the secret plan, which threatened a major source of town livelihood, and they rose up against the auction. Houston relented and Texas kept its navy until it joined the Union.

A series of treaties with the Native Americans was more successful in saving money by allowing for smaller military expenditures. In 1843 the Waco and Tawakoni tribes signed a treaty at Bird's Fort. In the next year, Houston and Chief Buffalo Hump of the Penateka Comanches signed the Treaty of Tehuacana Creek. While peace seemed ready to descend on the western frontier, the southern borders continued to be a scene of discord.

CONTINUED CONFLICT WITH MEXICO

In 1842 Santa Anna, again ruler of Mexico, sent a small army into Texas. The Mexicans attacked and captured San Antonio, Goliad, and Refugio but retreated after occupying these towns for about a day. Texans were outraged and demanded that Houston send forces into Mexico. But when the legislature appropriated land to pay for an army, the president vetoed the bill as inadequate. Meanwhile another, larger Mexican army took San Antonio again and held it for nine days. When the Mexican army finally retreated, they took several prisoners, including the entire jury of a district court, the judge, and attorneys.

Even the frugal Houston had to respond to this provocation and he sent General Alexander Somerville and about 750 men south to make sure the Mexican army had indeed left Texas. They reached Laredo in a month and found no Mexican army, so Somerville and his men crossed the Rio Grande looking for a fight. When they didn't find one, Somerville ordered his men to return to Gonzales. About 300 of the volunteers refused to return and organized themselves under the command of Colonel W.S. Fisher. On Christmas Day they crossed the Rio Grande and occupied the village of Mier.

Suddenly, the Mexican army re-appeared and an intense battle followed. On the day after Christmas, Fisher and his forces surrendered. They were marched to Mexico City where Santa Anna ordered their execution. Officers in charge of the captives refused to carry out these orders. Santa Anna changed his demand to the execution of one-tenth of the men with the losers chosen by draw. A large pot of uncooked beans was put in front of the men, and each one who drew a black bean was slated for execution. The survivors joined the captives of Santa Fe and San Antonio in the prisons of Castle Perote and languished there until British and U.S. pressure and the overthrow of Santa Anna resulted in their release.

Both the Santa Fe and Mier expeditions re-awakened U.S. interest in Texas. Once again, Houston brought up annexation. A new president, John Tyler, was willing to consider the issue. Houston had two conditions for negotiations: The United States had to protect the Texas-Mexico border and the negotiations had to be secret. The United States sent ships to the Gulf and army troops to its borders with Texas.

ANNEXATION AND THE MEXICAN WAR

In June 1844 the U.S. Senate again rejected Texas annexation. Most of the opposition came from antislavery forces. Annexation became an issue in the 1844 U.S. presidential election in which James K. Polk, a supporter, was the Democratic nominee. The party platform proposed a compromise that would allow Texas to enter the Union as a slave state while admitting Oregon as a free state. Polk was elected and in February 1845 the congress approved annexation.

Texas kept its public lands but had to meet its public debts. The United States agreed to negotiate with Mexico to make the Rio Grande the Texas-Mexico border. All of Texas's forts, customs houses, and similar public properties were ceded to the federal government. The 1845 Constitution allowed married women to own property in their own right and increased the homestead exemption.

The state constitution solidified Texans' Jacksonian distrust of banks by prohibiting the chartering of banks, a provision that retarded economic development. Commercial and industrial development were impossible without dependable sources of financing. Before the Civil War, the state had only one chartered bank, a Galveston institution incorporated during Mexican rule. The lack of banks also made money scarce. Old U.S. money circulated, but most people depended on promissory notes, defaced Spanish and Mexican coins, and barter to fill their needs for exchange.

When the U.S. Congress accepted the state constitution on December 29, 1845, Texas became the 28th state. War with Mexico was now inescapable.

General Zachary Taylor and his troops had been stationed on the Nueces River before annexation. Immediately after formal annexation, he moved across that river and toward the Rio Grande. Mexico demanded that the army return to north of the Nueces. Taylor refused, and, on April 24, 1846, war was official. To many Americans, the Mexican War was unneeded and unwanted; Whigs, abolitionists, and New Englanders, especially, saw no need to spill American blood in order to acquire yet another slave state. Texans embraced the conflict enthusiastically: 5,000 to 7,000 Texans joined up.

Most of the war took place south of the Rio Grande. Militarily, this conflict seems like a dress rehearsal for the larger conflict of the next decade. New tactics and logistical methods were tried and a cadre of officers faced actual battle experience that prepared them for the Civil War. Ulysses S. Grant, Robert E. Lee, and other future Civil War leaders honed their battle skills in the Mexican War.

The renown of other fighting men also began in the Mexican War. Colonel Jack Hays commanded the First Regiment, Texas Mounted Volunteers. This very irregular band of fighters included such men as John S. ("Rip") Ford, Ben McCulloch, and Sam H. Walker and came to be called the Texas Rangers. Using unconventional fighting methods, they scouted efficiently and kept supply lines open. The popular press made them subjects of national fascination.

When General Winfield Scott captured Mexico City in March 1847, the war ended. But the Treaty of Guadalupe

Hidalgo, accepting the Rio Grande as the boundary between Texas and Mexico, was not signed until February 2, 1848. The United States assumed most debts Mexico owed to U.S. citizens, and Mexico ceded New Mexico and California to the United States.

CONFLICT OVER NEW MEXICO

But remember: Texas also claimed New Mexico. Having cleared up its border dispute with Mexico, Texas now faced a similar fight with the U.S. government, which had established a territorial government in New Mexico.

Anti-slavery forces strongly opposed Texas's claims to New Mexico. The inhabitants of the Santa Fe region were no happier with the idea of becoming Texans in 1848 than they had been in 1841, when they arrested President Lamar's expedition. On March 15, 1848, the new state government of Texas created a county—Santa Fe County—that included most of what is now eastern New Mexico. But when they sent out a county judge, a federal official escorted him back to Texas.

Mass meetings in Texas demanded a military response. Texas, only recently a state and the cause of a major U.S. war, was now threatening to secede from the Union. The state legislature met on August 12, 1850, to discuss military and other responses to the denial of the U.S. territorial claim. President Millard Fillmore announced that if Texas invaded New Mexico, federal troops stationed there would respond.

Sam Houston thought the United States had no business unilaterally deciding on the boundary between Texas and New Mexico, but he was not one to call for secession: "Think you, sir, that after the difficulties they have encountered to get into the Union, that you can whip them out of it? No sir. New Mexico can not whip them out of it, even with the aid of United States troops. No, sir!— no, sir! We shed our blood to get into it, and we have now no arms to turn against it. But we have not looked for aggression upon us from the Union."

The Compromise of 1850 offered a trade-off. In exchange for $10 million, Texas renounced all claims to New Mexico and was to use the money to pay off the republic's considerable debt.

PEOPLING THE NEW STATE

With the end of the Mexican War, settlers poured into Texas looking for cheap land. Between the beginning of the republic and the beginning of the Civil War—15 years— Texas population increased by more than 17 times, from 35,000 in 1836 to 604,000 in 1860.

White settlement into Texas followed certain patterns. Draw a line from Texarkana to Waco: People to the south and east of this line tended to come from the lower slave-owning south, while those to the north and west came from parts of the United States where slavery was not as strong—the old midwest and the upper south. The mix of attitudes made parts of Texas especially violent both before and after the war, and was further stirred by the addition of European migrants with little knowledge of how slavery worked and who were sometimes ideologically opposed to the "peculiar institution." In the far south, Texas antagonism toward Hispanic Texans led to a more or less constant state of siege and bad feeling often erupting into full-scale fighting.

WHITE–HISPANIC VIOLENCE

Hispanic Texans living in the Lower Rio Grande Valley found their ability to do business, to protect their land titles, and just to live as they pleased challenged by an influx of whites. In 1847 a court ruled against Hispanic land claimants and in favor of whites who had land certificates from the Republic of Texas. Another court, however, ruled in favor of Hispanic claimants. Obviously, land ownership in the Valley was going to become a sticky issue and the governor appointed a commission to deal with the claims.

Not everyone trusted the commission, however. In February 1850 a group of white and Hispanic Valley residents tried to establish an independent Rio Grande Territory. These rebels held that the Nueces Strip had never been part of Texas and that the state government was trying to force residents to turn to "expensive and ruinous lawsuits" to protect their land. A counter-movement recognized the power of Texas in the Valley and called for state tribunals to investigate land titles. The pro-Texas movement eventually triumphed but the fears of the separatists remained a part of Valley culture.

Pioneers constructed these dog trot cabins to take advantage of prevailing breezes. Wind whistling through the open space (the dog trot) cooled the rooms to either side. Courtesy Center for American History, UT-Austin

In July 1857 the Cart War broke out in southern Texas. Hispanic carters were successfully hauling food and other supplies from the port of Indianola to San Antonio. Their ox-drawn carts moved merchandise quickly and cheaply. White competitors responded by burning carts, stealing merchandise, and even killing some of the carters. The Mexican minister in Washington, D.C., protested, and the secretary of state urged the governor to end the hostilities. Governor Elisha M. Pease sent militia to protect the carts and the Cart War ended by December 1857. But hard feelings remained on both sides. Hispanic Texans worried that white forces wanted to destroy them. Some whites did.

The next outbreak of white-Hispanic conflict lasted longer. Juan Nepomuceno Cortina belonged to a family with extensive holdings north of the Rio Grande. In 1859 Robert Shears, a Brownsville marshal, arrested a former servant of the Cortina family. During the arrest, Shears pistol-whipped the detainee. Cortina witnessed the violence and protested. Events escalated and Cortina shot and wounded Shears. Cortina grabbed the servant and the two rode out of town on Cortina's horse.

A few months later, Cortina returned to Brownsville with about 80 men. They captured the town, raised the Mexican flag, released prisoners from the jail, and shot four men in the process. Cortina did not stay in Brownsville, but as he rode out of town he issued a proclamation that he was a citizen of Texas protesting for the rights of other citizens. Eventually, Cortina was forced to retreat into the mountains on the Mexican side of the border, but he was a hero to Hispanics on both sides of the Rio Grande. About 245 people died and distrust deepened. (Some say that the antagonism of this "first Cortina war" was exaggerated in an attempt to draw federal forces—and the money they spent—back to the Valley.)

Cortina ended up living on the south side of the river and Texas Rangers frequently crossed the border to look for him and his supporters. During the Civil War, Cortina supported the Union Army and even received ammunition and supplies to harass the Confederate forces in south Texas. After the war, some residents of south Texas petitioned the legislature to pardon Cortina because of his service to the Union. The legislature did not pass the necessary bill and in 1875, under U.S. pressure, the Mexican government arrested Cortina. He was removed to Mexico City and died in its suburbs in 1894.

OPENING WEST TEXAS

The commercial success of the Santa Fe Trail tempted Texans to create an alternative route. A major trail south of the Santa Fe, the thinking went, could bring commerce to San Antonio, Houston, and maybe even Corpus Christi. On August 27, 1848, former Texas Ranger Jack Coffee Hays lead a party out of San Antonio to El Paso. Samuel Maverick, San Antonio cattleman and entrepreneur, went along and kept a journal.

Things went well for the group at first, but when they reached the Big Bend their food ran out and game was scarce. Soon they were eating their mules and cactus pears. The expedition's doctor cracked, ran from the camp, and disappeared into the mountains, lost to the expedition (he reappeared within the year after friendly Native Americans cared for him and pointed him in the direction of home). On October 2, according to Maverick, the expedition killed a panther (mountain lion) and ate it. When they reached the village of San Carlos, south of the Rio Grande, they had been without food for 12 days. The villagers shared their bread

In 1854, Fort Davis was established near Limpia Creek at the eastern base of the Davis Mountains. The post was a component of a line of forts reaching from San Antonio to El Paso and set up to guard the southern route to California. The horseman is a re-enactor at today's Fort Davis National Historic Site. Jack Lewis, courtesy TxDOT and milk with the adventurers, who then moved on to Presidio where they bought mules and food from the pioneer rancher Ben Leaton. They also began to reconsider their goal of reaching El Paso.

The party took a vote and headed back to San Antonio. On the return trip they took a less difficult northern route. They did, however, encounter more Native Americans. In his report to the financial backers of the expedition, Hays recommended the northern route. It had Native Americans, but it also had water and was easier to traverse.

The discovery of gold in California in 1849 renewed the search for a southwestern trail. John S. "Rip" Ford, like Hays a former Texas Ranger, tried to forge a road from Austin to El Paso. The expedition's co-leader was Major Robert S. Neighbors, a Native American agent. The Ford-Neighbors Expedition also found the outward southerly trip harder than a northerly return.

At almost the same time, some Corpus Christi merchants decided to sponsor a wagon train that would link their port city to Chihuahua. For a week the city was full of wagons and carts preparing to move west. On July 17, 1849, General William L. Cazneau (he had been a Mexican War general) moved out with about $90,000 worth of goods, 50 wagons, and 100 men. They headed west and had a skirmish with Native Americans as they entered the Big Bend area. Then, as far as contemporary newspaper accounts go, they vanished. What happened to most of the party is unclear, but Cazneau went on to other things. He and his amazing wife, Jane McManus Storm Cazneau, later founded Eagle Pass as another experiment in improving trade with Mexico.

Other expeditions set out to find a quick and easy way over the Big Bend. No wonder they tried so hard: In 1850 such everyday products as tobacco and coffee were selling in Chihuahua for seven or eight times their Houston prices. Still, the passage was daunting. In 1849 Robert Hunter, in an expedition headed by a Captain Thompson, wrote to his wife: "We have travelled two hundred and forty miles without seeing any timber and at two different times we drove two days and nights without water over mountains and ravines on the route Jack Hays said he found water so plenty, and if he had been in sight he would not have lived one minute. Our mules suffered immensely, but the men done very well as we had gourds and kegs."

Eventually, two Trans-Pecos routes evolved. One went close to the present border between Texas and New Mexico, but the lower route followed the Rio Grande.

EUROPEAN IMMIGRATION

European immigration picked up during the republic and early statehood. According to the 1850 census, Germans made up the largest group of Texans not born in the United States or Texas. Early in the republic's history, Germans had settled in the Brazos River area, especially around the town of Industry and the cities of Galveston, San Antonio, and Houston.

After 1847, however, Germans congregated on the western frontier in the area between the Llano and Colorado rivers. Many of these settlers were farmers and craftsmen seeking a new life, but others came from a stratum not widely represented on the Texas frontier—intellectuals. Especially after the failed 1848 revolution in Germany, many educated Germans decided to make new lives in Texas. They started the so-called Latin communities, where everyone knew— and read—the classical languages. Whether these individuals were successful farmers is another issue.

The German settlers dealt successfully with the Native Americans, especially with Comanches. The Society for the Protection of German Immigrants had acquired the right to settle people between the Llano and Colorado rivers, traditional Comanche hunting grounds. Agreement terms required that the Germans survey and settle at least part of the area before the fall of 1847. In January 1847 a party of Germans, Mexicans, and U.S. surveyors—all armed—left Fredericksburg. Two days later John O. Meusebach, the man the immigration society had put in charge of negotiating with the Native Americans, joined them. Meusebach seemed to have good rapport with the Comanches, who called him El Sol Colorado (the red sun) after his flowing red beard. By March 2 the parties had agreed to a treaty that allowed the settlers to enter the territory and the Native Americans to enter the white settlements. The society also paid the Comanches $1,000 for surveying rights.

This treaty marked the western end of the German belt, which reached from Galveston on the coast to Kerrville,

The Fredericksburg Easter Fires

The Saturday before Easter can be impressive in the German Hill Country town of Fredericksburg. At a pre-arranged time, the bells of all the churches begin to peal, people turn off their lights, and fires appear on the tops of surrounding hills. The Easter fires are almost as old as the town itself; the first record of them is from 1847 and the town was established in 1846. The local story today goes this way: When John Meusebach was negotiating his treaty with the Comanches, the Native Americans would communicate with each other by signal fires. The fires frightened the children, and their parents tried to calm them by telling them that the Easter bunny and his helpers were cooking Easter eggs.

Several problems arise with this story. One is that Meusebach and the Comanches negotiated their treaty on March 1 and 2, 1847, and Easter that year fell almost a month later—on April 4. Easter eve would have been on April 3. Second, other Texas German towns used to have Easter fires, but the Fredericksburg tradition is the only one that is still alive.

Third, the custom of Easter bonfires is primeval in Germany. Lighting fires to mark the beginning of spring was a practice of Germanic pagans in the areas later called Westphalia and Lower Saxony. When these peoples converted to Christianity, they continued the custom but gave it a Christian explanation. About half of the original German settlers in the Hill Country came from these two provinces. These settlers probably brought the custom with them. The local tradition was probably added at some later time to connect the fires with the new country they now inhabited.

No matter how the custom started you can enjoy the Easter fires in Fredericksburg any year. A pageant, enshrining the Comanche origin story, is also enacted at the fairgrounds. Call the visitor's bureau at (830) 997-6523 or visit www.fredericksburg-texas.com.

Mason, and Hondo in the west. Most of this migration was formally organized with "America Letters," describing Texas as a paradise on earth, sent back to German newspapers and luring ever more settlers. The organized immigration ended around 1850, but the German belt was well-established by then and even expanded some when migration picked up again after the Civil War.

Just south of the eventual western end of the German belt and bordering the Comanche lands was a settlement of Alsatians. The colony centered on the village of Castroville, named for the empresario Henri Castro. In September 1844 Castro led his colonists out of San Antonio under the protection of the ubiquitous John C. Hays and five other Texas Rangers. They chose as the town site a level area near a bend in the Medina River teaming with pecan trees and game. In this idyllic setting, the settlers had to endure droughts, Native American raids, locusts, and a cholera epidemic.

Still, they persevered. The Alsatians continued their European habit of laying out towns so that farmers lived in the village and worked individual plots that surrounded the village. The buildings did not have the deep front porches common to other Texas houses, and the Alsatians tended to build from stone or a combination of stone and timber. Many of the houses had thatched roofs.

While most people associate Polish immigration to the United States with larger eastern seaboard and midwestern cities, the first permanent U.S. settlement of Polish immigrants was in the prairies of Texas. In what is now Karnes County, a party of Poles established the town of Panna Maria on December 24, 1854. Panna Maria was also the site of the first Polish Catholic church and school in the United States. While most Poles who migrated to Texas tended to settle in the confluence of the San Antonio River and Cibolo Creek where the first group had settled, many moved on up to San Antonio itself, Bandera, and other towns farther west. Many also stayed on the coast at Galveston.

In the early 1850s, many Czechs also moved to Texas. Cat Spring in Austin County was the first settlement. Growing Czech migration tended to concentrate in central Texas counties like Austin, Fayette, Lavaca, and Washington. Fayette County eventually became the hub of Czech settlement. Most of these settlers were from Moravia and the Czech that was spoken in Texas mirrored the dialect of this region. Formal education in Czech and German began in Cat Spring in 1855 and the first Catholic school was built in the settlement of Bluff in 1868.

Another Slavic group that moved to Texas was the Wends, who spoke a Slavic language written in Gothic letters, called Sorbian. The Wends have never had a country of their own and spent most of their history surrounded by Germans and harassed by the attacks of marauding tribes and invading armies. Texas had to be an improvement. But in some ways it wasn't. To get to Texas, the Wends endured shipwrecks, cholera outbreaks, yellow fever in Galveston, and an 85-mile walk from the coast to their new land.

European Immigrants brought their own customs and organizations. These gentlemen are the first Czech orchestra in Texas, but no record remains of who they were or where they played. Courtesy Center for American History, UT-Austin

Their walk took them to Industry, Texas, but their leaders walked on 30 more miles and purchased a league of land in the present Lee County. There they established the community of Serbin. Wends tended to stay in Lee and Fayette counties throughout the 19th century. In many ways they were an invisible ethnic group, since they usually spoke German in public. The Wends themselves, however, enforced informal rules that kept them unassimilated until the 20th century.

These European groups tended to be unconcerned about slavery and did not identify emotionally with the southern United States. The "peculiar institution" was of no use on their small family-run farms, nor was the issue of states' rights. Although some Germans and Czechs actively opposed the Civil War and fought for the Confederacy, most European settlers tried to stay uninvolved. Some, especially

among the Latin community Germans, publicly opposed slavery, but most feared the violence that could follow if they were labeled abolitionists. They wanted only to be left alone. Among the Poles, many of the men had left their homeland to escape the draft and were not going to join yet another army. When the war and conscription finally came, Wendish men tried to confuse passing Confederate sympathizers by wearing dresses when they worked in the fields.

The Battles of Palo Alto and Resaca de la Palma

Two Mexican War battles were fought north of the Rio Grande in Texas: the battles of Palo Alto and Resaca de la Palma. Today, you can explore these sites in two ways: From the top of the Port Isabel Lighthouse State Historical Park, you can survey the panorama of the battlefields. On the ground, you can visit but not enter the Palo Alto Battlefield National Historic Site or go to the interpretative center in downtown Brownsville. At the moment the battlefield site itself is closed to the public.

The Road to Big Bend

You can reach the Big Bend area by following Interstate Highway 10 and then heading south. The trip can still be isolated and lonely, but you won't have to eat cactus pears unless you want to (although it is a good idea to keep an eye on your gas gauge). The towns of Alpine, Fort Stockton, Marfa, Marathon, and other stops on the road offer places to sleep and eat. In Balmorhea, you can stop for a dip in a state park swimming pool fed by artesian springs.

West of Big Bend National Park is the largest state park in Texas, Big Bend Ranch State Natural Area. This land was once one of the ten largest working ranches in the state; it is now crossed by RM 170, also known as the Camino del Rio, possibly the most spectacular drive in Texas. Driving RM 170 west from Lajitas, you will end up in Presidio, where you can visit Ben Leaton's fort. Now called Fort Leaton Historic Site, this huge adobe construction originally had 40 rooms; 24 have been restored.

6

SLAVERY IN TEXAS

The first Europeans brought slavery to Texas with the shipwrecks of Cabeza de Vaca. Traveling with de Vaca were the slave Esteban and his owner (see p. 20). As a colonial power, however, the Spanish preferred to force indigenous peoples to work their plantations and mines rather than importing slaves. In 1751 the Spanish arrested three Frenchmen who had settled along the Red River with two African slaves. But the fluid and poorly policed borders allowed many people to move slaves surreptitiously into out-of-the-way corners of Spanish Texas. Fugitive slaves sometimes fled to Texas from other southern states in the belief—to be proved wrong—that they could live freely there.

The Mexican government officially disapproved of slavery but never enacted effective restrictions. An 1823 law outlawed selling or purchasing slaves and required that the children of slaves be freed at the age of 14. Additionally, in 1827 the state of Coahuila y Texas banned the introduction of new slaves and declared the children of slaves free at birth. Just like the Spanish, however, the Mexican administrations did not enforce antislavery laws. White settlers were consistently allowed to bring in their own slaves. After four years, Austin's colony had 443 slaves out of a population of 1,800.

The first constitution of the Republic of Texas allowed importation of slaves from the United States, although it did forbid bringing slaves directly from Africa. It also prohibited the Congress from ever restricting slaveowners' right to bring their human property to Texas. During the republic and after annexation, slavery increased dramatically, from 58,161 slaves in 1850 to 182,566 in 1860—30.2 percent of the population. During the same period, cotton production went from 58,000 bales to 431,000.

Some plantations in Brazoria and Matagorda counties concentrated on sugar cane, but for most white agriculturalists east of the Balcones Escarpment, the only cash crop worth the time and trouble was cotton. The editor of the *State Gazette*, an Austin paper, predicted that with the growth of cotton farming Texas would soon have more than 2 million slaves.

In reality, on the eve of the Civil War only one Texas family in four owned even one slave, and of these families most had fewer than five. A few influential planters held most of the state's slaves, in particular the Mills family who alone freed 800 slaves when the Civil War ended.

SLAVERY AND THE TEXAS ECONOMY

Although slave labor was the primary force behind the rapid expansion of agriculture in Texas, it negatively affected other sectors. The plantation economy (and the state's ban on banking) kept industry and commerce weak. With slaves readily available, planters did not need agricultural machinery, and those without slaves could not afford mechanization. Cotton was processed outside Texas, so even the technology for converting raw plant to fiber was not needed.

The only technology that interested the planters was the railroad. Lack of adequate transportation kept cotton production in check. Texas rivers were unreliable because they periodically dried up or silted over with logs and debris. The primitive roads were dangerous and difficult for carting cotton. While planters liked the idea of railroads to transport their cotton, they were unwilling to invest in the industry and instead tried to convince the state to pay for them. Haggling in the state legislature took the place of capital investment and by 1860 Texas had only 400 miles of track—and most of that was centered on Houston.

One reason planters did not have available money to invest in new technology was the price of slaves. Land was cheap, or even free, and excellent land for growing cotton could go for $6.00 an acre. Having purchased cheap land, however, planters needed people to work it. From the 1840s to 1860 the average price of a slave more than doubled from below $400 to $800. A male slave in his prime years could cost about $1,200, and skilled slaves, such as carpenters or blacksmiths, could go for more than $2,000.

Romanticized view of slave life. Oil painting "Cotton Picking" by Otto Berninghaus (1929). Courtesy Center for American History, UT-Austin

The major slave market serving Texas was New Orleans, but markets existed in Houston and Galveston and even some smaller towns. Since some slaveowners used subterfuges to mask the condition of old or infirm slaves, intimate inspections were carried out in public. Even without this added insult, slaves did not forget being on the auctioneer's block. Jeff Hamilton was 13 when he was auctioned: "I stood on the slaveblock in the blazing sun for at least two hours....my legs ached. My hunger had become almost unbearable....I was filled with terror, and did not know what was to become of me. I had been crying for a long time."

Slaves could bring their owners income in many ways. The ever-rising prices for slaves gave owners an additional profit source, but most made money through slave labor. In addition to working slaves on his or her own land, a slave owner could hire surplus slaves out to others. Widows frequently made their living by hiring out the slaves they had inherited, and slaves could be used as collateral for loans from private lenders.

Slave Life in Texas

Massa Earl Stielszen captured [my parents] in Africa and brought them to Georgia. He got killed and [we] went to his son. His son was a killer. He got in trouble in Georgia and got him two good-stepping horses and the covered wagon. Then he chained all his slaves around the necks and fastened the chains to the horses and made them walk all the way to Texas.... Somewhere on the road it went to snowing, and massa wouldn't let us wrap anything round our feet. We had to sleep on the ground, too, in all that snow.

Massa had a great, long whip platted out of rawhide, and when one of the niggers fell behind or gave out, he hit them with that whip. It took the hide everytime he hit a nigger. Mother, she gave out on the way, about the line of Texas. Her feet got raw and bleeding, and her legs swelled plumb out of shape. Then massa, he just took out his gun and shot her, and whilst she lay dying he kicked her two, three times, and said, "Damn nigger that can't stand nothing." Boss, you know that man, he wouldn't bury mother, just left her laying where he shot her at. You know there wasn't any law against killing nigger slaves.

He came plumb to Austin through that snow. He took up farming and changed his name to Alex Simpson, and changed our names, too....

—Ben Simpson, *The Slave Narratives of Texas* [all slave quotations are from this volume]

Alex Simpson sounds like a pathological extreme, but the conditions of life for all slaves depended only on the slaveowner's character. A legend has grown up that slaves were treated especially mildly in Texas, but little evidence supports this assertion.

Legally, slaves were personal property like horses, wagons, or furniture. An owner could treat them as he or she pleased. A wise owner would treat property humanely in the hope of having long and useful service, but slaves frequently had to endure inhumane owners.

Rational owners fed their slaves a diet with enough calories to give them the energy to work. Usually, corn and pork were the primary ingredients in owner-supplied meals. Molasses, bread, and hominy were also frequent staples. Slaves used what little free time they had to supplement their meals with sweet potatoes, greens, and other easily grown vegetables and with wild game and fish. Few owners made their slaves sleep in the open, but the cabins they provided were poorly made and badly chinked, so inhabitants had to suffer drafts and rain. Floors were dirt, and beds, if they existed, were wood planks attached to the wall. Clothing was coarse and usually had seen many other owners; shoes were rare and ill-fitting when they were provided. On well-run plantations, field hands received clothes twice a year, in the spring and fall. Each male got two shirts, two pants, a hat, and, in the fall, a winter coat. Women were given two dresses. But this norm for clothing supplies was frequently not met.

No law compelled slaveowners to treat their slaves with dignity. In Texas slaves could not be legally freed. Owners who tried to release favorite slaves were usually thwarted. In March 1837 an Austin County man named Benjamin Thomas wrote a will that freed two adult slaves and their five children and gave them all of his property in Texas. After Thomas died, the administrator of his will asked the county court to throw it out because its provisions were "contrary to law." In 1847 Tom and Rachel, the two adults mentioned in the will, and all their children and grandchildren were still slaves hired out to the profit of the estate.

Some free African Americans lived in Texas when it gained independence, but the new constitution made it illegal for them to stay in the republic without congressional permission. Whites regularly ignored this law when they had vested interests in keeping particular free African Americans, usually craftsmen of some sort, in their communities. In 1840 the legislature made the law more strict and gave all free African Americans two years to leave Texas or be sold into slavery. President Sam Houston managed to postpone enforcement of the law. When Texas became a state, the punishments that could be applied to slaves—whipping, branding, forced labor— were made applicable to free African Americans. In 1858 the state legislature passed a bizarre law that allowed free African Americans to choose their own masters when they became slaves again. In a few instances, freedmen actually took advantage of this opportunity, perhaps fearing they would be enslaved in any event and might as well find a relatively decent master.

The law treated slaves differently in many ways. Being property themselves, slaves could not own property. While slaves had a right to a jury trial, no African American, whether free or slave, could testify in court against a white, so the right to a jury was nullified.

Whipping was legal and in fact any form of discipline that did not kill or permanently maim the slave was legal. Few people were willing to pursue a slaveowner who had destroyed his or her property, although non-owners were convicted of mistreating slaves that belonged to others. Even owners regarded as "kind" resorted to the whip, and dogs were sometimes turned on slaves.

Legally, slaves had no right to marry and no parental rights regarding their children. Despite the law, most slaves did manage some kind of family life. Most slaveowners encouraged this breach of the law—slave children were a valuable resource. Owners also believed that the emotional investment of adult slaves with children and men with wives made them less likely to run away. At night, after the overseer had gone to his house, family life could offer slaves a chance to be human, to have some control over their own lives.

But even in the private arenas of sex and family life, some owners exercised complete control. Slaves, described as so-called "studs," moved from plantation to plantation to breed

William J.E. Heard started the Egypt Platation in 1832; his descendants occupied parts of the land until 1992. These old barn and grain elevators near Egypt are thought to have been part of the plantation. Jack Lewis, courtesy TxDOT

stronger field hands. Some owners forced specific female slaves to breed with or live with specific men, those the owners had identified as "good breeders." Owners often required enslaved males to live with "harems" of more than one woman in the hope of producing more children. Slaveowners themselves frequently demanded sexual relations from female slaves—no matter what other conjugal relations the slave or master had.

At the other extreme were owners who recognized and respected slaves' family lives. Some owners allowed slaves to take part in marriage ceremonies even though these rituals had no legal standing. In an 1860 bill of sale, Rueben Hornsby, Jr., of Austin described his purchase of a woman and her seven children as "a family of eight Negroes." Still, the father of this family was missing.

Most slaveowners felt no compunction about breaking up slave families. In May 1859, for example, James Strawther of Austin County sold a six-week-old female from a slave family for $75. The death of the owner was the most likely time for a slave family to be disrupted. Even if a will called for keeping families together, the hiring out process could result in their being legally together but actually apart. After the death of William B. Holloway of Rusk County, the six slaves in his estate were each hired out to different renters. The slaves included an adult man and woman and her three children. Each of them served different people from 1859 to 1862. One boy served four different masters before he was ten years old.

Slaves devised many ways of dealing with the harsh unpredictabilities of their lives. Families and friends, music and religion all brought some comforts. Informal resistance included working as slowly as possible, stealing food and other items, and even violence against whites. Of course, these forms of rebellion ran the risk of punishment. The fear of a slave revolt was omnipresent among owners. Rumors of planned uprisings frequently ran like wildfire from one plantation to another. While Texas documented less than a handful of slave revolts, rumors were constant.

Unique Characteristics of Texas Slavery

Many of these harsh realities were true for slaves all through the South, but slavery had some unique characteristics in Texas: One, the state was a perceived haven for slaveowners from other slave states, and, two, Mexico, a country that had outlawed slavery, was close enough to beckon especially brave or desperate slaves. Like most slaveowners, Texas planters constantly feared an uprising.

Beginning before and continuing throughout the Civil War, slaveowners moved their human property to Texas beyond, they hoped, the reach of Union invasion. Most slaves moved to Texas came from nearby states, like Arkansas, Louisiana, or the border state Missouri.

Early in the war, the owner of Van Moore moved his slaves from Virginia to Texas. Moore told interviewers: "When war began most folks back in Virginia who owned slaves moved further South, and lots to Louisiana and Texas, cause they said the Yankees would never get that far, and they wouldn't have to free the slaves if they came way over here." Caroline Wright's journey began closer to Texas, in Louisiana: "One day I saw a lot of men, and I asked the missus what they were doing. She told me they came to fight in the war. The war got so bad that Mr. Bob told us we were all going to Texas. We all started out on Christmas Day of the first year of Lincoln's war. We went in ox wagons, and we had mules to ride."

Unfamiliar with the Texas countryside, relocated slaves were thought to be less likely to escape. Their moves across country, however, may also have made them more resistant. Breaking apart slave families for the trip might have increased resentment. While no one knows whether these new slaves were more likely to rise up or run away, their presence fueled the white's fear of rebellion.

SLAVE REBELLIONS

Rebellion was always the slaveowner's secret fear. From the beginning of the republic, Texans believed their slaves were capable of rising up and overpowering their masters. As Santa Anna moved closer to the Brazos Valley, rumors of slave plots swept from plantation house to plantation house. Even after Texas declared itself free from Mexico, runaway slaves frequently joined with Native American and Mexican bands to wage guerrilla warfare on whites and their holdings.

Fear of slave uprising lessened to a murmur for several years after the revolution, but violence must have been an ever-present fear. In March 1841 a Houston newspaper reported that two slaves had attacked Benjamin Franklin Terry, a wealthy planter and eventually a commander of a volunteer unit in the Civil War. The slaves used knives and axes, but Terry fought them off.

In September 1856 people in Colorado County feared that a coalition of slaves and Mexicans was supposedly rising up in response to the presidential campaign of John C. Frémont, a Republican opposed to slavery. Allegedly, 200 slaves armed with pistols and knives planned to seize more arms, kill all who opposed them, and escape to Mexico. Three African Americans were executed, one white abolitionist was whipped, and the entire Mexican population was evicted from the county. In reality this campaign was probably more closely related to anti-Mexican feeling than to fear of slave insurrection.

In November 1856 whites in Lavaca, DeWitt, and Victoria counties thought they had also uncovered an uprising plan. This revolt was to begin with the killing of all dogs in the area.

An Ohioan named Davidson was given 100 lashes and two other whites were accused of collaboration in the plot.

Fear of slave uprisings reached its apogee just before the Civil War in a panic called the Texas Troubles. On July 8, 1860, fire destroyed the business district of the small town of Dallas; fires also were said to have broken out on the same day in Denton and other north Texas sites. The facts about the Texas Troubles are difficult to pin down. Some reports said the fires began at the same time in different locations, others that only the Dallas blaze really happened and the additional fires were figments of hysteria.

At first, the public blamed the fires on the introduction of phosphorous matches and the inhabitants' lack of familiarity with their use. Soon, though, Charles R. Pryor of the Dallas *Herald* and other extremist newspaper editors suggested that white abolitionists and slaves started the fires. Vigilante committees visited slave quarters to interrogate the inmates, reported finding slaves armed with weapons, and frequently obtained confessions or accusations, usually as a result of physical intimidation. Word spread among whites that an insurrection was slated for August 6, election day. When the day passed without an uprising, the whites' fear did not go away. Eventually, vigilantes murdered 10 whites and probably 30 slaves, although some reports indicate that around 100 might have been killed. The whites who were killed or seized included ministers of the northern Methodist church, tavern keepers, pharmacists, two salesmen, a wagon maker, and a blacksmith. One slave named Patrick went to his death saying that his action had been "the commencement of a good work." Governor Houston commented that the fire-eaters had used a series of accidents to create a mob mentality. The fires succeeded in whipping up whites' fear of slaves and increasing slaveowners' desire to secede from the Union.

RUNAWAYS

The ultimate slave revolt was to run away, therefore taking control of one's own life. Planters frequently advertised for the return of fugitives. One offered $1,200 for six slaves who had taken four blooded mares, a large pacing horse, and 20 other horses with them to Mexico. A Bastrop area planter advertised for the return of 25 well-armed slaves on good horses who had also run away to Mexico.

The nearness of Mexico was a constant lure to run for freedom. In 1836 slaves killed the sheriff of Gonzales and escaped over the Rio Grande. Slaves continued to slip away until the time of emancipation, sometimes going alone but most often traveling in small groups of two or three and frequently taking their master's horses to make the trip easier. Most runaways were field hands between the ages of 20 and 40, 90 percent of them men.

During the republic, fugitives increased their escape attempts to Mexico. Two of Sam Houston's own slaves ran away and Houston did not attempt to get them back, saying, "They were smart, intelligent fellows [who] would help to civilize and refine Mexico, as their associations in Texas had been remarkably good." Tom Green ran into the two slaves outside Matamoros where he was imprisoned after the Mier incident. He said of these two, named Tom and Esau, "These *gentlemen*, now of so much consequence as to ride three leagues in a coach to congratulate General Ampudia upon his *splendid victory*, were General Sam Houston's two barbers, so well known to the public of Texas. Tom treated us with marked respect and attention, spoke of his prospects in that country, his intended nuptials, invited us to the wedding, and said that General Ampudia was to stand godfather on the occasion."

The Mexican government established colonies of former slaves along the border with Texas, seeing these communities as buffers against Native American raids. Texans saw them as a provocation. In the early 1850s a band of Seminole Indians and African Americans living in Oklahoma migrated through Texas to Coahuila. Under the chiefdom of Wild Cat, also known as Coacoochee, they settled opposite Eagle Pass in Piedras Negras. Eventually pressure from the United States forced Wild Cat's band to settle further from the border in La Navajo. There they became farmers but still functioned as a border guard for the Mexican military. Their numbers were constantly replenished by fugitives from Texas, Louisiana, Florida, and other slave states.

Private Mexican citizens also helped slaves escape. One village rigged up a flatboat in the center of the Rio Grande. Any runaway who could make it to the boat could pull himself across to freedom. Word passed from slave to slave about freedom in Mexico. Felix Haywood told the WPA interviewers about Mexico:

Sometimes someone would come along and try to get us to run up North and be free. We used to laugh at that. There was no reason to run up North. All we had to do was walk, but walk south, and we'd be free as soon as we crossed the Rio Grande. In Mexico you could be free. They didn't care what color you were, black, white, yellow or blue. Hundreds of slaves did go to Mexico and got on all right. We would hear about them and how they were going to be Mexicans. They brought up their children to speak only Mexican.

Armed Texans frequently crossed the river to look for escaped slaves, and slaves sometimes crossed the border in the other direction to raid for provisions in sparsely settled areas of west Texas. In March 1850 the Mexican minister Luís de la Rosa formally protested that four or five soldiers had raided a Coahuila ranch where they beat two or three Mexican citizens and carried away a fugitive slave. In 1851 and 1855 formal military groups crossed the border to recapture fugitives but met strong resistance. In 1851 an estimated 400 Texans fought alongside José María Jesus Carvajal in his revolt against the Mexican government. Carvajal had promised that the Texans could keep any runaways they found and that, when he won, his Republic of Sierra Madre would return all runaway slaves. Wild Cat and his band of Native Americans and escaped slaves fought on the side of the Mexican government, and together the two forces were able to put down this revolt.

Some estimates put the number of escaped slaves in Mexico before the Civil War at 4,000. Once free across the Rio Grande, the former slaves often had hard economic times until they learned Spanish. Some never learned the language and lived in small villages of runaways strung along the northern Mexican border, making a subsistent but free living. Runaways with special skills like carpentry or smithing—or even barbering for Sam Houston—could establish prosperous lives across the border.

Wild Cat and his band from Oklahoma were not an anomaly. Many slaves tried to escape to the north. Distance

Wild Cat Passes through Eagle Pass

Jane McManus Storms Cazeneau witnessed the passage of Wild Cat and his band into Mexico and gave a colorful description of the event:

We were sipping our chocolate, with every door thrown wide to welcome the breeze. [when her servant Francesca hurried up and pointed toward the hills]. We looked out in surprise, for there, emerging from the broken ground in a direction that we knew was untraversed [sic] by any but wild and hostile Indians, came forth a procession of horsemen. The sun flashed back from a mixed array of arms and barbaric gear, but as this unexpected army, which seemed to have dropped upon us from the skies, drew nearer it grew less formidable in apparent numbers.... Some reasonably well-mounted Indians circled round a dark nucleus of female riders, who seemed objects of special care. ... Such an array of all manners and sizes of animals, mounted by all ages, sexes and sizes of negroes, piled up to a most bewildering height, on and among such a promiscuous assemblage of blankets, babies, cooking utensils, and savage traps, in general, never were or could be held together on horseback by any beings on earth but themselves and their red brothers. The party began to break away and vanish into the little ravines that dip down to the river edge, and we understood by these signs they were encamping among us.

The word soon circulated that it was Wild Cat, the famous Seminole chief.... His tribe had lands assigned to them in Nebrasca [sic].... He has won too much savage glory in his wars with the whites, and has in him too much of the restlessness of his race to stay cooped up among government forts and agents....Wild Cat has turned his back on all this and come out to the Mexican border, with his immediate servants, followers, and kinsmen, to find a home and a field more congenial to the heart of a Red warrior.

—Cazeneau, *Eagle Pass*

made it impossible for them to reach to Canada, as slaves in more eastern regions did. Instead, runaways who did not think they could make it to Mexico tried to find asylum with various Native American bands. In the 1850s Indian Territory was an attractive goal for slaves in north Texas, but as early as the 1820s some runways had joined east Texas tribes. These Native Americans did not treat the former slaves as equals but did treat them better than the white

population had. During the 1838 battle that resulted in the
Cherokees being driven from Texas, many former slaves
fought with the Native Americans and left Texas with them.
Some escaped slaves rose to positions of power among the
Native Americans of the plains because of their
understanding of white ways.

Not all runaways made it as far as Mexico or Oklahoma.
Some merely hid in woods nearby where friends would feed
them on the sly. Anna Miller described how her sister and a
slave man lived in the woods: "Just about a month before
freedom, my sister and…Horace ran off. They didn't get far,
and stayed in a dugout. Every night they'd sneak in and get
molasses and milk and what food they could. My sister had
a baby, and she nursed it every night when she came. They
ran off to keep from getting a whipping."

Some runaways worked things in the other direction.
Sarah Ford remembered that her father's devotion to his
family hampered his desire for freedom:

*One time he was gone a whole year.…Papa was mighty good
to mama and me, and that was the only reason he ever came back
from running away, to see us. He knew he'd get a whipping, but
he came anyway.…They knew papa was the best tanner around
that part of the country, so they couldn't sell him off the place. I
recollect papa saying there was one place special where he hid
with some German folks.…When he hid there, he tanned hides on
the sly like, and they fed him, and lots of mornings when we
opened the cabin door, on a shelf just above [the door] was food
for mama and me and sometimes store clothes. No one had seen
papa, but there it was. One time he brought us dresses, and Uncle
Big Jake [the slaveowner] heard about them, and he sure was mad
because he couldn't catch papa, and he said to mama that he was
going to whip her unless she told him where papa was. Mama
said, "Before God, Uncle Jake, I don't know, because I haven't
seen him since he ran away." And just then papa came around the
corner of the house. He saved mama from the whipping.*

The Civil War ended legal slavery in Texas, but vestiges
remained. Even after the war some slaves still had to run
away to find freedom. Susan Merritt was 87 when she was
interviewed and she described the days after freedom
came:

Lots of niggers were killed after freedom, cause the slaves in Harrison County were turned loose right at freedom, and those in Rusk County weren't. But they heard about it and ran away to freedom in Harrison County, and their owners had them bushwhacked, that's shot down. You could see lots of niggers hanging to trees in Sabine bottom right after freedom, cause they caught them swimming across the Sabine River and shot them. There sure are going to be lots of souls crying against them in Judgement!

Before freedom of any kind could come, however, a bloody gulf had to be crossed by everyone in Texas and the United States.

Must-See Plantations

Texas had few grand plantation houses, such as those in more eastern slave states. A few were built, however, and some of those that remain can give you an idea of how income from slavery was spent. The Goodman-LeGrand House as it now stands in Tyler is the result of much family remodeling but it retains some of the flavor of the original 1859 structure and the nine-acre grounds that surrounded the original Greek revival structure are still intact. The house is now a historical museum.

South of Tyler is the Dewberry Plantation, which was built in 1854. The original plantation may have included 20,000 to 30,000 acres in three counties. The main house was named Myrtle-Vale because of the crepe myrtles that lined the walkway to the front of the house. Myrtle-Vale has been restored either with original materials or with cypress milled by hand as it would have been in the 19th century.

In the Jefferson area you can find three houses from the period. Mimosa Hall, part of the Freeman Plantation, is outside of Jefferson. In the town are Sagamore and the Alley-McKay house. Call the chamber of commerce at (903) 665-2672.

You can also get a concrete idea of Texas slave life at an archeological site near the town of Brazoria. The Levi Jordan Plantation has given up more than 600,000 artifacts connected to slaves and has been called "the Black Pompeii." While many of the artifacts have been displayed at the Smithsonian Institute, a visitors' center is being built at the plantation site and will publicly display at least some of the collection. The site is not yet opened to the public, but tours are occasionally offered. A nonprofit organization is trying to restore the plantation house itself. You can learn more about the plantation at www.webarcharelogy.com.

SECESSION AND WAR

When the Civil War broke out, Texas could easily have become a border state, like Kentucky or Maryland—slave states that did not join the Confederacy.

Before the conflict, Texans had a mix of attitudes toward slavery and the Union. In the very recent past they had struggled mightily to join the Union; giving up that accomplishment was not an easy decision. Sam Houston, the sitting governor, had been elected on a pro-Union platform. Some historians estimate that before actual fighting began only about one-third of Texans supported the Confederacy; another third was neutral, and another third supported the Union either actively or passively. After war broke out, these proportions probably did not change much, except that those who actively supported the Union left the state, became mute, or supported the Confederacy out of loyalty to the secession vote or sentiment for their home.

Houston distrusted political organizations and refused to institute a formal, permanent Union party in Texas. He had campaigned for governor as an independent, touring the state in a buggy and, in a frontier touch, campaigning shirtless on hot days. He beat his opponent 35,257 to 27,500. Still, his victory was a personal one and did not build institutional support for his pro-Union stance. In contrast, in 1859 those who favored secession seized control of the Democratic party and used that organization to develop support for their cause. They held that Texas, as a sovereign state, could "withdraw from the [Union] and resume her place among the powers of the earth as a sovereign and independent nation."

The Texas Troubles further damaged the Unionist cause. Extreme secessionists used the example of the Troubles to whip up support for leaving the Union. They portrayed Republican presidential candidate Abraham Lincoln as an abolitionist who had plotted slave insurrections. Many moderates felt that the purported slave insurrections made it difficult for them to oppose secession and support the Union in public.

Even without the background of the Troubles, many Texans believed that Republicans and other Northerners had purposely threatened slavery, perceived as an economic necessity for Texas. White slaveholders with southern roots were the most influential and powerful group of Texans. Many white Texans—even those who did not have slaves—had moved from somewhere in the South or were the children of people who had made that move. Slavery was an engrained component of Texas life and economy for almost everyone, but Unionism was also a strong ideology. These difficult and confusing contradictions led to outbreaks of violence.

UNIONISM IN TEXAS

Opposition to secession was scattered throughout the state, but the strongest concentrations were found in the northern part of the state, in central Texas, and among the Hispanic population along the border, especially around Brownsville. Across the state, German immigrants and supporters of the Whig party, who had moved to Texas from the border states, tended to support the Union.

Settlers on the western frontier also trusted the Union to protect them from Native American attacks more effectively than either the state or a smaller, less powerful country, such as the Confederacy. In 1860 the frontier was less than 100 miles west of Austin. These frontier settlers knew the value of the Union in real terms. Not only did the string of tiny forts protect settlers from Comanches and other threats, they also helped the local economies, since the army paid soldiers salaries that were frequently spent in the immediate area. But trust in the federal army waned around 1858 when frontier people came to see the army more as a group of soldiers who protected reservation Native Americans than as a band pledged to keep them safe.

In cities and towns many believed that the Union offered a stable economic climate and could protect existing legal relationships better than other entities could. Many Unionists even saw the larger nation as the best safeguard of slavery. On December 30, 1860, a Galveston lawyer, William

Pitt Ballinger, wrote in his diary: "This [year] closes I fear most ominously—This Govt. will be overthrown & the Union destroyed. I hope for the best and it may be that public order & prosperity will not be weakened and that security will be given to the institution of slavery—But I have strong fears to the contrary, and my best judgement is that we are doing an unwise & may be a fatal thing."

But these pragmatic considerations paled beside the identification with the symbols and memories of the United States that kept some Texans loyal to the Union. The perception of a shared history and a common bond of civilization with the entire United States made leaving the Union a wrenching experience for many Texans, no matter what their attitudes toward slavery and states' rights.

Loyalty to the Union was not the same thing as supporting the abolition of slavery. No matter what their attitude toward secession, few Texans publicly called for abolition of slavery. Those who did expressed religious concerns about slavery and others wondered about its economic contribution to the state. Adolf Douai, the editor of the San Antonio *Zeitung*, spoke out against slavery so vehemently that he had to leave the state. Still, these principled questionings of slavery were rare enough to suggest that most Texans—Unionists and Secessionists alike—believed that slavery was a natural institution. Abolitionists were rare in Texas.

Even so, public hysteria over hidden abolitionists fueled panic and vigilantism. After the Texas Troubles, vigilante committees continued to exert mob justice in parts of the state. North Texas was a prime example. The recently opened Butterfield Stage line had brought new people from the Midwest and other non-slave areas into the northern tier of counties above Dallas. Eventually fewer than 10 percent of the people in these counties owned slaves. Most of the violence of the Troubles centered in these counties. In October 1862, after the Civil War had begun, this area was also the scene of a major lynching of African Americans and whites suspected of being abolitionists. Called the Great Hanging of Gainesville, this episode muted most north country opposition to the Confederacy.

Sam Houston

Sam Houston. Courtesy Center for American History, UT-Austin

No Texan of his time was more mysterious and, at the same time, more famous than Sam Houston. Born in Virginia, he was the fifth child and fifth son of his Scots-Irish parents. When Houston was 13, his father died and his mother moved the family, by now including three sisters, to eastern Tennessee.

When he was 16, Houston established a pattern that he would repeat throughout his life: He ran away from home and went to live with the Cherokees. Why he ran away is a mystery, although some stories indicate that Sam objected to his older brother's plans for him to work on the farm. For three years he lived on the wrong side of the Tennessee River with the people he came to consider his chosen family and the man he called his "Indian Father," Chief Oolooteka. The Cherokees called Houston "the Raven" and his experiences made him more sympathetic to Native Americans than most white Texans, or North Americans, of the time.

Just as suddenly as he had come, he left the Cherokees and returned to white society. He taught school for a while and joined the army for the War of 1812. At the Battle of Horseshoe Bend, Houston's courage brought him to the attention of General Andrew Jackson, who became his mentor and patron—and another father figure. Houston returned the attention and revered Jackson for the rest of his life.

Houston continued to receive military promotions and became an Indian agent to the Cherokees. In this position, he tried to ease the removal of Oolooteka's band to what is now Oklahoma, but he could not stop the exile of his friends. By 1818 Houston was a first lieutenant when he abruptly resigned both his army commission and his Indian agent position. Apparently, he and Secretary of War John C. Calhoun had differences.

For six months Houston read law in Nashville and then opened a practice in Lebanon, Tennessee. Jackson again guided the younger man's career and saw that he retained a post in the state militia where he could make contacts. Eventually, he was elected attorney general of the District of Nashville. He rose within the militia, where he was elected a major general, and also in the Masonic order, another politically useful affiliation. In 1823 he was elected to the U.S. House of Representatives and served two terms. He resigned to run for governor of Tennessee in 1827. Elected to that post, Houston was on the path to ever greater power in Jacksonian America; he was even mentioned as someone who would one day be president of the United States.

Then everything changed. In 1829 Houston announced that he would run for a second term as governor and he married Eliza Allen, a 19 year old from Gallatin. The marriage lasted eleven weeks. No one knows what caused the Houston marriage to disintegrate. Neither Sam nor Eliza ever talked about it. There were rumors that she "loved another," but those were only rumors (and likely to be untrue since she did try to resume the relationship a few years later). Distraught, Houston resigned from the governorship on April 16 and headed west to Indian Territory and his friends and protectors, the Cherokees.

During this sojourn, Houston's Native American name changed from "Raven" to "Big Drunk." He dressed as a Cherokee and, at first, cut himself off from contact with white society. Despite his drinking, the Cherokees frequently used Houston as a tribal ambassador and in that position he helped keep the peace among the various groups in Oklahoma. Despite the fact that, under U.S. law, he was still married to Eliza, Houston married Diana Rogers Gentry, a woman of mixed heritage, and together they opened a trading post near Fort Gibson. In those days Fort Gibson was called the "hellhole of the southwest" where gamblers, adventurers, and other fringe characters mingled with soldiers and Native Americans. Houston gambled and drank and occasionally wandered around the Indian Territory performing his tasks as tribal representative and, eventually, liaison between the Native Americans and the Jackson administration.

Gradually, Houston reestablished contact with Tennessee and points east. Then, on a visit to Washington, D.C. in April 1832, he became newsworthy again. On the evening of April 13, Houston brawled with a U.S. representative from Ohio, William Stanbery. Houston whipped the Ohioan with his hickory cane and was arrested and tried by the U.S. House of Representatives; his lawyer was Francis Scott Key, the author of the "Star-Spangled Banner." Houston was found guilty and given a reprimand and a fine. But something had changed in Houston's mind again.

In December 1832 Houston left the United States and, abandoning his second wife, moved into the Mexican state of Texas. He settled in Nacogdoches, set up law practice, and became active in the political ferment of the impending revolution. He chaired meetings, represented his town at the Convention of 1833, and in October 1835 became commander-in-chief of the troops of Nacogdoches Department. In November Houston became the major general of the nascent Texas army. When the convention at Washington-on-the-Brazos declared Texas independent, Houston was reaffirmed as head of the army.

Almost immediately, soldiers and civilians alike complained about Houston's military style, since his strategy was to move farther east and away from Santa Anna's army. Texans had not realized he would be so cautious a fighter, but he knew that his few troops were undisciplined and that his supplies were limited. Help would probably not come from the United States or any other country. He had to conserve what he had and use his resources wisely, not squander everything on theatrical bravery. The victory at San Jacinto was probably a surprise to Texans, Santa Anna, and just about everyone except Houston.

Victory erased memories of retreat and Houston easily defeated Stephen F. Austin, the "father of Texas," to become the first popularly elected president of the Republic of Texas. A new capital was established not far from the scene of his victory and named in his honor. When he could not succeed himself because of the Texas Constitution, he was elected to the Texas House of Representatives and used his position to criticize his successor Mirabeau B. Lamar.

Houston's relationships with women were still irregular. When Houston was 40, he courted Anna Raguet, who was 17 and the daughter of a prominent Nacogdoches family. Her family, however, was scandalized by his controversial divorce from Eliza—a divorce that involved allegations of fraud and political influence—and the relationship was called off. In 1838 Houston once again set up a household with a Native American woman. This time he lived with the daughter of his friend Chief Bowles, but that alliance soon ended. As usual in white marriages with Native Americans, no divorce was ever sought. Then in 1839 on a trip to Alabama, Houston met Margaret Moffette Lea, the young widow of a Baptist minister. On May 9, 1840—three years after he finally divorced Eliza—Houston married Margaret Lea. She was 21, Houston 47. Margaret's strict religious beliefs reined in his drinking and, in general, settled him down. His marriage to Margaret seemed to be the relationship he had been looking for, and they had a long and, to all appearances, happy life together with eight children.

Texas joined the Union in 1846 and Houston was one of its two U.S. senators (the other was Thomas Jefferson Rusk). He was in the Senate from February 1846 to March 1859 and strongly opposed the sectionalism of the period. Ever an ardent Unionist, he delivered speeches on the evils of sectional feelings and supported the Missouri Compromise (which banned slavery north of latitude 36'30'). A slaveowner himself, Houston voted for the 1848 bill that prohibited slavery in Oregon Territory. In 1849 his old nemesis John C. Calhoun protested this bill as "aggression" of the free states against slavery, but Houston refused to sign Calhoun's proclamation. Probably the coup de grace for ardent secessionists and pro-slavery Democrats came in 1854 when Houston voted against the Kansas-Nebraska bill, which opened to slavery lands what the Missouri Compromise had previously closed.

At this time, state legislatures still appointed each state's U.S. senators. Houston believed that the Senate would not send him to Washington again and so resigned from the Senate to run for governor of Texas. The campaign of 1857 was a nasty three-way race. Houston ran as an independent against Hardin Runnels and Louis T. Wigfall. Wigfall, extremely pro-slavery and an ardent secessionist, followed Houston around the state attacking him as a coward and traitor and countering his arguments in stump speeches almost as good as Houston's. Runnels won the election.

In 1859 Houston again ran for governor as a Unionist and won, defeating Runnels. Houston's name called out pro-Union voters, but he also capitalized on Runnels's inability to end frontier fighting with Native Americans. His reputation as a Union man resulted in his almost being nominated for U.S. president by the National Union party. He narrowly lost to John Bell.

With Texa's secession from the Union, Houston withdrew from public life. Occasionally, he would speak publicly on some victory of Texas forces. His son Sam, Jr., fought for the Confederacy and was wounded at Shiloh. He retired in Huntsville with Margaret and their younger children. This man of contradictions—slave owner and Unionist, cautious general and impetuous fighter, friend of the Native Americans and frontier governor, bigamist and upholder of the law, an ambitious politician who gave up his office and future for principle—died before the war ended of pneumonia on July 26, 1863.

The place to visit to remember Houston is not the eponymous city but Huntsville, about 50 miles north. The town borders the Sam Houston National Forest and includes the Sam Houston Memorial Park and Museum, which preserves his Steamboat House where he retired, another Houston home called Woodland, his law office, and other period buildings. In Oakwood Cemetery, you can find Houston's grave and monument, which carries a quotation from Andrew Jackson, "The world will take care of Houston's fame." The most commanding Houston presence in Huntsville, however, is the giant statue looming over the countryside. Said to be the tallest statue of an American hero, the 67-foot concrete and steel likeness of Sam Houston can be seen from six miles away.

SECESSION

With the election of Abraham Lincoln to the presidency of the United States, southern states began seriously to consider secession. Even before the presidential election, some extreme voices in Texas had been calling for secession and after the vote their voices grew louder. According to the state constitution, however, only the governor could convene the legislature in special session and only the legislature could call a convention to consider secession. Sam Houston, ever the pragmatic Unionist, did again what he had done so well as a military leader: He stalled for time. Houston believed the enthusiasm for secession would die down and so he refused to act. Others, however, took this battle away from Houston. Chief Justice Oran M. Roberts and other prominent Texans issued calls for a January 8, 1861 election to choose delegates to a convention.

Realizing that he could not stop this extra-legal process, Houston convened the legislature in the hope that it would declare a secession convention illegal. What evidence exists today indicates that the election of delegates to the convention did not meet minimum legal requirements of the day. Frequently, delegates were elected by voice vote in public meetings. Informal methods convinced Unionists not to attend these meetings and many chose not to take part in what they saw as an illegal process. In some areas, paramilitary groups like the newly formed Knights of the Golden Circle used the threat of violence to silence Union sympathizers. About 70 percent of those who attended the delegate election meetings were slaveholders, although not necessarily owners of large holdings.

Rather than declare this group of delegates an illegal convention, as Governor Houston had expected, the state legislature validated the convention. The delegates came together on January 28. On the next day, they voted 152 to 6 to secede from the Union. In the next two days, however, a motion to submit secession to popular vote was carried. On February 1, the convention voted 166 to 8 in favor of a referendum on secession.

The Secession Convention, having voted both to secede and to submit the matter to the voters, formed a Committee on Public Safety and sent seven delegates to Montgomery, Alabama, to the convention that would set up the

Confederacy. Before the popular vote could be held, the Committee on Public Safety took over all federal property in the state and forced federal troops to leave. The popular vote of 44,317 for secession to 13,020 against seemed beside the point in the face of these actions. On March 5 the convention reconvened and declared Texas independent of the United States and part of the Confederacy.

One of the most adamant of those voting against secession was James W. Throckmorton, a Tennessee Whig by birth, a strong Unionist, an advisor to Governor Houston, and representative of Collin County, north of Dallas. After war was declared, Throckmorton became a Confederate general. During Reconstruction, he was governor of Texas. In March 1861, Throckmorton expressed his ambivalence and devotion: "While my judgment dictates to me that we are not justified by the surroundings or the occasion, the majority of the people of Texas have declared in favor of secession; the die is cast; the step has been taken, and regardless of consequences I expect and intend to share the fortunes of my friends and neighbors." He exemplified the many Unionists for whom loyalty to Texas was more important than other considerations.

The leading Unionist, Sam Houston, still had a few scenes to play before his final curtain call. In its reshuffle of the state government, the Secession Convention had called on all sitting state officials to swear allegiance to the Confederacy. When his name was publicly called, Houston sat silent in his chair. With that, the convention declared the office of governor vacant and made the lieutenant governor, Edward Clark, the chief executive.

Houston retired to his home in Huntsville. Twice, President Lincoln sent word to the former governor that federal troops would be at his disposal if he wished to resist the convention and restore himself to office. Houston turned down Lincoln's offer. Throughout the rest of his life Houston made no secret of his contempt for Jefferson Davis, the president of the Confederacy, with whom he had served in the U.S. Senate—Houston called him "Little Jeffie"—or of his opposition to such Confederate actions as the draft and the imposition of martial law. Frequently, he voiced his belief that, given the North's superior resources, war would only result in many deaths and the ruin of the South. Once again, he was right. In his retirement he was reputed to have considered plots to overthrow the Confederate regime in Texas and re-establish the republic but, if he considered these intrigues, he never implemented them.

WAR PREPARATIONS

One of Governor Clark's first actions was to divide the state into six districts (later eleven) for recruiting soldiers. The two McCulloch brothers, Ben and Henry, and John F. "Rip" Ford recruited volunteer troops and by the end of 1861, around 25,000 Texans were in the Confederate Army. Almost all the volunteers, however, wanted to be in the cavalry. As the British observer Arthur Fremantle, lieutenant colonel in the Coldstream Guards, noted, "it was found very difficult to raise infantry in Texas, as no Texan walks a yard if he can help it."

Other problems arose in raising a Texas contingent for the Confederate army. For one thing, the Texans were oddly and disparately provisioned. Confederate regulations called for soldiers to carry sabers and carbines, but Texans brought their own weapons with them. They came armed with Bowie knives, hunting rifles, shotguns, squirrel guns, expensive plated handguns, Colt revolvers, and sometimes even lances. Artillery and other major weapons were cannibalized from the recently abandoned federal forts.

At first, uniforms were nonexistent and each Texan could express himself through his clothing. Captain Sam Richardson of the Walter P. Lane Rangers fancied leopard-skin pants. Others wore more sedate outfits, but most uniforms did not match those of other units. The Fourth Texas Infantry wore several shades of gray trimmed in black braid, while the Sixth Texas Infantry wore salt and pepper gray with green trim. Others wore uniforms trimmed in blue or with red stripes. Their headgear varied widely; many a Texan preferred, and wore, a wide-brimmed sombrero instead of the standard gray caps with visors. Eventually, the Confederacy opened shops to manufacture and distribute clothing, shoes, and other materials needed for war. Each day prisoners at the Texas state penitentiary turned out thousands of yards of cloth for uniforms.

What supplies each man carried was another matter of personal whim. William Heartsill, also of the Lane Rangers,

Cinco de Mayo

Contrary to popular belief, Cinco de Mayo is not Mexican Independence Day—that is September 16, Diez y Seis. Cinco de Mayo—May 5—commemorates a battle important to two countries.

In early 1862 French troops of the Emperor Napoleon III along with Spanish and British armies landed in Veracruz, Mexico. President Benito Juárez had suspended payments of foreign debt because the Mexican treasury was bankrupt, and the three armies were there to collect what was owed. The Spanish and British made separate agreements with the Mexican government and left, but the French stayed. Napoleon III's army was thought to be the best and most modern in the world, and now thousands of its soldiers were marching on Mexico City. The French army had not been defeated in 50 years.

On May 5, 1862, French and Mexican forces descended on Pueblo, about 100 miles east of Mexico City. General Ignazio Zaragoza, who had been born in Texas, and 2,000 troops protected the town. The Imperial forces charged across a muddy battlefield (a thunderstorm had struck the night before) only to be met by stampeding cattle urged on by local citizens armed with machetes. After two hours the French were forced to withdraw and the Battle of Pueblo became a source of Mexican pride.

A year later, a reinforced French army managed to fight its way to Mexico City. In May 1863 French troops drove President Juárez out of the capital and installed Archduke Maximilian of Hapsburg as ruler of Mexico. Archduke Maximilian (frequently called the "archdupe") was a patsy installed on a puppet throne by a coalition of counter-revolutionary landowners and clergy. Juárez managed to form provisional governments in various parts of Mexico and to engage the invading army.

As important as these events were to Mexico, they also affected the United States. Napoleon III's apparent intention, after conquering Mexico, was to continue north to Texas and to join up with the Confederate forces. But the Battle of Gettysburg took place 14 months after the Battle of Pueblo. After Lee's surrender at Appomattox, Union General Phil Sheridan was stationed on the Texas border to ensure that the Mexican army was supplied with ammunition and weapons to repulse the French.

A divided and weaker United States was part of the French strategy. By keeping the French at bay until the end of the Civil War, Juárez's forces ensured that the Union Army would not have to fight a much stronger foe than the Confederates.

Two miles south of Goliad is the General Zaragoza State Historic site. A three-room stone structure was built on existing foundations that local traditions held had been Zaragoza's house.

If you are in Texas on Cinco de Mayo, you owe it to yourself to attend one of the many celebrations. Probably the biggest is the party in San Antonio, but almost all Texas towns mark the day in some way.

described the load carried by his horse Pet: "myself, saddle, bridle, saddle-blanket, curry comb, horse brush, coffee pot, tin cup, 20 lbs ham, 200 biscuit, 5 lbs ground coffee, 5 lbs sugar, one large pound cake presented to me by Mrs. C E Talley, 6 shirts, 6 prs socks, 3 prs drawers, 2 prs. Pants, 2 jackets, 1 pr heavy mud boots, one Colt's revolver, one small dirk, four blankets, sixty feet of rope, with a twelve inch iron pin attached."

Individuals could organize military units. The wealthy sugar and cotton planter Benjamin F. Terry started probably the most famous private unit, the Eighth Cavalry—known informally as Terry's Texas Rangers. Terry was killed early in the war but his unit continued to fight under various leaders. They fought at Shiloh, Perryville, Murfreesboro, Chickamauga, and Chattanooga. Under General Nathan Bedford Forrest they were guerrilla raiders, and they joined other units of the Confederate Army to try unsuccessfully to stop Sherman's March to the Sea. Even after the war was over, elements of Terry's Texas Rangers continued to fight.

Terry's Texas Rangers prepare to leave Austin for the War between the States. The young lady is part of the send-off ceremony.
Courtesy Austin History Center, Austin Public Library

Texas Soldiers

About 80 percent of Texas soldiers in the Confederate Army were of English, Welsh, or Scots heritage. The Third Texas Infantry from south Texas did include many Hispanic and German men and was led by Lieutenant Colonel Augustus Buchel, a native of the Rhineland. Colonel Santos Benavides, the former mayor of Laredo, was the most well-known of the more than 2,500 Hispanic Texans who served in the Confederate Army.

As the war dragged on, however, enthusiasm waned and eventually the Confederate Congress passed a draft law. Governor Francis Lubbock, who had defeated Governor Clark in 1861, tried to contribute the state's share to the conflict. In November 1863 he reported to the state legislature that 90,000 men were serving in the army. When the age limits were extended to 17 and 50 in 1864, between 100,000 and 110,000 Texans became eligible to serve.

Texans could fight either in state military units or as part of the Confederate Army. About two-thirds of Texan soldiers stayed in the southwest to fight Native Americans or to repulse anticipated Union attacks. Most of the important battles of the war were fought far from Texas. Some soldiers from Texas fought at Shiloh under Texan Albert Sidney Johnston or at Chickamauga and Gettysburg in Hood's Texas Brigade, commanded by General John Bell Hood. Other Texas commanders who made names for themselves east of the Mississippi included General Lawrence Sullivan "Sul" Ross, General Mathew Duncan Ector, and Colonel Hiram B. Granbury. The first man had a west Texas university named after him, the second a county, and the last a town.

Not all required to serve did. The rich could hire substitutes to serve for them. Exemptions could be obtained by office holders, owners of large numbers of slaves, people involved in frontier defense, and those necessary for particular occupations, such as agriculture. Many Texans enlisted only to find that they lacked the taste for military discipline or merely wanted to be home with their families. By the end of the war, 4,664 Texans were officially listed as deserters.

Some Texans became Jayhawkers—Unionist guerrillas who operated behind Confederate lines. At first this appellation was applied only to fighters from Kansas and Missouri, but soon the nickname was given to any Unionist fighter in the South—especially west of the Mississippi River. Jayhawkers tended to hide out in the timbered areas of north Texas and in the depths of the east Texas swamps. The difference between Jayhawkers and deserters was often difficult to describe—except that the Jayhawkers were more likely to engage in battles, at least in theory.

Others who favored the Union joined—or tried to join—the Union forces. For example, a former attorney general and representative from Texas to the U.S. House of Representatives was Unionist Andrew Jackson Hamilton. When other southern congressmen had walked out of the Congress, Hamilton had stayed in his seat. He returned to Texas and was elected to the Texas legislature as a Unionist. When he refused to take the oath to the Confederacy, he believed his life was in jeopardy and was forced to hide out in the hills west of Austin. In the spring of 1862 he made his way to Mexico where he gathered other refugees around him to prepare to fight for the Union in Texas. In November 1862 Lincoln appointed him military governor of the state.

Not all Texans who supported the Union were as well known, or as fortunate, as Hamilton. In August 1862 Major Fritz Tegener led a party of between 60 and 70 German Texans toward Mexico to volunteer for service in the Union Army. Near the Nueces River in Kinney County, Lieutenant C.D. McRae and a band of 94 Confederates overtook the would-be Unionists. The Unionists were not on guard because they believed they had eluded Confederate outposts, but they had been betrayed by one of their party—a man named Charles Bergmann. In the Battle of the Nueces, 32 of the Unionists were killed immediately and an unknown number were shot and hanged later by the Confederate forces. The dead were left where they fell and three years later family and friends gathered their bones for burial in Comfort, a village in Kendall County. They later built a monument, *Treue Der Union* [True to the Union], to their memory. It is reputed to be the only monument to the Union dead south of the Mason-Dixon Line.

Some who just wanted to ignore the war tried to stay in Texas and avoid the greater conflict. One avenue for avoidance was to volunteer to serve in the frontier militias, organized under such names as the Minute Men, the Gillespie Rifles, and the Frontier Defense Company. Since the Texas government held that men engaged in frontier defense were not subject to the draft, militia service was a convenient way to avoid army service. In 1861 some Hill Country Germans started an organization provocatively named the Union Loyal League as a purported frontier defense mechanism. With more than 500 members in the Hill Country counties of Gillespie, Kerr, and Kendall, the Loyal League was eventually forced to disband.

A little more than 2,000 Texans made it out of Texas (usually to Mexico) and joined the Union Army. Of these men, 47 were African American and 958 were Hispanic. They formed the First Texas Cavalry (Union), which fought in the Louisiana campaign and, toward the war's end, in Brownsville. Eventually a Second Texas Cavalry (Union) was formed.

War for the Coast

The first battles in Texas centered on ports, lifelines to the outside world. The Union Navy blockaded Texas ports in July 1861, and in the spring of the next year, Captain Henry Eagle demanded that Galveston surrender. His demand was a bluff, however. General Paul O. Hébert, after evacuating civilians and livestock, refused to surrender and Eagle backed down. Hébert informed Governor Lubbuck that the city had been lucky this time but was inherently indefensible.

The next attempt on a Texas port came in August 1862 farther south, at Corpus Christi. A naval attack led by Lieutenant John W. Kittredge was repulsed by troops commanded by Major Alfred M. Hobby. The Confederates used old earthen works that General Zachary Taylor's troops had constructed during the Mexican War. In September Kittredge and his men went ashore near Flour Bluff south of Corpus and were captured. Federal ships controlled the harbor, but the city was not occupied until the end of the war.

Two failures on the lower coast pushed the federal navy farther north to Sabine Pass, where initially the Union forces fared better. In July 1862 Confederate reports had pointed out that Sabine Pass—which is on the Gulf below Port Arthur—was not adequately defended, but before improvements could be made, Union forces shelled the outpost. The

The Sabine Pass Lighthouse is on the Louisiana side of the river because the highest ground is on that side. As a U.S. senator, Sam Houston saw to it that this and other lighthouses were built along the Texas coast. Bob Parvin, courtesy TxDOT

Confederate defenders spiked their cannon and abandoned the area. The Union sailors came ashore and destroyed what remained of the position and a railway bridge and depot.

Buoyed by this success, the Union navy turned its attention once again to Galveston. Working on his conviction that Galveston was indefensible, General Hébert had removed almost all heavy artillery from the town, over vocal protest from the citizens of Galveston. Now only one cannon remained to greet Commander William B. Renshaw and his forces when they sailed into Galveston harbor on October 4. A four-day truce was called and all civilians were evacuated. On October 8 General Hébert surrendered the island.

Victory, however, placed Renshaw and his men in a precarious position. Even after they were reinforced by three companies of Massachusetts men, the Union forces in Galveston numbered fewer than 400. To add to Union woes, General Hébert had been replaced by John B. Magruder, an experienced soldier with a love of action. Magruder had sworn to relieve Galveston. Magruder swathed two gunboats in protective bales of cotton and sent them into Galveston Bay while a land force concentrated opposite the town. On January 1, 1863, the Confederates regained Galveston.

When the federal forces withdrew, the Confederates were able to refortify Fort Griffin at Sabine Pass. The Union forces, however, were planning to retake the Texas coast with Sabine Pass as their major attack point. In early September, four gunboats, 23 transports, and 5,000 troops prepared to land at Fort Griffin. The defending forces consisted of Lieutenant Dick Dowling, one gunboat, and 46 members of the Davis Guard.

On September 8 the federal gunboat *Clifton*, commanded by Lieutenant Frederick Crocker, entered the channel and fired on the fort. The *Clifton* fired 26 shells but the range kept them from being effective. Dowling simply kept his men under cover. In the afternoon, the battle enlarged with the addition of two gunboats from the Louisiana side of the Sabine and a continuation of the *Clifton*'s attack from the Texas side; another ship also trailed the *Clifton*. When the ships were within 1,200 yards of the fort, the defenders opened fire. The steam mechanism of one ship was pierced and scalding steam and water covered the crew. The *Clifton*'s boiler was blown apart by a direct hit and someone on the ship hauled up the white flag of surrender. Crew members, thinking the ship was about to blow up, jumped ship and straggled to shore where they were arrested by Dowling and his men. Believing that the Confederate defenders were stronger and more numerous than they were, the federal forces withdrew to their home base in New Orleans.

In one hour, a Confederate force of fewer than 50 men had captured two gunboats and captured or killed 350 federal fighters. With perhaps a bit of exaggeration, Magruder called Dowling and his men "the greatest heroes that history has recorded." Jeff Davis, a little more modestly, called the battle "one of the most brilliant and heroic achievements in the history of this war." In any event, the second Battle of Sabine Pass is one of the most astounding upsets of the war.

In the fall of 1863 Union forces once again turned their attention to the southern ports of Texas. On November 2, 1863, 7,000 federal troops commanded by General Nathaniel P. Banks and carried in 26 ships landed near the mouth of the Rio Grande. The Confederate forces under the command of Brigadier General Hamilton P. Bee numbered fewer than 100. Bee abandoned the city and loaded up 45 wagons with supplies. Before they left, the Confederate troops burned cotton supplies and other material that could not be evacuated. Union troops occupied Brownsville on November 6.

Banks's troops used Brownsville as a base for taking other points on the coast. Soon they occupied Mustang, St. Joseph, and Matagorda islands. Confederate troops spiked their guns at Fort Esperanza on Matagorda and then set everything on fire before pulling out. Indianola and Port Lavaca were the next to fall to the federal forces. At the same time Colonel Edmund J. Davis and Colonel John L. Haynes occupied the Ringgold Barracks near Rio Grande City. Confederate troops destroyed the San Antonio and Gulf Coast Railroad and left the area to the federals.

General Magruder decided that he could not stop the Union forces in the Rio Grande area and turned his attention to the lower Brazos River where he was convinced the next attack would come. But General Banks's next campaign began farther to the east.

WAR ON THE RED RIVER

Banks was convinced that taking the agricultural country of east Texas and the military storehouses and shops in Marshall and Henderson would destroy Confederate morale and cut the southern armies off from needed material. So his next move came on the Red River rather than the Brazos. In March 1864 General Banks and 25,000 soldiers set up the Red River accompanied by a mass of gunboats. Meanwhile

Civil War Prison Camp

General Frederick Steele was moving his federal forces of about 15,000 down from Little Rock, Arkansas. The two armies were to merge and destroy all opposition in north Louisiana, south Arkansas, and east Texas.

The general in charge of the Confederate armies of the Trans-Mississippi Department was E. Kirby Smith. He called on the armies of General Magruder, who sent all the troops he could spare, including a new brigade under the command of General Bee, fresh from the Brownsville surrender, and another brigade under the French aristocrat Camille Armand Jules Marie, the Prince de Polignac. Lieutenant General Richard Taylor, the field commander of the Confederate troops, pushed back Banks's army near Mansfield, Louisiana. The Confederates took 2,500 prisoners in that battle on April 8. The next day the federal forces counterattacked and pushed back the Confederates.

Camp Ford began as a training camp for conscripts and was named for John S. "Rip" Ford, who was at that time in charge of conscription. In July 1863 the Confederate Trans-Mississippi Department ordered that prisoners of war in Shreveport, Louisiana, be moved to Camp Ford. Eventually, it became the largest prisoner-of-war camp west of the Mississippi. Located near Tyler, the camp had passable conditions before the Red River Campaign when the capture of so many of Banks's soldiers filled it past reasonable limits.

Prisoners had to build their own shelters, and before the Red River Campaign many constructed shelters out of wood and other materials. They also made clothes, furniture, dishes, baskets, and other items that they traded with locals. After April 1864, living conditions became wretched. The population suddenly tripled with the addition of 3,000 captured Yankees. Food, clothing, and shelter became scarce.

Timber in the area had all been used. The new prisoners constructed shelter out of brush or blankets. Many ended up living in holes in the ground to protect themselves. For many, the clothes they were wearing when captured were all they had during their imprisonment; the federal blockade and the end of local manufacturing in the South had cut off the supply of clothing for everyone. Union officers at Camp Ford wrote to the U.S. government, which sent two shipments of clothes for the prisoners.

Over the two years the camp was in existence, around 6,000 prisoners lived there. Of these, 286 died. After the war, Union soldiers destroyed the camp and little remains of it.

Smith County now operates an interpretive historical and archeological park on the site of Camp Ford. Archeological investigations have uncovered the perimeters of the camp and brought some artifacts to earth. An interpretative kiosk and some walking trails can be found at the site, about two miles northeast of Tyler.

General Smith had a difficult decision to make. He needed to stop General Steele's southward march through Arkansas, but he also had to commit troops to the battle with Banks's army. In the end, he sent two divisions from Taylor's army to join General Sterling Price, the Confederate commander in Arkansas. This army managed to stop Steele's troops, but Taylor was never able to engage Banks in a definitive battle. Instead, for six weeks the two armies harassed each other up and down the Louisiana and east Texas bayous. The loss of life was staggering. The Confederates lost 4,300 soldiers, including 2,852 Texans. The federal forces lost 5,400. Several thousand Union soldiers were taken prisoner and sent to Camp Ford near Tyler. Later some were moved to Camp Groce near Hempstead.

Taylor was never able to defeat Banks definitively, but the campaign did keep federal forces from occupying north Louisiana and east Texas. Fighting did not stop in the Trans-Mississippi Department. A Texas cavalry brigade commanded by Brigadier General Richard Gano and a band of Confederate Native Americans led by Stand Watie attacked federal outposts in Oklahoma. These combined forces won a major victory at the Battle of Cabin Creek.

War on the Frontier

People on the frontier and in the northeastern counties of Texas had more immediate concerns than the possible invasion of Union forces. Comanches and other Native American groups took advantage of the absence of troops from the frontier forts to stage raids.

Around Christmas of 1863, about 300 Comanches raided Montague and Cooke Counties, killing about a dozen Texans, burning ten houses, and carrying off horses and women. Troops gave chase, but the Comanches got away. The spring and summer of 1864 saw many small raids, but nothing major occurred until October 1864. The Comanche Little Buffalo led a group of more than 500 Kiowas and Comanches into Young County. Forming themselves into small raiding parties, the group attacked isolated ranches and farms along Elm Creek, a tributary of the Brazos River. Some families took refuge in two small forts, where troopers found the refugees after they arrived. The troops gave chase but never found the Native Americans.

Abandoned hill country barn. © Carol M. Sander

The Battle of Elm Creek gave rise to two stories, the stranger of which involved a man named John Wooten whose horse was shot out from under him. Wooten started running away with two Native American riders chasing him. Every time he stopped running, one of his pursuers would call him by name and tell him to keep moving. He ran for three miles and escaped. Wooten had once worked as a butcher at a reservation in Throckmorton County and he assumed that the two pursuers had recognized him and spared his life because he had fed them. The second story involves Brit Johnson, a slave whose son was killed in the fight and whose wife and surviving children were captured. According to the narrative, Johnson joined the Comanches in Oklahoma. He gained the respect of the tribe and convinced them to release all their captives.

After Elm Creek, patrols increased and settlers were encouraged to "fort up" at the slightest indication of a problem. Increased awareness of danger probably contributed to a battle with a band of peaceful Kickapoos crossing Texas to escape the chaos of the Civil War. A combined force of about 325 state militia and 161 Confederate troops set out in January of 1865 to find hostile Comanches and Kiowas. Command was never well coordinated between the militia, under the leadership of Captain S.S. Totten, and the Confederates, led by Captain Henry Fossett.

Around January 7, Fossett's scouts found a camp of
Native Americans they assumed were Comanches. The
Native Americans were camped in woods along the banks of
Dove Creek, a tributary of the Concho River. Totten's militia
caught up with the Confederates early on the morning of
January 8, and the two commanders came up with a hasty
plan that assumed the Native Americans were hostile.

The attack did not go well. For one thing, the Native
Americans were in a strong defensive position covered by
dense woods. The attackers had to wade a creek and cross
over dense cover filled with briars while being shot at. The
Confederate troops captured the Native American horses,
but the Kickapoo recaptured the animals. During the night a
storm drenched the survivors; by morning snow was falling.

The Kickapoos managed to get away and make it to
Mexico, but the Battle of Dove Creek so embittered this
formerly peaceful tribe that they took to making revenge
attacks on the Texans along the Rio Grande.

Only one other major Civil War engagement involved
Native Americans and soldiers. In November 1864, Union
troops under Colonel Christopher "Kit" Carson left New
Mexico and entered the Texas Panhandle to stop Comanche
and Kiowa raids on the Santa Fe Trail. Just north of the
Canadian River, near the ruins of an abandoned adobe fort,
Native Americans attacked the soldiers. Carson and his men
took shelter behind the walls of the old fort and managed to
fight off the attackers in what became known as the First
Battle of Adobe Walls.

War along the Rio Grande

John S. "Rip" Ford had seen battle in the Mexican War, was
once a Texas Ranger, and had led expeditions into the Big
Bend. He was not pleased with his first Civil War
assignment, recruiting volunteers for the Confederate Army
and overseeing conscripts. Being a man of action, Ford was
overjoyed when General Magruder ordered him to form an
expeditionary force to liberate the Lower Rio Grande Valley
from the Union forces. Not only did this assignment give
Ford the chance to see battle once again and to fight against
the federal army, but it also brought him the possibility of
one more encounter with an old enemy—Juan Cortina, who
was fighting on the Union side.

Colonel Ford recruited for the Cavalry of the West in December 1863 in San Antonio. On March 18, 1864, Ford led his troops out to search for the enemy. While camped at a Confederate outpost, Ford received a call for reinforcements from Colonel Santos Benavides in Laredo, where a federal raid had been repulsed. Drought had left the Nueces Strip grassless and barren. To cross it, Ford would need more water and horses. He told Benavides that Laredo would have to continue to defend itself. This cautious desire to ensure his supply base, however, cost Ford the element of surprise.

In the last week of March, Ford finally decided that, even without new supplies, he had to continue on or the campaign would fall apart. After a grueling march across the coastal plains, the Cavalry of the West reached Ringgold Barracks to discover that Ford's caution had been misplaced. The federal forces had apparently long ago left this upper Rio Grande position and returned to Brownsville. The area from Rio Grande City to El Paso was free of federal soldiers. Ford and his forces now cautiously approached Brownsville, skirmishing with some companies of the First Texas Cavalry (Union) near Las Rucias. On July 30, 1864, a patrol rode into Brownsville to find that the federals had left two days before.

Ford established Confederate control over the town, but unrest continued to flare up along the border. Just as eager as Ford to resume their rivalry, Juan Cortina, now a Mexican general, attacked Brownsville with artillery fire in September 1864. Cortina was beaten back when Imperialist armies attacked him from the Mexican side. For several months, south Texas was relatively calm.

On April 9, 1865, General Robert E. Lee surrendered the Army of Northern Virginia at Appomattox Court House. The army he relinquished included the last remnants of Hood's Texas Brigade—617 men out of the original 5,000. Over April, other Confederates surrendered in bits and pieces, but General Kirby Smith, the commander of the Trans-Mississippi Department; General Magruder, the commander in Texas; and Governor Pendelton Murrah all called on troops and civilians to resist and continue to defend the state. Gradually, the urge to resist waned. Tired soldiers began walking home.

Meanwhile, Rip Ford and his troops were preparing to fight the last battle of the Civil War. On May 11 a federal force of white and African American troops left the island of Brazos Santiago and crossed over to the Texas mainland. They skirmished with Confederates near Palmito Ranch, but neither side won decisively and both made camp. The next day Ford and about 300 troops arrived with field artillery and, after several charges, broke the enemy lines. The federals retreated, but Ford decided his men were too tired to follow. A few days later the two sides parlayed and Ford decided further fighting was useless. He released his men, and Ford and his wife crossed the Mexican border into Matamoros to stay with friends.

Texas descended into anarchy. Kirby Smith tried to concentrate his forces in Houston, but his soldiers deserted their units and went home. Riots broke out in Houston, Galveston, Austin, and San Antonio. Unpaid for months, soldiers looted Confederate warehouses. Some reports said that children in Galveston stole gun powder and cartridges and exploded them in the streets. On May 23 the Washington County planter Thomas Affleck wrote to his friend John Anderson, "The army has entirely disbanded & are sacking as they go….We have no Govt. or country. God help us."

Must-See Civil War Battlegrounds

At Sabine Pass Battleground State Historical Park in Jefferson County a series of markers indicate important aspects of the battles there and identify some of the participants. The fifty-acre plus park also has an open-air pavilion with explanations of the battle. Since Fort Griffin was a "mud fort," no original fortifications remain. A monument is topped by a bronze statue of Dick Dowling.

A historical marker also describes the battle at the Palmito Ranch, east of Brownsville. Ringgold Barracks, east of Rio Grande City, was an active army post until 1906. Civil War period buildings that survive at the site include the post hospital and the building alleged to have been Robert E. Lee's house when he commanded the pre-war Department of Texas. Other Texas forts with Civil War associations include Fort Davis National Historic Site in Jeff Davis County in west Texas, Fort Bliss in El Paso, Fort Duncan at Eagle Pass, Fort Mason at Mason, Fort McIntosh at Laredo, and Fort Belknap at Newcastle.

Reconstruction

On June 19, 1865, General Gordon Granger and 1,800 federal troops landed in Galveston. General Granger announced that all slaves in Texas were free, the acts of the Texas government since secession illegal, and officers and men who had served in the Confederate forces paroled. He urged former slaves to "remain at their present homes and work for wages" and reminded them not to congregate at military posts. Unfortunately, General Granger's statements were not as easy to enforce as they were to announce.

War's End

On June 2, 1865, General Kirby Smith formally surrendered his army, but peace did not come. Texas was sunk in chaos—politically, economically, and socially. Like other southerners, Texans had to create a new economic system based on free labor instead of slave labor. Land values and cotton prices plummeted. No administration existed to run the state. War emotions left neighbors distrusting, or even hating, each other. Native American raids continued to threaten the frontier. During the Civil War, the inability to protect western settlers had caused the frontier to contract about 100 miles to the east.

Shortages of imported commodities and even of some staples had left their mark on those who had stayed in Texas during the fighting. Using roasted sweet potatoes and peanuts as coffee substitutes probably was wearing, although not life-threatening, and the large numbers of refugees pushing into Texas from other southern states swamped what few resources were left.

Texas fared better than many other Confederate states. No major battles were fought in Texas; battling armies did not trample crops, steal household goods, and ravage infrastructure—at least not to the extent that they did in states like Georgia and South Carolina. Nonetheless, returning soldiers were exhausted, hungry, and traumatized by violence. They and their family members probably looked forward to a return to normal, but it would be a long while before that would happen. First, Texas had to re-establish civil government and try to create a new economy.

PRESIDENTIAL RECONSTRUCTION

Even within the victorious federal government, opinions differed over how to treat the states and people of the defeated Confederacy. President Lincoln held that, since secession was illegal, reconstruction of the rebel states was a matter for his—the executive—branch of the government. In the U.S. Congress, however, some elements of his own party—the Radical Republicans—believed that since the southern states had forfeited statehood, they could return to the Union only as new states and only through the legislative branch.

Lincoln made the first move. On December 8, 1863, he announced that, when 10 percent of the 1860 voting population of any seceded state could take the oath of allegiance to the United States and accept all laws regarding slavery, a government could be established. Under his plan, Lincoln restored statehood to Tennessee, Louisiana, and Arkansas.

But everything changed when Lincoln was assassinated. Andrew Johnson, who succeeded Lincoln, was not in as strong a position as his predecessor had been. A Tennessee Democrat who remained loyal to the Union, he was not trusted by the Republicans and had no leverage for controlling congressional radicals. On June 17, 1865, Johnson appointed Andrew Jackson Hamilton provisional governor of Texas. But General George A. Custer commanded the federal troops in Texas, and he believed that the military should remain the predominant force in governing the state.

Congress established the Freedmen's Bureau in March 1865. Responsible for establishing schools and relief aid for freed slaves, the bureau also oversaw labor agreements that involved freed people and protected them in the courts. Probably the bureau was most successful in overseeing schools—a definite necessity for the newly freed slave population, of whom 95 percent were illiterate at the end of the war.

General George Custer, his wife and dog, and various officers and friends pose in front of his headquarters in Austin. The University of Texas has refurbished this handsome building at the corner of Red River and Martin Luther King, next to the Erwin Special Events Center.
Courtesy Center for American History, UT-Austin

In September 1865, General E.M. Gregory was put in charge of the Texas Freedmen's Bureau. The vast distances in the state made the bureau's job difficult. In addition, few of the 50,000 federal soldiers in Texas could help the bureau's agents. Instead of being stationed in interior areas with large freed slave populations, most U.S. soldiers were strung along the Rio Grande to support Mexican President Benito Juárez in his showdown with the French and Mexican Imperialist forces. Without military backup, agents could not force recalcitrant former slaveowners to abide by labor agreements or treat freed slaves as liberated.

Provisional Governor Hamilton set about trying to build a working state government. As fast as he could, Hamilton filled almost all state, district, county, and local offices with Union sympathizers. In keeping with President Johnson's reconstruction plans, Hamilton called for an election on January 8, 1866, to select delegates to a constitutional convention. He made it clear that the convention had to fulfill four conditions: Slavery had to be declared finished and the 13th Amendment outlawing it accepted. Freed slaves' civil rights (but not necessarily the right to vote) had to be secured, the secession ordinance rejected, and state and Confederate debt incurred as part of the war repudiated.

When the convention assembled in Austin on February 7, 1866, the delegates were divided into three factions. At the extremes were dedicated Unionists and secessionists; in the middle were the majority, committed to neither. This last group elected as president of the convention J. W. Throckmorton, the Unionist who had served as a Confederate brigadier general.

While the convention did acknowledge that slavery had ended and that freed slaves had civil rights, African Americans were still denied the right to vote and hold office and could not testify against whites in trials. The delegates also refused to approve the 13th Amendment, holding that their approval was unnecessary since the amendment had already been ratified. In one regard the convention went further than asked; it repudiated all state debts incurred since secession—not just debts incurred in the conduct of war. This denial of all debts was supported by Unionists, secessionists, and moderates, but not by those who held outstanding loans to Texas.

The resulting constitution closely followed the 1845 Texas Constitution. An election was called for June 25, 1866. The candidates for governor included Throckmorton, who upheld the reconstruction aims of President Johnson and opposed allowing African Americans to vote, and E.M. Pease, a Unionist who favored allowing literate African American males to vote. Throckmorton won 49,277 to 12,168; the constitutional amendments passed by a narrower margin.

The Eleventh Legislature convened on August 6 and Throckmorton was inaugurated on August 9. President Johnson declared rebellion at an end in Texas on August 20—Texas was the last state to be returned to the Union under presidential reconstruction.

Immediately, the legislature created a new world somewhere between the old and the emerging one envisioned by the national government—a Texas in which African Americans were no longer slaves but not quite free and still inferior. John H. Reagan, the highest-ranking Texan in the Confederate government, warned the legislators that the Radical Republicans were prepared to overturn presidential reconstruction and they should tread

This map of the proposed reoccupation of south Texas appeared in the New York Herald on 28 March 1863. Courtesy of Texas General Land Office

softly. The legislators ignored his advice.

Instead, they passed a series of laws we now call the "black codes," seriously limiting the rights of African Americans in Texas. The laws regarding vagrancy, apprenticeship, and labor seemed especially designed to keep former slaves in a state of peonage, requiring, for instance, that laborers be obedient and respectful. Employers were given the final word in all labor disputes and could deduct

Band prepares to celebrate Emancipation Day, also known as Juneteenth, in 1900. Courtesy Austin History Center, Austin Public Library

Juneteenth

Liberated slaves in Texas marked General Gordon Granger's June 19 announcement of the Emancipation Proclamation as a holiday called Juneteenth. No one is sure when freedmen began formally celebrating Juneteenth, but the day is generally thought to be the oldest observance of the end of slavery.

Whites often resisted freedmen's attempts to celebrate the day. Landowners would demand that tenant farmers and sharecroppers return to the fields on Juneteenth; urban employers refused to recognize the day. Often civil authorities would not allow African Americans to use public property, such as parks, to mark the day. The food, parades, and attempts at fancy dressing were objects of white humor, when in fact they were almost all the same as the trappings of other ceremonies in the country, such as the Fourth of July.

Usually, the day would begin with a reading of the Emancipation Proclamation, a prayer service, sometimes a parade, and testimonies from former slaves. Food was often lavish because each family brought at least one dish, including rarely available beef, lamb, or other meat for barbecue.

Some African American institutions bought property to ensure that they would be able to mark Juneteenth without interference from white-controlled civil authorities. In Mexia in 1898, a group of former slaves bought land called Comanche Crossing for a Juneteenth park. According to legend, slaves at a large plantation walked two miles from their former master's land to a crossing on the Navasota River. There, they met a band of Comanches and shared a meal with them. The original name of the site

commemorated this feast. Later, the park was named Booker T. Washington Emancipation Park, and at its height in the 1970s, the Juneteenth celebration in the park attracted 20,000 people. A 1981 incident when three young African Americans drowned while in police custody cut back on attendance.

At some point in the 1920s, celebration of Juneteenth is said to have fallen off. Some point to the use of nationally produced textbooks, which gave January 1 as the day of the Emancipation Proclamation and did not mention Juneteenth, as a cause of this decline. Others believe African Americans no longer considered Juneteenth a "real holiday" as they tried to blend in with white society. A more likely explanation is that white media and white society in general came to ignore the holiday—no longer finding it either threatening or humorous.

The holiday had a publicity resurgence in the late 1940s and early 1950s and then went underground again until the 1970s. Some attribute the renewed interest to the Reverend Ralph Abernathy's 1968 Poor Peoples March to Washington. In 1974, a Juneteenth celebration in Keist Park in Dallas drew thousands of people. The following year the mayor proclaimed Juneteenth Day in Dallas. In 1979 the Republican governor of Texas signed a bill making Juneteenth an official state holiday.

As Juneteenth has grown in popularity Texas towns and cities have begun official celebrations. For listings of selected Juneteenth celebrations, go to www.juneteenth.com/2texas_us.htm.

from wages for such infractions as disobedience, wasting time, or leaving home without permission. A major attempt to treat free labor as if it were coerced labor involved using the vagrancy law to label a person as idle, arresting him or her, and then contracting out the convicted person's labor. Eventually, anyone sentenced to jail for any misdemeanor could face similar treatment. Although these laws were often framed without mentioning race, they were designed to control African American labor.

The black codes affected more aspects of life than just work. African Americans were cut off from a major economic reward of the period since they could not claim free land under the Texas Homestead Law. They could not serve on juries, testify in court against whites, hold office, or vote. Interracial marriage was officially outlawed.

Finally, the legislature tried to cut off education for African American children by limiting their school funding to what African American taxpayers could raise. Since freed slaves still had no land or jobs, this provision essentially ended public education for their children.

The black codes did not accomplish their goals, however. On January 3, 1867, General Joseph B. Kiddoo, who had replaced General Gregory as head of the Freedmen's Bureau, declared one of the laws—the contract law—biased against freedmen. Without this key law, the other laws lost their importance. Still, during the rest of Reconstruction— and on after it had ended—tension existed between the goal of truly freeing the former slaves and the desire of many landowners to use African American laborers as if their status had changed little, if at all. Without their own land, former slaves ended up as sharecroppers or tenant farmers, often for their former masters.

Governor Throckmorton held that President Johnson's proclamation that rebellion had ended in Texas made military rule unnecessary. The president, however, was fighting for his political life and the Radical Republicans in the U.S. Congress were growing stronger. In the national election of 1866, the Radical Republicans gained control of the U.S. Congress and began their own reconstruction program. On March 2, 1887, they passed, over President Johnson's veto, the First Reconstruction Act.

CONGRESSIONAL RECONSTRUCTION

The First Reconstruction Act held existing governments in the former Confederate states inadequate and divided the Confederacy into five military districts. The commanding generals in each district had powers superior to those of state laws and officials. Southern states had to call new constitutional conventions with delegates drawn from the entire male population—except for unpardoned Confederates. These conventions were to draw up new constitutions to submit to the voting population. The new constitution had to be acceptable to Congress and, especially, had to grant African American males the right to vote. New legislatures had to ratify the 14th Amendment granting that vote.

Congress appointed General Philip Sheridan the military commander of the Fifth District, which included Texas.

General Charles Griffin was in immediate charge of Texas. Governor Throckmorton told Griffin that he would cooperate with him, but both generals saw the governor as a man who would not protect freedmen's interests. In August 1887, Sheridan removed Throckmorton from office and replaced him with E. M. Pease, who had been governor of the state from 1853 to 1857 but who had been handily defeated by Throckmorton. The military then replaced officials at all levels.

The U.S. Congress had framed an "iron-clad oath" for all officials and voters in the old Confederacy to take. A man had to swear that he had never before held an elected office, or any other position that required pledging to uphold the Constitution, and then rebelled against the Union. Sheridan interpreted this oath rigidly; even men who had held relatively minor offices were banned from serving again— often they were even forbidden to serve on juries.

In November 1867, however, the more moderate General Winfield S. Hancock replaced Sheridan. He allowed local officials to re-open registration for voting for delegates to the constitutional convention. A majority of those registered had to vote in the election before the convention could convene, and African American males were allowed to vote for delegates and to serve in the convention. The election was held over five days in February 1868. The Union League tried to get out the votes of former slaves, but the Ku Klux Klan and similar organizations tried to keep African Americans and Unionists from voting. Most registered white voters failed to vote: 52,964 registered voters, mostly whites, boycotted the election. The vote was 7,757 white voters and 36,932 African American voters for the convention and 10,622 white voters and 818 African Americans against.

The convention met in Austin on June 1, 1868. Of the 94 delegates, two had helped to draft the Constitution of 1845 and six had served on the 1866 Constitution. One had been in the German National Assembly. George Ruby, the president of the Union Leagues of Texas, was one of ten African American delegates. The convention bogged down on extremely divisive issues and did not complete its work until the winter of 1869. All in all it spent $200,000 on its deliberations—an incredibly high sum for the time.

One of the divisive issues was partition. When Texas had first entered the Union in 1845, it retained the right to

Freedom

When freedom came, released slaves had many different reactions, according to later interviews with freedmen:

After I was traded off, my new massa wasn't so good to me. He thought all the time the South would win the war, and he treated us mean. He kept telling us a black nigger never would be free. When it came, he said to us, 'Well you black _____, you are just as free as I am.' He turned us loose with nothing to eat and almost no clothes. He said if he got up next morning and found a nigger on his place, he'd horsewhip him.

—Eli Davison, born in Dunbar West Virginia, 1844;
moved to Madison County, Texas, 1858

The surrender came, and Massa Jim read the long paper. He said, 'I'll explain it to you. It's the order from the government which makes it against the law to keep you as slaves.' You should have seen those colored folks. They just shook. Their faces were as long as their arms, and so pestered they didn't know what to say or do.

Massa never said another word and walked away. The colored folk said, 'Where are we going to live?' 'What are we going to do?' Uncle John said, 'When do we have to go?' Then massa laughed heartily and said they could stay for wages or work on halves. Well, sir, there were a bunch of happy colored folks after they learned they could stay and work.

—Elsie Reece, born in Grimes County, Texas, 1847

During the war Marster Charley cussed everything and everybody, and we had to watch and keep out of his way. After two years he got a letter from Marster Billy, and he said he would be home soon and that John was killed. Missy started crying and marster jumped up and started cursing the war, and he picked up a hot poker and said, 'Free the nigger, will they, I'll free them.' And he hit my mammy on the neck, and she started moaning and crying and dropped to the floor. There they were, the missy a-moaning, my mammy a moaning, and the marster cussing as loud as he could. He took the gun off the rack and started for the field where the niggers were working. My sister and I saw that, and we started running and screaming because we had brothers and sisters in the field. But the good Lord took a hand in that mess, and the marster hadn't gone far in the field when he dropped all of a sudden. The death set in on the marster, and the niggers came running to him. He couldn't talk or move, and they toted him in the house. The doctor came, and the next day marster died.

Then Marster Billy came home, and he broke up the place with the freedom for the niggers. Most of them left as soon as they could.

The missy got very condescending after freedom. The women were in the spinning house, and we expected another whipping and scolding, cause that was the usual doing when she came. She came in and said, "Good morning, women," and she never said such before. She said she would pay wages to all who stayed and told how good she would treat them. But my pappy came and took us over to the widow Perry's land to work for shares.

After that, the missy found Marster Billy dead in the shed, with his throat cut and that razor beside him. There was a piece of paper saying he did not care to live because the niggers were free and they were all broken up.

—Annie Row, born on a plantation near Rusk, Texas, 86 when interviewed

Everybody went wild. We all felt like heroes, and nobody had made us that way but ourselves. We were free. Just like that, we were free. It didn't seem to make the whites mad, either. They went right on giving us food just the same. Nobody took our homes, but right off colored folks started on the move. They seemed to want to get closer to freedom, so they knew what it was—like it was a place or a city.

We knew freedom was on us, but we didn't know what was to come with it. We thought we were going to get rich like the white folks. We thought we were going to be richer than the white folks, because we were stronger and knew how to work, and the whites didn't, and we didn't have to work for them any more. But it didn't turn out that way. We soon found out that freedom could make folks proud but it didn't make them rich.

—Felix Haywood, born in Bexar County, 92 when interviewed

—*The Slave Narratives of Texas*, Ed. Ron Tyler and Lawrence R. Murphy

divide itself into not more than four states. The 1868-69 constitutional convention was one of the few assemblies actually to consider this possibility. The first suggestion came from Pease who proposed that Texas sell to the United States all land west of a line from the mouth of the Pecos to the northwest corner of Hardeman County, giving away the Panhandle and a broad swath of the Llano Estacado. A counter-proposal called for dividing Texas into three states: East Texas, Texas, and South Texas. In January 1869 the constitutional convention rejected a Constitution of the State of West Texas and the idea of dividing the state died. Another proposal that went nowhere was voting for women. The bill proposing this idea did make it through committee but was voted down in the full convention by a margin of four to one. The constitution included voting rights for African American men, a much more centralized government than had existed previously, a stronger governor than usual in Texas, and much stronger support for public education. Sale of public lands went to support schools for all children from 6 to 18 years old, regardless of race or color.

An election was scheduled for November 16, 1869. Moderate Republicans and Democrats supported A. J. Hamilton, the former provisional governor, and radical Republicans supported E.J. Davis, who had been a brigadier general in the Union Army. Disgusted with the convention and angry with the military leaders of Texas, Pease resigned as governor on September 20. From that date until January 8, 1870, Texas had no civilian governor and was run by General J. J. Reynolds, who had become military commander of the state. When the election results were announced, the Radical Republican E.J. Davis received 39,901 votes and the more moderate Hamilton 39,092. Hamilton always believed that he had won the election and was denied the governorship by corrupt methods. Certainly, the election was flawed: New African American voters were intimidated by one side and coerced by the other. Many white voters stayed away from the polls. On the other hand, the constitution was adopted by a majority—7,246 to 4,928. Davis, however, became the most unpopular governor in the history of the state.

Ratification of the new constitution and election of state officers made Texas once again ready to be declared reconstructed. On February 8, the legislature ratified the 14th and 15th amendments and elected two U.S. senators. At the end of March, President U.S. Grant admitted the Texas

The Waco Suspension Bridge is thought to be the first permanent span over the Brazos River. The Waco Bridge Company was chartered in 1866 and contracted with John A. Roebling, who would later design and build the Brooklyn Bridge. Many believe that the Waco bridge, opened for traffic in 1870, was a prototype for the more famous New York bridge. Today the Waco Bridge is used for pedestrian traffic in Indian Springs Park. Jack Lewis, courtesy TxDOT

Secret Organizations

Even before the Civil War, whites in the South established secret organizations to support and further slavery. The Knights of the Golden Circle was organized in 1854 to ensure the continued strength of slavery in the southern United States and to expand it into Mexico, the West Indies, and Central America.

While the KGC officially disbanded during the war, rumors held that it continued as a spy organization in the North during the fighting and was reborn after the conflict. No evidence shows any kind of KGC activity in the North.

The Knights of the White Camellia was organized in New Orleans in May of 1867 and soon reached into central Texas in one direction and into the Carolinas in the other. In Texas, however, membership was concentrated in the eastern part of the state, especially in counties along the Louisiana border. Although they were frequently confused with the Ku Klux Klan, the KWC were better organized than the Reconstruction Klan and not as violent. In fact, the KWC is often thought of as the KKK for the more respectable strata of society. The Knights began to disband by 1869, and essentially ceased to exist by 1870, possibly absorbed by the KKK.

Six Confederate veterans founded the Ku Klux Klan in 1866 in Pulaski, Tennessee. Originally, the organization was social and recreational, but it soon came to be associated with vigilante violence against African Americans and Reconstruction. By the late 1860s, members swore to support white supremacy, oppose race mixing, resist carpetbaggers, and restore white control of government.

The KKK probably reached Texas by March 1868. Early on, most activities consisted of parades, cryptic newspaper notices, and midnight cemetery meetings, but gradually violence against freedmen and Republicans became more common. From Houston to the Red River, a band of about 20 counties was home to KKK intimidation of many forms. In Trinity County, for example, Klansmen killed several freedmen, intimidated others into registering as Democrats, and threatened federal officials.

During the Davis administration, the state legislature made it illegal to be armed and disguised. The grand wizard of Texas announced that the KKK was disbanding and apparently the state organization did dissolve. Some local groups also went out of business, but others continued. In May or June 1870, a KKK parade was held in McKinney, and in Bastrop the next year, masked men beat a white teacher of African American students. In April 1871 the Ku Klux Klan Act gave the president of the United States the power to suspend the writ of habeas corpus when a secret conspiracy was involved. The Reconstruction Klan seems to have ended with this act. After World War I a new Klan revived, but the Reconstruction Klan left a legacy in Texas of intimidation against African Americans and strengthened the belief among some Texans that vigilantism was an acceptable method of social control.

senators and representatives to congress. On April 16, 1870, General Reynolds declared military rule of Texas ended. Many Texans, however, did not consider Reconstruction over until a Democratic governor was elected—four years later.

One of the major actions of the Twelfth Legislature was the creation of a integrated public school system, supported by one-fourth of the state's annual revenues and a poll tax. Attendance was mandatory for at least four months of the year.

The Reconstruction legislatures also crafted a system of public higher education. Many in the old Confederacy saw the Morrill Land Grant College Act, a federal law establishing land grant colleges in each state, as a northern plot to take over the minds of southerners. Still, the Eleventh Legislature accepted the terms of the act and the Twelfth established the Texas land grant college and named it the Agricultural and Mechanical College of Texas—later to be Texas A&M University. The land grant colleges were funded by the sale of millions of acres of federal land. Since the state made the institution segregated, another land grant college had to be established for African Americans; it became known as Prairie View State Normal and Industrial College.

The Twelfth Legislature also postponed the 1870 elections to 1872 and gave the governor the power to appoint more than 8,000 local officials. Railroad construction was encouraged by issuing bonds. To try to control violence, the legislature created a state militia and a state police force—both under the governor's control.

When the postponed elections rolled around in 1872, Democrats and moderate Republicans controlled the legislature and immediately cut back the governor's powers. In 1873 Richard Coke easily defeated Davis. In one last unpopular move, Davis appealed to President Grant for troops to keep him in office. Grant refused.

In 1875 another convention was called to write the third state constitution in nine years and to rid Texas of any vestiges of Reconstruction. The first issue, however, was money. When Coke took office, state income could not cover half the expenses of legislated programs. To save money, state offices were reduced and the salaries paid to the remaining officials slashed. The state road program was cut back, and judges were made elected rather than appointed officials. Most far-reaching, the public education system was gutted. Schools became part of a "community system," segregated by race and lacking the power to tax.

Governor Coke turned to a problem that had bedeviled his predecessor also—the incredible lawlessness of Reconstruction Texas. The state militia and police, however, had been dissolved as hated vestiges of the Davis administration. Coke resurrected the Texas Rangers in 1874. The rangers included several white men who had been in the former state police, but none of the former African American policemen.

Violence in Post-War Texas

After the Civil War, Texas was beset by riots, feuds, lynchings, and random violence. Interracial violence, continuing warfare with the Comanches and their allies, lingering hatred fed by the ideologies of the war, the breakdown in administration and distrust of the Reconstruction administrations, economic and social uneasiness, and clashes over ownership of cattle (both wild and assumed to be wild) and other livestock all fed the rising lawlessness. How many people died during this period is impossible to say, since many deaths were never reported—especially when African Americans were killed by whites. Even after some order was established, bad feelings continued to affect people's attitudes throughout the 20th century.

While Kentucky has the national reputation for feuds, Texas feuds were probably more numerous, more bitter, and longer-lived. During Reconstruction, feuding became a major Texas outlet. The 1870s was the most lawless period in Texas history with outlaws, vigilantes, and counter-vigilantes marauding throughout the state. The Early-Hasley, Mason County, Sutton-Taylor, Horrell-Higgins, and other feuds arose from war-related enmities. Many of these conflicts occurred in frontier areas or in counties where Union and Confederate sympathizers found themselves living close to each other.

The Sutton-Taylor feud is one example, and probably the longest and bloodiest of the Reconstruction feuds. Those on the Taylor side were all related to Josiah Taylor who was originally from Virginia and pro-Confederacy. The Sutton

Buffalo Bayou at the foot of Main St. in Houston, 1867.
Courtesy Center for American History, UT-Austin

faction was drawn from the Reconstruction-era Texas State Police. In 1866 Buck Taylor shot an African American sergeant who had showed up at a dance held in a Taylor family home. In the same year Hays Taylor shot an African American soldier in a saloon in Indianola. In the next year, two Taylor brothers shot two federal soldiers in Mason.

William Sutton was a deputy sheriff when, in March 1868, he led a posse after some horse thieves. In Bastrop, the posse caught up with Charley Taylor and killed him. They took another man captive and shot him as he "tried to escape." Later in the year, Buck Taylor accused Sutton of cheating in some horse dealings. On Christmas Eve, 1868, persons unknown shot and killed Buck. On August 23, 1869, a large posse of state police killed Hays Taylor. Police under the control of Captain Jack Helm took two sons-in-law of Pitkin Taylor from their homes in August of 1870 and killed them. Helm was removed from the state police, but in June or July of 1873 Jim Taylor and the famous outlaw John Wesley Hardin killed Helm as he was leaving a blacksmith shop in Wilson County.

The day after Helm's murder, the local sheriff convinced both parties to sign a truce, but it only lasted a few months. Sutton decided it was time to leave De Witt County. First, he moved to Victoria, but that wasn't far enough. On March 11, 1874, Sutton was boarding a steamship in Indianola when Jim and Bill Taylor rode up and shot him and another man. More lynchings, murders, jail escapes, and cattle rustling followed until 1876 when the Texas Rangers were finally called in. Eight men were charged with murder. In the end, however, only one man was ever convicted for any of the Sutton-Taylor killings and he was pardoned.

Over more or less the same years, the Mason County War followed much the same pattern of accusations of cattle and horse rustling, killings, and lynchings. In Mason County, ethnic overtones surfaced more predominately since local Germans were seen to be fighting other whites. This feud was topped off by the burning of the Mason County courthouse and the consequent destruction of all legal papers about the feud. Many feuds raged in other parts of the state and remained a part of Texas culture deep into the twentieth century.

Racial violence during Reconstruction followed different patterns. Accusations of cattle rustling were seldom part of this violence. Instead, both white and African American communities were tense about social, political, and economic changes. Any perceived racial transgression could set off days and nights of destruction. In 1868 the commander of the Fifth Military District said that "The murder of negroes is so common as to render it impossible to keep an accurate account."

In far west Texas, violence mixed political loyalties, economics, and racial animosity. The El Paso Salt War (also known as the Salt War of San Elizario) involved mineral deposits 100 miles east of El Paso. Hispanics on both sides of the border considered these salt lakes public property and the salt free to all.

In 1872 Charles Howard, a Democrat and former Confederate officer from Missouri, joined forces with Louis Cardis, who controlled the Hispanic vote, to break the Republican control of the salt deposits. This alliance was short lived. After he was made a district judge in 1874,

Howard filed for titles to the salt lakes in the name of his father-in-law. In 1877 Howard arrested two men who had declared their intention to collect salt, but a furious mob captured Howard and held him captive for three days. He gained his freedom by pledging to give up his claim to the salt lakes and leave the area. Four friends signed a $12,000 bond guaranteeing he would fulfill his pledge.

Howard moved to New Mexico, but within a month he returned to El Paso and killed Cardis. The Hispanics of the area demanded Howard's arrest and the Texas Ranger Frontier Battalion arrived to keep the peace. In early December, 16 wagons set out for the lakes to collect salt. Howard confronted the people he described as trespassers, but the angry mob besieged Howard and the rangers for four days. Two whites died during the siege. On the fifth day, Howard and the rangers surrendered. While the rangers were allowed to leave—without their guns—Howard and two others were executed by firing squad.

Several detachments of U.S. army troops were sent into the town. The fighting killed and wounded many, but most of the leaders of the mob made it over the border. While some of them were indicted, none were ever arrested and no one was ever brought to trial. The U.S. Congress investigated the incident, but the only action to result from the Salt War was the re-opening of Fort Bliss in El Paso.

LAND AND RAILROADS

While the governments of the 1870s struggled to re-establish law and order, they also had to deal with a collapsed economy. Across the nation, money supplies contracted. The effect of this decline in bank note circulation was most devastating in the South. Land value and farm prices—the main source of wealth in Texas—plummeted. Still, land was the main source of income for the state.

When Oran M. Roberts succeeded Richard Coke as governor, he insisted that the legislature sell public land for 50 cents an acre. Roberts wanted to fill up state coffers, but all he did was lower land prices. Soon land was selling for 15 cents an acre. Critics of Roberts's policy pointed out that it invited speculation. To counteract this problem, the next governor, John Ireland, instituted a rule requiring each purchaser to swear an oath that the land was being bought

Today the Tarantula Steam Engine plies the 21 miles from the Grapevine Station to the Fort Worth Stockyards. This route covers part of the original Cotton Belt Line. The builders of this line intended to extend their route from St. Louis, Missouri, to Eagle Pass and on into Mexico City. By 1877, the line had reached Fort Worth; by 1888 it was in Grapevine. Kevin Stillman, courtesy TxDOT

"for a home." According to subsequent investigations, this rule only added perjury to speculation. Enormous grants of public land ended up feeding the growth of large ranches.

Public land also subsidized the construction of railroads. Before the Civil War, Texas had only a few rail lines radiating out of Houston; no lines connected Texas to other states before 1872. To Texans of the late 19th century, the railroads seemed the technological quick fix for their economic woes. The state legislature and individual towns offered railroads any kind of incentive. The people of Brenham, for example, not only gave the railroad right of way through their town, they also paid the company

$150,000 in cash. Fort Worth gave bonuses to any railroad that would connect to the city. Many formerly thriving settlements withered after railroads passed them by for other towns. The state legislature gave away the most to railroads, however—a total of 32,150,000 acres of state land.

The railroads connected Texas to the rest of the country and opened new markets for agricultural products. The citizens of the small town of Dallas threw a buffalo barbecue when the railroad came through in 1872. They and the farmers of the region saw the new transportation lines as a way to move from subsistence living to a market economy. The railroads and cheap land helped write the next, mythic chapter in Texas history.

9

Cowboys and Indians

The images most identified with the popular idea of Texas come from a very short period: roughly the two decades following the Civil War. During that time, the cattle drive shaped the idea of the Texas cowboy, and attempts to push back Native Americans and exterminate the buffalo fed the frontier battle myth. The real story of cattle trailing and ranching, however, springs from railroads, cheap land, eastern appetites, and a glut of cattle.

Cattle drives had been tried before the 1870s. Under Spanish and Mexican rule, cattle were often trailed to the south to be sold in Mexican markets. The first recorded large cattle drive to the north went from Texas to Ohio in 1846. During the 1840s and 1850s, Texas cattlemen drove animals north over the Shawnee Trail, which crossed Missouri, Illinois, Indiana, Iowa, and Ohio. By the mid-1850s, however, farmers along this trail noticed that soon after Texas cattle came through their own cattle came down with a mysterious disease, and an often fatal one. This "Texas fever," identified later as the tick-bourne babesiosis, frightened both Missouri and Kansas enough for the states to set up quarantines against "southern cattle."

Some livestock owners experimented with other ways to market cattle. South Texas coastal ranchers occasionally tried sending cattle to market on steamers. During the Gold Rush, a few enterprising Texans drove herds west to feed hungry miners. During the 1850s, cattle worth $14 apiece in Texas could be sold for more than $100 in California.

Before the Civil War, stockmen practiced a form of round up known as the "cow hunt." According to old trail driver George W. Saunders, in the days "before the chuck wagon," men would agree on a time and place for a cow hunt. Each was responsible for his own bedding, a coffee pot, tin cup, salt, sugar, and "a wallet of biscuit." Individuals would also bring four or five horses for themselves.

The cattle had been wandering on the open range for months, bearing calves along the way. While the different herds mixed together, only the cattle brands identified owners. The unbranded calves would be penned until a frantic and bawling mother cow claimed her young one, both returning to the owner shown by the mother cow's brand. Usually these cow hunts took 10 to 15 days.

During the Civil War, cow hunts ceased and cattle wandered the range for years with little intervention from their supposed owners. Four million cattle are estimated to have roamed Texas after the war, far more than postwar Texas needed. A market for beef did exist, however, in the growing eastern and midwestern cities. After the war, the cattle owners had to figure out who owned specific animals first and then how to get them to eager urban mouths. Along the way, owners also had to extend the lands available for pasturing their stock—to accomplish this, cattlemen, settlers, and the U.S. Army forced the remaining Native Americans onto reservations and exterminated the buffalo their economy depended on.

COMANCHE MOON

During and immediately after the Civil War, most white settlers on the unprotected western edge of Texas escaped Native American attacks by moving from their exposed and isolated ranches into forts and other secured areas. The withdrawal of federal troops and the failure of the Confederate government to protect the frontier left the settlers vulnerable to attack. On moonlit nights, especially during the full moon of late summer and early fall (later called a "Comanche Moon"), the Comanches and their allies would raid cattle and horse herds. In April 1866, a Waco newspaper held that only one-fifth of frontier ranches were still occupied. In reaction, in the fall of that year, the Reconstruction authorities stationed 4,000 federal troops in frontier forts. But the forts were not an immediate solution to the settlers' protection problems. The distances between these outposts were great, and frequently the troops in them were untrained in Native American warfare and lacked discipline.

In October 1867, Native Americans of the southern plains and commissioners of the federal government met at Medicine Lodge Creek in Kansas. The Kiowa and

Comanche argued that west Texas belonged to them and that they should be allowed to continue their nomadic life there. The treaty that resulted from the meeting, however, forced the Native Americans who signed it to move onto reservations and halt their raids. In return, the federal government agreed to supply the reservations with food, clothing, and agricultural implements. Whites were banned from reservation lands. The treaty had no effect on the Native Americans not in attendence, however, and about half the Comanches and many Kiowa refused the agreement.

From its very beginnings, the reservation system did not work. The U.S. Congress took its time in debating the appropriations for the promised supplies, and not until July of 1868 was $500,000 set aside. In the meantime, those tribes that had agreed to the treaties were living in wretched poverty on the reservations. White buffalo hunters also encroached on reservation lands and the military showed little inclination to do anything about them.

In May 1871, William Tecumseh Sherman, the general of the army, and Randolph B. Marcy, army inspector general, toured the frontier. Marcy was convinced the Native Americans could soon drive whites from the area, but Sherman did not believe conditions were as bad as the settlers portrayed them. The inspection tour set out from San Antonio on May 2 and traveled to Fort Richardson, just south of Jacksboro in the northern Cross Timbers, without seeing a single Native American. The party reached Fort Richardson on May 18 and Sherman went to sleep still thinking the Texans' fear of Native American attacks was exaggerated. Sherman's view changed abruptly overnight.

During that night a wounded teamster, Thomas Brazeal, crawled into the fort and described an ambush along Salt Creek about 20 miles west of the fort. Sherman's party had passed along the same trail under the watchful eyes of the Kiowa, who had let the military group go unmolested. They attacked the more lucrative supply wagon caravan that came next, killing seven of the 12 teamsters in the government-contracted wagon train and stealing 41 mules.

The Battle of Salt Creek led directly to a new offensive against the Native Americans of west Texas. First, Sherman advocated some policy changes. In particular, he wanted the families of raiders who used the reservations as their bases to

Buffalo Soldiers

After the Civil War, the U.S. Congress reorganized the regular army and set aside the 9th and 10th Cavalry and the 24th and 25th Infantry for African American soldiers. These regiments were sent west to help fight the Native American wars of the late 19th century. The story is that the Native Americans named these soldiers after the totemic animals either because they were brave and strong like buffaloes or because their hair reminded the Native Americans of the buffalo's fur.

Stationed for the most part at isolated posts, buffalo soldiers performed regular garrison tasks, escorted mail trains, built roads, and fought major frontier battles. In Texas they served at, among others, Forts Richardson, Concho, Davis, and McKavett. During the Indian wars, 13 enlisted men and six officers from the buffalo soldier regiments earned the Medal of Honor. Even so, their hardest battles may well have been within the army.

With only one exception, the officers of these units were white. Ranald Mackenzie, William Rufus Shafter, and Abner Doubleday—he of baseball fame—among others, all commanded these units at one time or another. The exception to the rule was Henry O. Flipper, the first African American graduate of West Point and a lieutenant stationed on the southwestern frontier.

Flipper was first stationed at Fort Sill, in Oklahoma. There he supervised the construction of a drainage ditch designed to rid the post of malaria, helped string telegraph lines, scouted on the Llano Estacado, and took part in battles against Quanah Parker. As a reward for his field service, Flipper was made a quartermaster at Fort Davis in Jeff Davis County. This position gave him control of supplies and the physical plant at the fort.

When Shafter became commanding officer at Fort Davis, he immediately relieved Flipper of some of his duties. Local civilians warned Flipper that white officers were out to destroy his career, and in 1882 he found post funds missing from his quarters. Flipper concealed the loss in an attempt to find the missing money. Shaftner found out about the discrepancy, however, and immediately filed charges against him. A court-martial acquitted Flipper of embezzlement but found him guilty of conduct unbecoming an officer.

Flipper fought to clear his name but died in 1940 without vindication. In 1976 the army granted him an honorable discharge and stated that his dismissal had been the result of racial hostility. President Bill Clinton issued a full pardon for Flipper in 1999.

Fort Davis National Historic Site is west of the town of Fort Davis. The site has a restored barracks with a museum and five other restored buildings and offers reenactments. Call (915) 426-3225.

lose the right to receive government supplies. Sherman also wanted soldiers to be able to enter reservations when pursuing raiders or when looking for stolen possessions. Previously, he had given Colonel Ranald Slidell Mackenzie command of the Fourth Cavalry; Ulysses S. Grant considered Mackenzie the most promising young officer in the postwar army, and this young officer would play an important role in the coming military campaign against the Kiowa and Comanches.

In October 1871, Mackenzie led about 600 men, including 20 Tonkawa scouts, from the Clear Fork of the Brazos toward Blanco Canyon where a Comanche band headed by Quanah Parker was camped. The cavalry reached the canyon on October 9. After the soldiers had bedded down, Parker and a small Comanche force hurtled through the camp and scattered 66 horses. When the sun came up, a detachment of soldiers followed the horses and the small group of Native Americans herding them. Climbing to the top of the canyon, the soldiers were surprised to find a much larger band of Comanches waiting in ambush. While Lieutenant Robert Goldthwaite Carter and five other men stayed and fought a rearguard action, the rest of the cavalry retreated and went for help. Carter, who received the Medal of Honor for this action, and his men were saved by the timely arrival of the Tonkawas and Mackenzie's main troops. Shouting taunts at the Tonkawas, the Comanches disappeared over the Caprock and into the forbidding Llano Estacado.

For six days Mackenzie and his troops pursued the Comanches, forcing them to abandon shelters and other possessions. On October 12, the two forces finally came into direct contact, but nature intervened with an early, blinding snowstorm. The cavalry was forced to camp, and Parker and his band escaped again. Returning to camp, the soldiers skirmished with Comanche spies. In the fight Mackenzie was wounded, the weather worsened, and the soldiers and their horses grew weary. Mackenzie ordered the campaign ended. The troops returned to their forts in mid-November.

While not a triumph, this initial campaign gave the soldiers experience in fighting Native Americans and some knowledge of the Llano Estacado's natural conditions. Soon they would secure the information that would make crossing the forbidding plains possible.

In March 1872 in the southeast part of present-day

Borden County, Sergeant William H. Wilson, with a detachment of scouts from Fort Concho, surprised a band of Comancheros (native New Mexican traders who supplied Native Americans in the Llano Estacado with guns, horses, and whatever else they could deal). In the ensuing conflict, the soldiers captured a New Mexican named Polonis Ortiz. Back at Fort Concho, Ortiz told the astonished commanding officer, Major John P. Hatch, that he and other Comancheros regularly crossed the Llano Estacado along a series of trails with adequate water. Until Ortiz revealed the secret water sources of the arid plains, whites had assumed that maintaining life on the Staked Plains would be waterless and impossible. Ortiz, however, showed them tributaries of the Canadian River, Tierra Blanca Creek, the Gallinos River, and other streams that offered steady water supplies. His information gave the soldiers intelligence for future battles and furthered the subsequent white settlement of the plains.

Sherman must have been dismayed when he read Ortiz's descriptions of horse and cattle thieving, trading with both Kiowa and Comanche, and other Comanchero exploits on the Llano Estacado. On April 20, 1872, Sherman wrote to General C.C. Augur, who was now commander of the Department of Texas, "I fully authorize you to break up the illicit traffic with Indians on the Staked Plains and if any of the parties engaged in it are caught they should be turned over to the United States Civil authorities of the State of Texas." Mackenzie prepared for an offensive against the plains tribes.

In July, as Mackenzie and his troops were looking unsuccessfully for Native Americans along the Freshwater Fork of the Brazos, his scouts sent word that they and Polonis Ortiz had found a cattle trail leading west across the Llano Estacado. Mackenzie's orders included breaking up cattle-stealing rings as well as fighting Native Americans, so he led his troops out onto the plain toward New Mexico. Reaching present-day Santa Rosa, New Mexico, they became the first U.S. military force to cross the Llano Estacado and return to Texas, but they found no cattle thieves and no Native Americans. On their return trip, Mackenzie and his men scouted Palo Duro, Cita, and Tule canyons. Mackenzie would use this reconnoitering within two years.

Mackenzie believed this expedition was a failure and set

Soldiers from Fort Concho contributed to the emergence of west Texas by mapping large parts of the region, building roads and telegraph lines, and escorting stagecoaches, cattle drives, and railroad surveyors. This structure is the Officers Quarters at Fort Concho National Historical Landmark, San Angelo. Jack Lewis, courtesy TxDOT

out again in September, marching toward the upper tributaries of the Red River. On September 29, 1872, the soldiers came upon a large Comanche encampment on the south bank of the North Fork of the Red River. Mackenzie divided his forces to ensure that the camp was surrounded and charged. Taken completely by surprise, the Comanches fought valiantly but to no avail. The village was destroyed, many braves killed (some sources say 50), and about a hundred captives sent back to Fort Concho.

The soldiers also seized the entire Comanche horse and mule herd—from 800 to 3,000 animals. That night Mackenzie and his men camped about two miles from the battle site and sheltered the captured horses and mules in a depression a mile from their tents. During the night the sentinels guarding the animals must have fallen asleep, because Comanches managed to stampede most of the herd. After a repeat performance the next night, the Comanches retrieved almost all of their mounts.

Each side learned something from the Battle of the North Fork. Mackenzie decided that the key to victory was to unhorse the Native Americans. The Comanches realized that their Panhandle camping places were no longer inviolate. Finding safe campgrounds for the winter would no longer be as easy as it had been in the past. Following North Forks, a period of calm descended on the frontier area with each side gathering strength and thinking out its strategy.

During 1873 and early 1874, Native American and white tensions increased. Contributing to the situation were the Native American desire for revenge and culture of raiding and the activities of white horse thieves, whiskey peddlers, and buffalo hunters. Two charismatic Comanche leaders, Isa-tai and Quanah Parker, now rallied their forces for a last attempt to preserve their ancestral way of life.

In late June Comanches laid siege to a settlement of buffalo hunters at Adobe Walls. The hunters had been systematically destroying the herds and had set up a permanent camp consisting of several stores, a restaurant, a saloon, and a blacksmith shop. The entourage included 28 men and one woman, the wife of William Olds, who ran the restaurant. In the initial attack on June 27, two buffalo hunters were killed and a third fatally wounded. The Comanches besieged the complex until July 1. During that time Olds died when he accidentally shot himself in the head while coming down from a lookout position. A young guide, Billy Dixon, made a name for himself with his "long shot" of 1,538 yards that killed a war chief. The battle ended when Quanah Parker withdrew as white reinforcements arrived. Adobe Walls was abandoned and buffalo hunting slacked off for a while, but the real result of the battle was the Red River War of 1874–1875 that destroyed the buffalo herds and relocated the Native Americans of the southern plains to Oklahoma reservations.

The Red River War followed Sherman's proven strategies for Native American fighting—push from all directions at once. By July 25 five columns of troops had entered the Llano Estacado and the Panhandle in an attempt to drive the Native American bands into their traditional canyon campgrounds. There, the thinking was, they could be forced to surrender or be killed. The five columns converged on the Panhandle from all over the region: Major William A. Price moved east from Fort Union in New Mexico, Lieutenant Colonel John W. Davidson moved west from Fort Sill in Oklahoma, and Colonel Nelson A. Miles and his men marched south from Fort Dodge, Kansas. Two columns came from Texas:

The Mysterious Kid

Samuel Dunn Houston of San Antonio told this story to an old trail drivers meeting; the incident happened in 1888. The crew was short of hands when they arrived in Clayton, New Mexico. Houston went into town to hire two or three trail men but could find no one looking for work. A friend remembered that a young boy had been in town looking to hire on a trail drive and had gone to work at the livery stable. Houston hired the kid to work with the crew's horses. He continues the story:

I got along fine [with the kid] for three or four months. The kid would get up the darkest stormy nights and stay with the cattle until the storm was over. He was good natured, very modest, didn't use cuss words or tobacco, and always pleasant. His name was Willie Mathews, was nineteen years old, and weighed one hundred and twenty-five pounds....I was so pleased with him that I wished many times that I could find two or three more like him.

[Around noon when they reached Hugo, Colorado, near the Colorado-Wyoming line, the kid asked Houston if he could quit.] He insisted, said he was homesick and I had to let him go.... About sundown we were all sitting around camp and the old herd was coming in on the bed ground. I looked up toward town and saw a lady, all dressed up, coming toward the camp, walking.... I couldn't imagine why a woman would be coming on foot to a cow camp, but she kept right on coming. [When she was about 50 feet from the camp, Houston went out to meet her] When she got within about twenty feet of me, she began to laugh, and said, "Mr. Houston, you don't know me do you?" Well, for one minute I couldn't speak. She reached her hand to me, to shake hands, and I said, "Kid, is it possible that you are a lady?".... The kid sat down and I said, "Now I want you to explain yourself." "Well," she said, "...my papa is an old-time trail driver from Southern Texas.... I used to hear papa talk so much about the old cow trail and I made up my mind that when I was grown I was going up the trail if I had to run off.

When she read in the paper that Houston's herds were passing Clayton, which was not far from her home, she saddled her pony, took some of her brother's clothes and a pair of his boots, and left. She told her brother to tell their father she would be gone for a week and not to worry. It took her three or four days to get to Clayton. "Now, Mr. Houston, I am glad I found you to make the trip with, for I have enjoyed it." The train departed at 11:20 PM and Houston left one man with the herd while he and the rest of the men went to Hugo to see her off. After Houston returned home, he received many letters from the girl and her father "thanking me for the kindness toward Willie and begging me to visit them."

—George W. Saunders, *Trail Drivers of Texas*

Mackenzie's men from Fort Concho and a contingent commanded by Lieutenant Colonel George P. Buell from Fort Richardson.

Each of these columns pushed forward, engaging in skirmishes and battles with the desperate Native American tribes. Two major battles were fought in Palo Duro Canyon, the first in stifling heat and drought as soldiers commanded by Colonel Miles pushed a mixed band of Cheyenne, Comanche, and Kiowa warriors out of the lower reaches of the Palo Duro and onto the Llano Estacado. Miles had to call off the advance when he outran his supply lines. A Cheyenne village with much-needed supplies was destroyed, but otherwise this battle was inconclusive. The second Palo Duro battle would come at the end of the fighting and would seal the doom of the Native Americans on the plains.

To fetch supplies, Miles sent Captain Wyllys Lyman to Oklahoma. On the return trip, some 400 Kiowa warriors beseiged the 36-wagon train from September 9 to the afternoon of September 15 when reinforcements arrived. At about the same time, six soldiers and civilian scouts were pinned down in a buffalo wallow by a mixed band of Comanches and Kiowas, many of them returning from the Lyman's Wagon Train fight. The small scouting detail managed to repulse their attackers for two days until relief arrived. Their misery was increased by an afternoon thunderstorm that filled the wallow with water; that night they made beds out of tumble weeds. All of the defenders were awarded the Medal of Honor, but Billy Dixon, the "long-shot" hero of Adobe Walls, and Amos Chapman were ordered to return their medals when officials realized that the two men were civilians. Dixon refused.

All through the Panhandle, troops kept coming upon Native American paths with fresh marks indicating the riders were moving south. The push of the out-of-state troops seemed to be having an effect. Small units of troops broke off from their larger columns to scout streams and canyons where Native Americans might be hiding. These strategies kept the Native American bands always on the move with no rest.

Mackenzie reestablished his old supply camp near Blanco Canyon for his northward thrust. On September 26 his troops camped near the head of Tule Canyon. Since scouts reported

Cowboys had to improvise services such as barbering. Note the log and dirt cabin that is partially underground. Courtesy Center for American History, UT-Austin.

Native Americans in the area, the soldiers secured the horses against an attack. Despite every attempt to start a stampede, the Native Americans could not budge the horses. In the morning Mackenzie and his men followed the attackers for a while, but the colonel's goal lay in another direction.

Scouts had brought word of a large encampment in Palo Duro Canyon. Marching north all of the 27th, soldiers rested and then, at 4:00 AM on the 28th, descended to the canyon floor, where they could see many lodges. Daylight had broken by the time they reached the bottom and the encamped Comanche, Cheyenne, and Kiowa took to the ravines and rocks along the canyon walls. From these protected locations, they fired on the soldiers below. But Mackenzie's strategy no longer involved killing large numbers of warriors; he systematically destroyed the shelters and possessions that had been abandoned in camp. By 3:00 PM the cavalry left the canyon. They took with them around 2,000 Native American horses. Remembering the daring rescue of their horses after the Battle of North Fork, Mackenzie ordered that all of the horses be shot. Tonkawa scouts managed to save a few, but troops killed most of the animals.

The combined Native American forces faced winter without shelter, horses, winter clothing, or stored food, and they had nowhere to turn except the reservations. A few skirmishes and battles remained to be fought, but the Red River War was essentially over. On June 2, 1875, the last holdouts, Comanches led by Quanah Parker, surrendered to Mackenzie at Fort Sill. The Comanches and buffalo were gone; the Panhandle and Llano Estacado were now ready for the next migration. Whites pushed into the area; first came transitory cattle drivers, but more permanent settlers—ranchers and farmers—followed. Towns and cities came next.

TRAILING NORTH

Even after the Civil War, fear of Texas fever in Missouri, Kansas, and eastward states cut off the possibility of Texans trailing their cattle to markets in that direction. With the Native Americans of the southern plains confined to reservations and the buffalo essentially extinct in Texas, trailing to the north became possible. Markets were in the east, however, not the north. The war had depleted the eastern cattle herds. Longhorns that were worth $2.00 each in Texas could be sold for $40.00 in large cities. How could Texans take advantage of this market? Joseph G. McCoy had the answer.

In 1867 McCoy, a livestock dealer from Illinois, sold the Kansas and Pacific Railway on setting up a cattle-shipping facility in Abilene, Kansas. McCoy persuaded the Kansas legislature that Abilene was so far away from settled areas that cattle quarantine laws did not need to be enforced there. (Later, he convinced the Illinois legislature that Texas cattle overwintered in Kansas could safely enter Illinois.) Texans only needed to get their cattle to this railhead and ship them east from there. To reach Kansas, cattlemen would follow a trail blazed by Jesse Chisholm, the son of a Scots trader and a Cherokee mother—a man who moved not only over territory but also between cultures.

Since the days of the Texas Republic, Chisholm had traveled between present-day Oklahoma and Texas. Married into a white family of traders in eastern Indian Territory, Chisholm traded with the Native Americans to the south and west of the family's trading post. Soon he had learned a dozen languages, established branch posts, and had a side business as a guide and interpreter. The route he followed as he went about his various businesses became known as the Chisholm Trail.

The first cattle driver known to follow the Chisholm Trail was O.W. Wheeler. In 1867 he and his partners bought more than 2,000 cattle in San Antonio. Wheeler's plan was to overwinter the animals on the plains and then to move them west to the California markets. At the North Canadian River, however, they found wagon tracks and followed them. The tracks were Chisholm's. The cattlemen realized that Jesse's trail was far enough west to avoid trouble with settlers. Of course until the mid-1870s, Native American attacks were still a problem for anyone trying to trail cattle north.

It is a mistake to envision the Chisholm, or any of the other cattle trails, as a well-marked single pathway, as if it were some 19th-century interstate highway. The cattle moved over a broad area to avoid overgrazing. River crossings were often the only common points of a trail, since an easy crossing with no quicksand or rapids was a very useful find. Usually herds crossed the Red River at Spanish Fort or Red River Station.

Few ranchers drove their own cattle to market. Contractors did most of the actual trailing and usually charged between $1.00 and $1.50 a head to herd cattle north. Contractors probably moved about 90 percent of the cattle that went to Kansas from Texas between 1866 and 1890.

About a dozen people were necessary to control a herd of around 3,000 cattle. The trail boss organized the event and gathered the other drovers. He was in charge of selecting the route and suitable campgrounds and usually rode ahead of the herd looking for water and good grazing. The cook also moved ahead of the herd in his chuckwagon. A wrangler took care of the extra horses (called the *remuda*). Each cowboy riding the herd had a particular function: The point riders were at the head of the herd watching and controlling the lead steer. The swing riders rode alongside the herd to keep it moving in the right direction. Flank riders rode farther back on the side of the herd and made sure it did not spread out. At least two drag riders came last, riding at the back of the herd to keep it moving. These drag riders constantly ate dust, and their position was reserved for newcomers or riders in need of punishment.

Longhorns prospered on their own on the open range where they developed natural immunity to Texas fever. Their long legs, hard hooves, and ability to gain weight while walking all day made them perfect for the trail drive. © Terrence Comeron

Maybe two-thirds of cowboys were white males, but African Americans, Hispanics, and Native Americans also rode the trails. Women also trailed cattle. A few, such as Lizzie Johnson of Austin and Margaret Bouland of Victoria, ran their own herds to Kansas, but some women disguised themselves as boys and rode as part of the crew. No matter what Hollywood may lead you to believe, few trail bosses allowed cowboys to carry guns. One accidental shot could stampede the herd, losing time and cattle for the trail drivers. The trail boss needed to get as many of the cattle as possible to the railhead, part of his pay being a share of the profits.

Most drives began in the early spring, moving about 10 to 15 miles a day. At this pace, the trip from home pasture to market took about six weeks. With luck the cattle would travel from water hole to water hole. Weather, fires, and predatory animals could wreck the best-laid plans. In 1876, for example, a thunderstorm near Waco stampeded 15,000 Longhorns. The animals hurtled into a ravine and several thousand died.

Settlers began to move into the Chisholm Trail area, and by 1876 most of the trail drivers had moved their cattle to the Western, or Fort Dodge, Trail. The end of the Red River War and defeat of the Native Americans of the plains made this route more attractive. The Western Trail gathered many feeder routes from south Texas that converged in Kerrville and proceeded north across the James, Llano, San Saba, Colorado, and Brazos rivers. It left Texas at Doan's Crossing on the Prairie Dog Town Fork of the Red River. While some of the herds were delivered to reservations in Oklahoma and a few went on to Ogallala, Nebraska, most were transferred to cars of the Santa Fe Railroad in Dodge City, Kansas.

James T. Lytle, a rancher and drover from the Castroville area, blazed the Western Trail. In 1871 he formed a trailing partnership with his cousin Thomas M. McDaniel. The two became contract drovers for ranchers in their area. Lytle was frequently the trail boss for his partnership's drives. In 1874 the firm received a boost in capital and prestige when Charles A. Schreiner—a Kerrville merchant, banker, and rancher—joined the partnership. He brought John W. Light of Kimble County into the organization. The Lytle-Schreiner-Light partnership was not an informal cowboy arrangement, but an organized capital-intensive company. In 1887 Schreiner became the full owner of the firm, and Lytle became general manager of the American Cattle Syndicate, as the operation was then called. The cattle drive was becoming big business.

OPEN RANGE INTO BIG PASTURE

Trail drives were changing in many ways. Settlers kept pushing farther west and encroaching on the trails. Newly erected barbed wire fences blocked the cattle routes. Texas fever again frightened farmers, and Kansas tightened its quarantine on Texas cattle. As railroads began to reach into the western parts of Texas, owners of large ranches found it easier to take their herds to local railheads than to trail

Barbed wire has taken many forms since it was invented in the 1870s and has become an object of collectors. This panel is part of the Mulkey Owens' barbed wire collection. Kevin Stillman, courtesy TxDOT

Barbed Wire

People moving into Texas were used to making fences out of wood or stone. Out on the high plains wood was scarce. There may have been a few more stones than trees, but not enough to make stone walls practical. Some settlers experimented with ditches and mud walls to enclose crops. Thorny brush had been used in south Texas, but none of these fencing substitutes was satisfactory. The thorny brush, however, was the prototype for the invention that would fence the West.

In 1873 three men—Joseph Glidden, Isaac Ellwood, and Jacob Haish—separately stumbled on an exhibit at the DeKalb (Illinois) County Fair. A local farmer named Henry M. Rose was showing his contraption: a regular wooden rail with sharp wire points sticking out of it. Rose intended his device to be attached to existing fencing as a deterrent for particularly difficult cattle, but his concept appealed to each of the three men in different ways. Ellwood's customers were always pestering him in his hardware store for better fencing. Glidden was a farmer and Haish a lumberman and both needed better and cheaper fencing. Each man tinkered on his own to improve on Rose's idea.

Glidden was the first to apply for a patent. He and his wife had worked nights in the family kitchen twisting barbs onto smooth wire, but the barbs kept sliding about on the wire. Glidden whipped out the family coffee mill and used it to wrap the wire around the barb. He then added a second strand of wire that further secured the barbs. Ellwood had also been messing up the kitchen with wire pieces. When he heard village gossip that Glidden was working on the same idea, he and his wife hitched up the buggy and drove over to Glidden's farm. Mrs. Ellwood immediately blurted out that Glidden's invention was better than anything her husband had come up with. The next day Glidden and Ellwood became partners. Haish, however, applied for patents on both wire and a wire stretcher and was the first actually to receive a patent. In July 1874 Haish served legal papers on Glidden and began years of patent wars.

While the inventors thrashed out their rights back east, enterprising salesmen hit the Texas market. In 1876 one of the more flamboyant, John "Bet-a-Million" Gates, staged a demonstration in San Antonio's Military Plaza. The story goes that Gates penned a herd of wild Longhorns in the plaza and proved that barbed wire could restrain even the biggest and meanest of bulls. Gates extolled his product to the assembled Texans as "light as air, stronger than whiskey, and cheap as dirt."

Price was part of barbed wire's success. In 1874 a pound cost $4.50 and four pounds could fence an acre. By the late 1890s the cost was one-tenth of that. Gates contributed to the falling price by organizing manufacturers of nonpatented barbed wire into a "moonshine wire" group. The ever-decreasing cost of fencing allowed sedentary farmers to protect their crops and farm animals and eventually let them replace the traveling cowboy. Together barbed wire and the steady water supply of windmills made agriculture possible in west Texas. Influential cattlemen, such as Shanghai Pierce and Charles Goodnight, fenced in their immense pastures.

By the 1890s a thousand kinds of barbed wire were selling under a wild assortment of names: Split Diamond, Hold-Fast, Twist Oval, Necktie, and Arrow Plate amid many others. Today, fanciers collect the old forms of barbed wire and meet in regular swaps and auctions to enlarge their collections and tell each other tall tales about the fencing of the West.

You can visit the Devil's Rope Museum in McLean. Be sure not to miss the two balls of barbed wire on top of limestone pedestals in front of the museum. Each ball weighs more than 370 pounds. Texas A&M University has a significant collection of barbed wire. The 269-piece collection is housed in the Animal Industries Building on the College Station campus and is open to the public.

them north. The ranchers experimented with new breeds of cattle and set up fences to ensure that their newly purchased purebreds remained that way. The railroads made sure that the supply of barbed wire was never-ending. In 1893 John Rufus Blocker made the last drive on the Western Trail, delivering a herd to Deadwood, South Dakota.

Cowmen began to accumulate large land holdings so they could more easily link up with railheads on their own properties. While these enormous ranches were often individual or family holdings, they were just as often investments put together by syndicates of easterners or Europeans.

In 1879 the legislature set aside three million acres of land to be sold to finance the construction of a new capitol building. In November 1881, the need for a new building became more urgent when the existing capitol burned. The Capitol Syndicate, made up mostly of wealthy Illinois investors, took over the entire contract when the original investor bowed out after being accused of bribery. The syndicate paid the state $3,244,593.45 for the land, over $1.00 an acre, though the cost of the capitol when it was finished in 1888 was $3,744,630.60. Taxpayers had to come up with the rest.

The syndicate planned to run cattle on the land until it could be subdivided and sold off to settlers. They needed a name for their initial venture and settled on calling it the XIT Ranch. In 1884 the syndicate formed the Capitol Freehold Land and Investment Company of London to gain access to English capital. The Earl of Aberdeen, members of Parliament, and other wealthy British investors chipped in about $5 million.

Colonel Amos C. Babcock, one of the original Illinois investors, made an important early decision. He and several surveyors looked over the land and decided it needed to be fenced. The first pasture fence was finished in 1885. By the end of 1886, XIT had used barbed wire to fence in 781 miles of range to enclose 110,271 cattle valued at $1,322,587. By 1900, 325 windmills and 100 dams ensured that the fenced-in cattle had enough water. These large fenced-in pastures sealed the coffin of the open range.

WIRE CUTTERS AND STRIKERS

The range did not die a quiet death, however. In 1883, a

pivotal year, drought made easy access to water a dire necessity, fence cutting reached a peak, and the cowboys of five west Texas ranches went on strike.

And that wasn't all. Many Texans, still fighting the Civil War, saw the fencing of the open range as a Yankee attempt to destroy a Texan tradition. In the popular view, large companies controlled by eastern and foreign capitalists were changing the face of the high plains and driving out small owners. Public institutions also went on the record against fencing: For example, the commissioners' court of San Saba County called on the state legislature to outlaw barbed wire fences, and the Nolan and Fisher county stockmen's association passed a resolution that land west of the 100th Meridian should never be fenced.

Landless cattlemen resented barbed wire deeply. The first land to be enclosed was always the best—with the best grass and the most accessible water. A dry spell in 1883 made it harder for landless livestock owners to find water for their animals and many of them took to cutting fences in order to reach streams and rivers. But those who had fenced in land were not blameless, frequently caring little to differentiate between their own land and public land or someone else's private land.

Fences were destroyed in more than half of Texas counties. Usually groups calling themselves names like the Blue Devils or the Javelinas struck at night, wrecking fences and warning the owners against rebuilding them. Some prospective settlers were frightened away by the violence, and the Fort Worth *Gazette* claimed that fence cutting had forced tax valuations to fall by $30 million.

Governor John Ireland called a special session of the legislature to deal with the problem. Rather than outlawing barbed wire as the San Sabans had wanted, the legislature made fence cutting a felony calling for one to five years in prison. Pasture arson was made punishable by two to five years. Fencing in public lands or lands that belonged to others, on the other hand, became a misdemeanor with the constructors given six months for removal. Ranchers were also allowed to build fences across public roads if they installed gates every three miles and kept them in working order. Fence cutting continued to be a problem in Texas, but it never again reached the acute state of 1883.

The cowboy strike arose from many of the same problems that had caused fence-cutting. The conditions of cowboy work changed as absentee owners gained greater control of the ranching industry and made it less migratory. Traditionally, cowboys had kept small herds of their own. They were often paid in calves, branding and keeping "mavericks," the unbranded cows named after Samuel Maverick who claimed his brand was no brand. The new capital-intensive owners, however, put cowhands on wages only—an average of $40 a month—and claimed mavericks as company property. These owners did not want cowboys running their own herds, a practice they saw as an invitation to rustling.

In late February 1883, men from five ranches presented owners with a demand for higher wages and set March 31 as the strike deadline. Tom Harris of the LS Ranch appears to have been the main organizer of the strike—certainly owners called him "bold and bad." It is unclear how many men took part, since people regularly joined and walked away from the work action. While newspapers and ranch owners warned that the strikers planned fence cuttings, pasture burnings, and the mass killing of cattle, no violence occurred.

The strike did not succeed. Owners of the T-Anchor and LE ranches fired all striking cowboys, while those at the LS and LIT raised wages a little and then fired all workers who would not accept the increase. Replacement workers were hired at temporarily increased wages. The May roundup took place without incident; the strike had lasted almost two and a half months. Afterward, rustling increased in the Panhandle, a crime often attributed to disgruntled workers.

The reputation of barbed wire fencing suffered from the 1885-1887 Big Die-Up. In winter, cattle in northern Texas pastures tended to drift to the south seeking shelter in the canyons and valleys away from the cutting Panhandle winds. Ranchers built so-called drift fences to keep the cattle contained. The Panhandle Stock Association ran a cooperative drift fence that reached for more than 30 miles into New Mexico across the Panhandle and into Oklahoma. But the winter of 1885 was unusually harsh. As the cattle moved south to get away from the snow and cold, they ran up against the drift fences. Unable to escape, they smothered or froze to death. When the thaw came in January 1886,

The Wind

Dorothy Scarborough's novel *The Wind* was published in New York City in 1925, but the setting is 1880s west Texas. The novel tells the story of a woman driven insane by the physical conditions of the frontier. The silent screen star Lillian Gish liked the story so much that she played the protagonist in the 1927 movie. The excerpt below is the beginning of *The Wind*:

The wind was the cause of it all. The sand, too, had a share in it, and human beings were involved, but the wind was the primal force, and but for it the whole series of events would not have happened. It took place in West Texas, years and years ago, before the great ranges had begun to be cut up into farms and ploughed and planted to crops, when there was nothing to break the sweep of the wind across the treeless prairies, when the sand blew in blinding fury across the plains, or lay in mocking waves that never broke on any howsoever-distant beach, or piled in mounds that fickle gusts removed almost as soon as they were erected—when for endless miles there seemed nothing but wind and sand and empty, far off sky.

But perhaps you do not understand the winds of West Texas. And even if you knew them as they are now, that would mean little, for today they are not as they used to be. Civilization has changed them, has tamed them, as the vacqueros and the cowboys changed and gentled the wild horses that roamed the prairies long ago. Civilization has taken from them something of their fiery, elemental force, has humbled their spirit. Man by building their houses here and there upon the plains, by stretching fences, by planting trees, has broken the sweep of the wind—by ploughing the land into farms where green things grow has lessened its power to hurl the sand in fury across the wide and empty plains. Man has encroached on the domain of the winds, and gradually, very gradually, is conquering them.

But long ago it was different. The winds were wild and free, and they were more powerful than human beings....

ranchers found thousands of cattle piled dead against the drift fences. The next winter, with another giant blizzard, was the same, and in some counties, the losses reached 75 percent of the herd. One cowboy reported skinning 250 bodies a mile along a 35-mile sector of fence. When the following summer brought a severe drought to the area, marginal outfits folded up.

Larger ranches could absorb their failing neighbors. Climate, strikes, and fence cutters did not stop the trend toward ever bigger ranches. The King Ranch was a south

Texas family-owned giant; the Waggoner and Burnett families both owned north Texas ranches with more than 400,000 acres each. Charles Goodnight established the 700,000-acre JA Ranch along Palo Duro Canyon, and Thomas Sherman Bugbee started ranching above the Canadian River until he had 450,000 acres in his Shoe Bar Ranch. Corporate ownership took off too. The foreign syndicates continued to grow. A Scottish syndicate owned the 861,000 acres of the Matador Ranch, while a British company controlled the Spur Ranch with more than 400,000 acres.

FARMERS, SHEEP, AND RAILROADS

While ranchers tended to despise farmers (they called the settlers "nesters"), they also needed these newcomers. For one thing, the ranchers could make extra money by selling land to farmers. Usually, the farmer would go bust and the rancher could get the land back for resale. Ranchers also needed farmers to populate the new counties forming in the west. The legislature had mapped out nice square counties for the region, but none of them could be officially organized until 150 signatures of residents had been collected.

This roundup and branding took place at the Hooper Ranch near Marble Falls in 1902. It is timeless in the cowboy way of life.
Courtesy Austin History Center, Austin Public Library

A small group of Quakers from Indiana became the first white settlers to farm above the Caprock. Their leader was Paris Cox, who had been born in North Carolina and left the state rather than face the Confederate draft. Traveling later with a group of buffalo hunters through the Llano Estacado, Cox fell in love with the landscape and vowed to return and make the region his home. In 1876 he obtained authority from the state to sell land at 25 cents an acre.

In 1878 Cox hired a local cowboy to drill a well and to plow 30 acres for planting. Cox, his wife, their two sons, and three other families moved onto the site in Crosby County. Cox built his family a sod house, but the others elected to live in tents. In early spring, after a difficult winter, the winds whipped through the settlement and blew away the tents. The three other families decided to return home, but Cox and his family stayed and planted grains, melons, potatoes, and vegetables. Soon another son and a daughter were born, a succession of crops was harvested, and eventually other families joined them.

By 1882, 10 families lived in the settlement.

By 1884 the Cox settlement had a post office and a name—Estacado. As long as Paris Cox lived, the town did well, growing to 200 residents by 1890. After Cox died, however, the town was leaderless, and in 1892 grasshoppers and drought finished the settlement off. Others took its place, however, as farmers and small towns moved out over the Caprock and populated the Llano Estacado.

While cattle ranchers still did not like farmers much, they despised sheep ranchers. By the 1880s the sheep culture that had taken hold in the German Hill Country moved west. The prosperous Kerrville merchant and banker Charles Schreiner encouraged sheep by forcing mortgage holders to agree to raise a flock. He also provided warehouses for wool and a commission system.

Always looking for better pastures, sheepmen moved their herds about throughout the year. In 1881, however, the legislature passed a law that sheep could not graze on land without the owner's permission. No such law existed for cattle or horses. Sheepmen were forced to buy land and fence it, and fencing only made cattlemen resent them more. In December 1883, Horace Starkweather found his wires cut and his sheepfolds, herders' huts, and 2,000 cedar posts burned. Within three weeks he replaced the fencing with a five-wire fence with rocks along the bottom, but again someone cut 30 miles of the new fencing and let scabby sheep in with his flocks.

As more sheep—and eventually goat—raisers moved to the west Texas plains, they mixed their herds. Spreads were soon running sheep, goats, and cattle on the same pastures. The landscape would never look like the farming lands of other parts of the country. Soon conglomerations of houses sprang up along railroad tracks. Cattlemen and sheep herders took to staying over when they dropped their animals off at the railhead. Hotels, saloons, stores, and even churches and schools served the needs of west Texans, and soon towns dotted the plains.

The railroads made it easier for farmers and ranchers to sell their products and to buy needed supplies. In return the railroads sold land to both nesters and cowboys. After the legislature authorized the sale of public lands to the rail companies to encourage railroad building, the Texas and

Pacific Railroad soon owned more than five million acres in Texas. As towns grew, they also tried to entice railroads to come through their communities by offering the lines more land and other incentives. The railroads would then sell this land to settlers in the hope of profiting from their commerce.

Most rail companies, however, did not do as well as they had hoped. Many could not sell their land, which had to compete with cheap public land, and the companies became "land poor." Undercapitalized, they often ended up bankrupt. The land they held was sold at cut rate prices, driving the price of land down even further.

The remaining railroads laid tracks as fast as they could. The locations of tracks could dictate whether a community would thrive and prosper or fade away into a ghost town. While the new lines could bring prosperity, they also made farmers and ranchers part of the national economy and broke up local patterns of economic control and benefit. Customers became dependent on the railroad's services, and the lines often exercised this power in a less than benevolent manner. Farmers and others believed that the railroads discriminated among their customers. Secret agreements among railroad magnates divided up markets, fixed prices, and pooled assets. Railroad companies also had unfair advantage in the state legislature, where their lobbyists used money and other enticements to kill bills the lines disliked. State legislators and other influential people also received free railroad passes, an unsubtle economic bribe. Resentment of the companies' power led to unrest and, eventually, organized protest movements.

The railroads were another nail on the coffin of the cowboy way of life. Cattle were herded onto railway cars, not along the trail; railheads became settlements, then towns, then cities. The cattle drive west was over, but its mystique lingered. The cowboy—not the sheep herder, the dirt farmer, or the train engineer—became the icon that Texans plastered all over their state, from sports teams to pickup ads. Even as they zip along freeways and hurtle up skyscrapers, Texans still yearn for the memory of a period that barely existed in the grand scheme of history. A scant three decades in the life of a centuries-old land have forever etched themselves into our idea of Texas and given the state a claim on a western rather than southern identity.

Each day a cattle drive is re-enacted at the Fort Worth Stockyards Historic District. Weather permitting, the cattle begin in the late morning at the east end of Exchange Avenue and travel west past the Stockyard Visitor's center to the Cowtown Coliseum. There they can be viewed from the Herd Observation Deck. The cattle then make the return trip in the afternoon. J. Griffis Smith, courtesy TxDOT

Must-See Sites

Dixon's Medal of Honor

You can see the unreturned Medal of Honor of Billy Dixon, the "long-shot" hero of Adobe Walls, at the Panhandle-Plains Historical Museum in Canyon. The oldest history museum in Texas, the Panhandle-Plains has a varied collection, including a pioneer village with hands-on experiences. Call (806) 651-2244 or go to www.wtamu.edu/museum.

Palo Duro Canyon

The Palo Duro Canyon, famous for the Red River War and for being the second largest canyon in the United States, was formed by the main branch of the Red River (called the Prairie Dog Town Fork). Randolph B. Marcy, who came upon the canyon in 1852, was the first white to describe it. Today, the Palo Duro State Park, east of Canyon, includes about 16,000 acres and offers camping, horseback riding, and other recreational opportunities. Call (806) 488-2227 or go to www.palodurocanyon.com.

Life of the Cowboy

You can still get some idea of life on the cattle drive in Fort Worth. Every day "cowboys" drive a herd of Longhorns through the historic stockyards area in downtown. Also in the same area, the Texas Cowboy Hall of Fame, the Cattle Raisers Museum, and the National Cowgirl Museum and Hall of Fame offer glimpses of western life. Go to www.fortworth.com/01visitors for more information.

In Texas, the town of Kerrville grew as both a meeting point for those following the Western Trail and a marketing center for area ranchers. Today you can relive some of the scenes of the cattle drives at the Cowboy Artists of America Museum, which also houses a western Americana library. Call (830) 896-2553 or go to www.caamuseum.com.

According to J. W. Williams in *The Big Ranch Country*, old cowhands on the large ranches found themselves fenced off from the buddies they had made when herds moved over the open range. To renew their friendships, they organized a cowboy reunion in Seymour in 1896 and again in 1897. Today, the Texas Cowboy Reunion takes place in Stamford on a weekend near the Fourth of July and includes rodeo events, a chuckwagon cookoff, and a cowboy poetry reading. Call (325) 773-3614 for information. You might return to the area at Christmas time and attend the Cowboy Christmas Ball in Anson, a big dance based on a poem by Lawrence Chittenden that was first published in 1890.

The Capitol

The new 1888 capitol building paid for by west Texas land was made of pink granite hewed from Hill Country quarries. Today the old building still commands the view of Congress Avenue in Austin, but newer underground additions offer their own attractions, including exhibits, a gift shop, and a cafeteria. Call (512) 463-0063 or visit www.capitol.state.tx.us.

Railroading

At several sites you can experience railroading as it was in late 19th-century Texas. The Texas State Railroad State Historical Park offers train rides between Palestine and Rusk. The Tarantula Train, which goes from the Fort Worth Stockyards to a depot in Grapevine, and the Hill Country Flyer, which connects Cedar Park, north of Austin, to Burnet also let you experience old-time railroading. Several towns have converted old depots into museums and other cities have built special museums such as Age of Steam Museum in Fair Park in Dallas, Red River Railroad Museum in Dension, Gulf Coast Railroad Museum in Houston, Texas and Pacific Railroad Museum in Marshall, and B-RI Railroad Museum in Teague. The Texas Panhandle Railroad Historical Society keeps a Santa Fe steam locomotive on display in Amarillo. You can find an extensive list of Texas railroad museums and historical societies at home.earthlink.net/~bkroger.

10

CHANGING WORK WAYS

Farmers moving out onto the plains were a vanguard of agriculturalists in a state that was still predominately rural. (In 1900, 83 percent of Texans lived in rural areas.) Most Texans were farmers, but they were also profoundly dissatisfied. Cotton was still the staple cash crop, tying Texas to the depressed economy of the Old South. The price of cotton, which had been 35 cents a pound in 1865, was 5 cents in 1898. Equipment prices, taxes, and interest payments on mortgaged land had not gone down. Railroads charged what seemed to be exorbitant prices to haul crops and animals to market. Middlemen, farmers thought, were getting rich while the source of wealth—the tillers of the soil—grew impoverished.

Not everyone who farmed owned land. Many poor whites, most Hispanics, and almost all recently freed slaves worked other people's land. An agricultural hierarchy existed, and at the bottom was the migratory farm worker who had no set place to work and moved from area to area selling labor for some form of direct payment—money, food, shelter.

Just above the migratory worker was the sharecropper, who stayed in one place for at least one growing season and worked another person's land in return for a portion of the profit on the crop's sale (usually half, another name for a sharecropper was a "halver"). The land owner provided the sharecropper with the tools and animals needed to bring in crops, a house or other form of shelter, and, most importantly, credit at the local store. Often the same person owned the store and the sharecropper's land. At the store the sharecropper could buy food, clothing, and other necessities. While land owners occasionally supplied seeds, most 'croppers had to buy their own seeds at the store. When the crops were sold, the amount owed the store was deducted from the sharecropper's part of the profit; it was a rare sharecropper who managed to come out ahead—even when the land owner played fair in adjusting profit against credit.

Next up on the ladder of farm workers was the tenant farmer, almost always a landless white person. Tenant farmers provided their own tools, seeds, and other supplies and usually could keep three-fourths of the cotton and two-thirds of the grain for themselves. Since they gave the land owner one-fourth of cotton and one-third of grain, they were said to work on "thirds and fourths." Tenant farmers made their own credit arrangements. Even though tenants had a little more control of their economic relations and could at least claim to have an investment in tools, animals, or other items, they often had to mortgage their belongings to pay the merchants who gave credit on seeds and supplies. For the system to work to the benefit of the tenants and sharecroppers—not to mention the land owners—the price of cotton had to keep pace with the prices of other provisions. With cotton prices falling, tenants and sharecroppers were declining deeper into debt and despair. Even the owners of agricultural land felt the effects of the moribund market. All agriculturalists agreed that powerful outside interests were impoverishing agrarians.

WORKING-CLASS PROTESTS

Several organizations gave voice to the farmers' dissatisfaction—the Grange, the Greenback party, and the Knights of Labor—but the Farmers' Alliance took off among Texas agrarians. Eventually, the alliance grew into a national organization of three million, making it one of the largest protest organizations in the history of the United States. The alliance began with a September 1877 gathering in Lampasas County. Growth was slow, but in 1883 S.O. Daws was made the alliance's full-time lecturer. Daws toured the state with the message that "the capitalist holds your confidence in one hand, while with the other he rifles your pocket." Membership increased.

In 1886 the alliance met in Cleburne and condemned the "shameful abuses" farmers and workers were suffering "at the hands of arrogant capitalists and powerful corporations." They called for the federal government to pass an interstate commerce act and to revamp the currency system with money (greenbacks) circulation based on population rather than a metal standard (such as gold). With cheaper money available, alliance members believed farmers could remedy declining crop prices.

Both the Farmers' Alliance and the Knights of Labor, an early labor union, were galvanized by opposition to the railroads. Farmers saw the railroads as a major impediment to higher profits, and the Knights' most memorable action in Texas was against the railroads. The Knights had first organized in the state in 1882 and were unique in allowing women, farmers, and African Americans to join their union.

The Knights' defining moment—and their death blow—in Texas came with the Great Southwest Strike of 1886. In 1885 the Knights won their demands in a strike against the Wabash Railroad, which was owned by the railroad baron Jay Gould. Membership shot up. In March 1886 a foreman on the Gould-owned Texas and Pacific Railway was fired on the suspicion that he was a member of the Knights. Martin Irons, a master workman and chair of the executive committee of the Knights' District Assembly 101, called a strike.

The work action soon spread to other rail lines and violence followed. Gould hired replacement workers and Pinkerton detectives, and Texas Governor John Ireland called out state militia and Texas Rangers to push back the striking union members. Gould's 1885 settlement began to look like a strategic capitulation; he would use the Great Southwest Strike to destroy the Knights. The railroad magnate held out and public opinion turned against the union. Eventually the strike was broken, and the Knights of Labor never recovered in Texas. Martin Irons also never recovered. He was blacklisted and could not find work under his real name. He died in 1900 and was buried in Bruceville, south of Waco. A monument marks his grave.

The collapse of the Knights of Labor left the Farmers' Alliance as the main voice for reform in Texas. In 1890 the alliance supported James Stephen Hogg as the Democratic nominee for governor. Hogg was a reformer who championed many of the same goals as the leaders of the alliance, but he lost their support when he refused to support the alliance's idea for "subtreasuries," which would involve the government in making land and commodity loans directly to farmers. In April 1892 alliance members left the

Democratic party, and the Populist party came to Texas.

In the 1892 election, the Populists nominated candidates who seriously challenged the Democrats' dominance of the state. The Populists floundered, however, on the issue of race. For one thing, despite the fact that they had African American members (John Rayner sat on the executive committee), the Populists could not woo African American voters away from the Republican party. More importantly, the rank and file maintained their racial prejudices. Given the choice between white supremacy and Populism, they chose white supremacy, leading them to the Democrats.

The 1892 Election

When the time came for Governor Hogg to run for his second two-year term, farmers were dissatisfied with the results of his reforms. For example, his new railroad commission, which was supposed to regulate the rail lines and end at least some of their abuses, did not have a single farmer on it. But Hogg had also gone too far for some conservative Democrats. The election promised to be exciting.

Hogg's supporters kept the conservatives out of the Democratic convention in Houston. The conservatives, or Gold Democrats, left the party and nominated their own candidate for governor—George Clark, a railroad attorney. The Populists nominated Thomas L. Nugent, who had been a Democratic judge. Meanwhile, the Republican party splintered just as the Democratic party had.

With the death of the former governor E.J. Davis, control of the Republican party had passed to Norris Wright Cuney, an African American and one of the savviest politicians of his time. Cuney held a federal job, customs collector in Galveston, and this position gave him control of federal patronage in the state. At this time the Republican party's power in Texas came from African American voters. In some counties on the Gulf Coast, African American voters were the majority and the Jim Crow laws that would eventually check African American voting were not yet in force. While few African American office holders existed, African Americans could make a difference in power, especially among the Republicans.

Unhappy white Republicans revolted against Cuney's leadership. The "lily-whites" withdrew from the party and nominated Andrew Jackson Houston, Sam Houston's son, for governor. Cuney realized that the African American Republicans had little chance on their own and, distrusting the regular Democratic party, he threw his support to George Clark, the Gold Democrat. Governor Hogg, however, turned his attention to African American voters, especially farmers. Hogg's supporters formed clubs for African American voters and the governor assiduously courted them. Many African Americans clung to the Republican party as their only political base in the state, but Hogg managed to lure away about half of them. He won re-election with 43 percent of all votes in a field of five candidates.

The Democrats took over the issues that the Farmers' Alliance and the Populists had championed, and farmers deserted the Populists. But even after Hogg left office, his party kept some of his reforms alive. A much more conservative period was coming for all voters in the state, however. While Texas remained an agricultural state, farmers' influence declined, and with that decline went a major force for reform. In the early 1890s farmers made up about one-half of the state legislature; after 1900 they were about one-third. Other interests were influencing the state's politics and economy as new industries assumed importance. Lumbering was one of these interests; oil was another.

Logging out East Texas

The open range was not confined to the plains. Fences were few and far between in the forests of deep east Texas. Since the first white settlements, stock owners had exercised the right to range their cattle and hogs over any and all unfenced land and most people fenced only the most necessary areas—vegetable gardens and other delicate crops. Not only could domestic animals roam as they pleased, people could hunt, fish, gather nuts and wood, even build emergency stock pens wherever they rambled. Unlike west Texans, farmers in the Piney Woods saw no reason to own more land than was absolutely necessary. Each man figured he could always use the neighbor's land when needed or the forests that belonged to no one.

Trees were considered common property. Anyone could go into a stand of cypress or white oak and cut what he

The Hogg Family

Many historians think that James Stephen Hogg, the first Texas-born governor, was the best governor Texas ever had. He was too young to have been a Confederate soldier, and he was not tied to the party outlooks of the past.

He was born in Rusk. His father had been a brigadier general in the Civil War and died in battle. A year later Hogg's mother died and made Jim Hogg an orphan at the age of 12. The five Hogg children—three boys and two girls—were left to run the plantation. The family estate was sold off piecemeal to pay for daily necessities and to help the boys obtain the education they needed to earn their livings as adults.

James Stephen Hogg, probably around 1900. Courtesy Center for American History, UT-Austin.

Hogg combined newspaper work and the law. He was a typesetter for a Rusk newspaper and also worked with the sheriff in Quitman. In the latter job, he was ambushed and shot in the back by a band of outlaws. After he recovered from this attack, Hogg went to work for a Tyler newspaper and eventually had his own newspapers in Longview and Quitman. His newspapers opposed local outlaws, subsidies for railroads, and the corruption of the Grant administration. In 1875 Hogg became a practicing lawyer. From 1878 to 1884, he made a reputation for himself as a county attorney and then a district attorney. He managed to woo enough African American voters away from the Republicans to ensure Democratic control of Smith County.

Friends urged Hogg to seek statewide office, but at first he refused. Finally, in 1886 he ran for state attorney general and won. To Hogg the overriding problem for Texas at that time was regulating corporations, especially railroads. As attorney general he enforced the laws that required railroads and other corporations to sell their land grants to settlers within a reasonable time. He broke up a railroad association that had been formed to pool traffic, fix rates, and, in general, hobble competition. He was also responsible for the second antitrust law in the nation.

Despite his victories, Hogg became convinced that neither the state legislature nor the attorney general's office had the power to control corporations, especially the railroads. To achieve control over these companies, he proposed the creation of a state railroad commission, and he ran for governor with this idea as one of his major planks.

Hogg was a dynamic campaigner and a thrilling stump speaker. He was not above using "earthy" language in his stump speeches and, like Sam Houston before him, would doff his shirt in the heat of summer oratory while pulling gulps of water from a bucket at his side. Most importantly, he could find the words that explained exactly how a railroad commission would benefit the daily lives of farmers and mechanics.

In his years as governor, 1891 to 1895, Hogg cracked down on the corporate practice of selling inflated stocks, impeded the practice of selling state lands to foreign corporations, and limited the indebtedness cities and counties could take on. His over-riding goal was to ensure that individual settlers held onto Texas lands and were treated fairly by corporations.

After Hogg's death in 1906, other family members carried on his legacy. He taught his children that wealth carries responsibility. His only daughter, Ima, ensured that the family name continued to be attached to Texas philanthropy. Her first interest was music, and she helped start the Houston Symphony Orchestra. But her life took a different turn after she suffered some kind of breakdown. In 1929 she founded the Houston Child Guidance Center and in 1940 started the Hogg Foundation for Mental Health. Also in the 1940s she was elected to the Houston school board where she fought for equal pay for teachers regardless of sex or race. Later she bacame interested in historic preservation and the arts and founded city and state institutions to carry on her concerns. While her father was an outstanding governmor, Ima may have made the more permanent contribution to the state. Many of her donations are open to the public today.

In 1957 Ima donated the land that would become the Varner-Hogg Plantation State Historical Park north of West Columbia. Two other Hogg homes are open to the public, although they are not state parks. The town of Quitman owns and operates the Governor Hogg Shrine Historic Site. It has three museums connected to the Hogg family: The Stinson House belonged to the family of Jim Hogg's wife, the Honeymoon Cottage was the first home of the future governor and his wife, and the Miss Ima Hogg Museum has displays related to the history of northeast Texas. The Jim Hogg Historic Site in Rusk includes a replica of Hogg's birthplace, a museum, and a family cemetery.

needed for shingles or barrel staves. Excess would be floated down the nearest river and sold in Houston, Beaumont, or Orange. No one argued about the ownership of the lumber. Life in the Piney Woods was hard scrabble, but the people were individualistic and lived with little regard for other's rules or opinions.

After the Civil War things changed. The state sold public lands to all newcomers. Not all of this land was in west Texas, and large companies from outside the state saw the possibilities for putting together vast forested tracts in the eastern part of the state. Speculators moved into the Piney Woods and bought virgin timberland for $1.25 an acre. Some farmers also sold "stumpage" rights to their lands, whereby buyers could cut all the marketable timber. To the farmers, this deal seemed heaven-sent. Most of them saw the pine as a big weed that impeded plowing; by selling stumpage they could get their land cleared and be paid for it.

By 1902 a few large timber companies had bought up most of the deep east Texas timberland. In one decade, the region went from an economy dominated by subsistence farming to one based on cutting and selling timber. The timber companies and the railroads depended on each other. Railroads used timber for tracks, and the lumber companies shipped their product by rail. A railroad pushing into the forest made it possible for a lumber company to establish a company town—one in which the company owned everything from the sawmill to the smallest house. The town then needed a railroad to carry cut timber to market. In 1904, 62 sawmills operated along the Gulf, Colorado and Santa Fe railroad. By 1906, there were 230. Local lives were changing swiftly.

The timber companies seemed to offer east Texans a better life than they had found in subsistence farming and hunting. The companies would buy up land, bring in rail lines and skilled workers, set up a town, and hire unskilled workers, African American and white, from the immediate area. The companies built housing for workers and paid them in company scrip. The scrip could only be redeemed at the company store, which often charged inflated prices, but to the farmers of the region the housing and pay often seemed an improvement over the impoverished lives they had been living. Sons of farmers, and often the farmers themselves, deserted their plows for a chance at pushing saws.

The move from farm to sawmill involved more than relocating and taking on a new occupation. Farmers were used to setting their own hours and work rules, within the confines of nature. As timbermen, they rose in the dark to the shriek of the mill whistle and spent the day working to the foreman's schedule. The whistle blew for everything—there was even a whistle to send the women back home to start cooking lunch.

The individualistic forest dwellers often found the switch to employee life difficult, and sometimes violence resulted. Timber towns developed reputations for off-hour drinking and fighting. Gambling, prostitution (the "ladies" came in on the railroad and left the same way), and other vices proliferated. Fights blew up not only because of immediate tensions but also because of long-standing east Texas feuds that followed families into the timber mill towns.

Despite the violence and the often chaotic conditions of daily living, a mill town was an exercise in hierarchy. The style and placement of houses clearly indicated the status of the inhabitants. The superintendent's house would be close to the mill office, painted, and relatively spacious. Farther away from the office, the houses decreased in size and such amenities as paint, indoor plumbing, and electricity disappeared. In some mill towns, those at the higher end of the hierarchy had electricity 24 hours a day, while skilled blue-collar workers might have it for only 12, and unskilled workers for even less, often using only oil lamps and wood stoves. Some companies did not bother to paint unskilled workers' houses; others painted unskilled white workers' houses white and the African American workers' houses brown.

But segregation went further. European workers perceived as "darker" were also set apart. Companies that hired Hispanic, Italian, Irish, or workers from other ethnicities tried to separate each group's housing. Sometimes the segregation included separate company stores, but often the groups had separate sections or entrances to the same store. At one mill commissary, the meat market sold pork chops and other better cuts at the "white" door, while at the "black" entrance the butchers sold hog jowls and chitterlings. If a white person had a hankering for chitterlings, all he had to do was ask an African American co-worker to buy them for him and he could return the favor when his colleague wanted pork chops. One mill town had a theater for its workers, but status was preserved there, too. White-collar workers and their families sat in the front downstairs, while other white workers filled out the lower floor. Up above were two balconies: African Americans had one and Hispanics the other.

Unmarried employees lived in company hotels—and none were female. Like everything else, the hotels were segregated. At the very least one hotel would be set aside for white managers and another for everyone else. Most companies tried to divide their unmarried workers by the caste rules, so they would have to erect separate hotels, or boardinghouses, for unskilled white workers, African Americans, Hispanics, Italians, Irish, Slavs, and whomever else they hired. Expense was not laid out for the unskilled workers' living quarters. Bedbugs were a perpetual problem. The pests were controlled by dissolving three bags of mothballs in five gallons of gasoline and washing down every mattress once a week. No smoking in bed.

The food in these hotels varied. Some, such as the Antlers in Diboll, were known for fine cooking. Some of the workers' boardinghouses were run by women with reputations for good simple cooking. Most of the tables set for workingmen, however, depended heavily on the pioneer diet of cornbread, bacon, beans, and syrup.

Whites filled management and administration and most skilled positions, Irish and Hispanics laid and repaired track, and Italians worked in the lumber yard. The hardest and most dangerous work went to African Americans.

When a lumber company turned its attention to a forest, work crews came through in an ordained order. First to move through a new stand of wood would be the turpentiners, men who were said to be the most unruly and violent of all timber workers. Working alone or in small groups, they made V-shaped chips in the pine bark and set up buckets to catch the leaking sap, which would be distilled into turpentine and resin. The next workers to come through were the engineers, who methodically calculated the best places to lay rail tracks. Their plans would be carried out by right-of-way and grading crews. The steel gang would complete the tracks that the logging crew would then use to send out timber.

After a tree had fallen, a "tong man" would attach tongs and cables to the log and a steam-powered "skidder" would pull the fallen tree toward the cars waiting on the rail track. Most tong men were African American.

Logging was filled with danger. In some sawmill counties, the rate of disability among adult men was double the state average, not counting, of course, the many who died. The "drum man" who operated the controls of the skidder faced a special kind of danger. The steam-powered skidder was an enormous machine—two stories tall—that pulled in logs from four directions. The drum man either powered the pulling chains or braked them. Any failure of communication between the drum and tong men could result in the death or maiming of the latter. A tong man had to be ready to jump to safety at the first sign of a breakdown in the system, or a fast-moving giant log could crush him.

The skidder-pulled logs also snapped and obliterated smaller trees. For every log a mechanized skidder pulled, estimates held, three younger trees were killed. The dragged logs also tore giant trenches in the earth—trenches that would crumble with the next rain and erode the land. When the timber crew moved on, the landscape was moonlike, with the earth full of gouges and holes and stripped of all vegetation.

Lumber companies built up mill towns, stripped the countryside, and then moved on. Replanting made no economic sense, especially since cheap new forests were always available. "Cut-out" was inevitable. Anyone paying attention could chart the impending death of a mill town. Crews would go out each day into the very forest their labor was shrinking. When the last tree was cut, the logs would be shipped out, the boiler fires extinguished, and the people would move on—to the next mill town.

Often, companies pulled out of an area not because the lumber had reached cut-out, but because fire had destroyed the mill. Stacks of wood and piles of dry sawdust made kindling of sawmills. If a major fire burst through a mill or town toward the end of a forest's economic life, the company would often just pull up stakes and leave.

Writing of a village called Ewing, Angelina County historian Bob Bowman could have been speaking about most of the mill towns: All that remained in the town, he described, were "a few concrete leftovers from the town's sawmill, some forgotten graves hidden in the forests, a few water cisterns that mark Ewing's homesites, and an old wooden residence." Such ghost towns still dot the Piney Woods.

GUSHERS

At almost the same time as the lumber companies were mining east Texas for above-ground resources, Texans discovered the economic possibilities of the hidden resource that would become identified with Texas for most of the 20th century: oil.

Oil had been a part of Texas life since people first lived there, but it was often more of a nuisance than a commodity. Native Americans used oil for medicine, waterproofing, and in other applications. White settlers cursed the oil they found seeping into their water wells. Some of the cannier used it in snake-oil medicines and other scams. For a long time oil was useful only as a waterproofing caulk. But eventually a new market was created when kerosene lamps became available to households.

The first Texas oil well appeared in Nagadoches County in 1866, and in the 1890s Corsicana in Navarro County was the center of Texas oil activity, with 300 wells and a crude refinery by the end of the decade. By 1900 the Corsicana field was producing 836,000 barrels a day—more oil than anyone in north central Texas needed. The producers stored the oil in open tanks and much of it slopped over into surrounding creeks. Pollution became a problem. The city fathers took to spraying the substance on dirt roads to keep the dust down. Looking for a way to use the stuff up, the leaders of Corsicana in 1897 asked J.S. Cullinan of Pennsylvania to come up with better uses. Cullinan convinced the Cotton Belt Railroad that oil could power a steam locomotive. Other railroads soon switched from coal to oil and a market was born. Cullinan later merged his company with two others and the result was named the Magnolia Petroleum Company; later it became the Mobil Oil Company.

At the turn of the century, John D. Rockefeller's Standard Oil controlled 90 percent of the U.S. oil supply; one company

These pump jacks for shallow oil wells were found in the Big Thicket in Hardin County. John Suhrstedt, courtesy TxDOT

Derrick workers

Gerald Lynch worked in the oil fields of Texas for 33 years. He began as a teenager in Corsicana in 1925 and worked his way through many specialties, including derrick man and tool pusher, the pinnacle of his career. Here he describes the men who built the derricks:

The old wooden derricks were erected by a very special breed of men. They were called "rig builders." They were highly paid men, drawing $18–$24 a day, and were exceedingly strong, ambidextrous, tough, and skillful. They had to be because the work that they did was beyond the capacity of the average able-bodied man. They could hold up and steady a 3-by-12 inch board in a corner of a derrick they were building, then nail it in place with sixty-penny spikes. They used instead of a hammer a long-handled hatchet with a round serrated head opposed to the blade. They would usually sink a sixty-penny spike in three blows, and had to be able to nail left-handed in order to keep up, as the work was fast and furious. Those tough old boys prided themselves on being stronger, tougher, faster, and meaner than anybody, and were just that. The total elapsed time it usually took to build a derrick from starting legs to crown was three days, working off scaffold boards and pounding thousands of nails. They were much men, and even though they pre-sawed the "derrick patterns" in town, everything had to be laid out to pattern on the job. The old-time rig builders are all gone, but they were kings in their day. They had the grace and balance of tightwire artists, and more guts than they needed. One of them would "go in the hole," i.e., fall to his death, occasionally. His friends would grieve, wonder what happened, go to his funeral, then go out the next day and build another derrick.

—Gerald Lynch, *Roughnecks, Drillers, and Tool Pushers: Thirty-Three Years in the Oil Fields*

executive confidently stated that no oil reserves would be found west of the Mississippi. Pattillo Higgins, however, believed otherwise. Against the reigning geologic belief of the time, Higgins thought that the salt domes of the Texas Gulf Coast harbored petroleum. In 1892 he, Emma E. John, and several other partners started the Gladys City Oil, Gas, and Manufacturing Company and drilled into a salt dome formation south of Beaumont. Previously, the lonely hilltop had only been used as an asylum for isolating plague victims, but now the partners of Gladys City Oil were convinced the hill called Spindletop hid valuable resources. The sands of the area, however, made drilling tricky, and the cable-based drilling equipment the company used did not help. Three shallow wells were dry. Two of the partners left the company.

In 1899 Anthony F. Lucas, a man knowledgeable about salt domes, joined with Higgins and the two tried to drill more wells. The partners approached financers who were backed by Andrew Mellon money. The Mellon interests came through with cash, but more importantly they insisted that seasoned drillers from the Corsicana field be called in. Higgins was pushed out of the partnership and Lucas's share was diminished, but obsessed with proving that his theories were correct, Lucas hung onto the project.

The Corsicana drillers, Al and Curt Hamill, used a rotary drill bit that was heavier and more efficient than those Higgins had been using. From October 1900 to the following January, Lucas and the Hamills struggled with the sticky sands. Suddenly, on January 10, 1901, mud bubbled up through the hole they had drilled. The mud was followed by a rush of drilling pipe—six tons of it—and then more mud. Soon oil shot 100 feet into the sky. The Lucas geyser had released the potential of Spindletop Oilfield and changed the economic history of Texas.

For nine days the well gushed 100,000 barrels of oil a day. Finally Lucas and the Hamills figured out a way to cap the well but not before a huge pool of oil had built up around it. Even with this hazard, townspeople from Beaumont and folks from around the country braved the black sludge to come and gawk. Some did more than gawk. By September, six other wells on Gladys City land had come in successfully.

Oil was not the only thing shooting into the sky—land prices took off as well. An area resident who had been trying for three years to sell his land for $150 found a buyer willing to shell out $20,000. That speculator turned the property around in 15 minutes—for $50,000. In that first year, the population of Beaumont went from 10,000 to 50,000, and an estimated $235 million was invested in oil. In 1901 the state chartered 491 oil companies.

The same region yielded other strikes. In 1903 Sour Lake came in, followed later by Bateson and Humble. Speculators poured into the Gulf Coast. Working men also came looking for their fortunes, even though their goals were often modest. Most of the oil field workforce had been agricultural

What Makes Meat Texas Barbecue?

Every region of Texas, and sometimes it seems every person, has a different idea of barbecue. In certain times and places, arguing about the topic might have gotten you shot, or at least roughed up. One reason for this contentious disagreement is that Texas barbecue is true fusion food. Texas barbecue is made up of Mexican shepherds' food; the cuisine of slaves and liberated African Americans; cowboy vittles; and European, especially German, meat market practices; but different regions of the state have different affinities.

In east Texas, for example, traditional barbecue is pork of some kind that has been marinated or basted with lots of sauce and cooked over oak, hickory, or pecan. West Texans and most Hispanic Texans prefer mesquite and cook goat or beef over it. In central Texas, people might give you some sauce if you ask for it with your cooked beef, but the request marks you as someone who "doesn't know barbecue." If you go far enough south in the state, you come upon *barbacoa*, a cow head sealed in leaves or, in more recent times, aluminum foil and buried in hot coals.

Until the beginning of the 20th century, Texas barbecue styles did not mingle much. In the German-influenced areas of the state, butchers would smoke leftover pieces of meat or grind them up into sausages and then smoke them. Customers would buy these meats and take them home to be part of a regular meal. Things changed when some new customers came by the meat markets.

Itinerant cotton pickers made barbecue what it is today—a big business and part of the state's identity. Throughout the summer the pickers would work their way across the state from south to north. Pickers— whether white, Hispanic, or African American—were not allowed inside restaurants, so they got their food at the meat markets. Even at the markets, pickers would buy their meat at the back door, and maybe pick up some crackers and pickles. They ate the whole meal under a nearby live oak. No plates, no forks, no side dishes. The meat markets became de facto restaurants or, to be more exact, barbecue joints.

During the Depression, people who would not normally have been pickers joined the agricultural work force. When they returned to their homes across the state, they took their new understanding of barbecue with them. Soon regional ideas about barbecue merged. Today the typical barbecue place anywhere in the state may have started as a meat market or grocery store (if it is old enough), but now it sells smoked beef, pork, and sausages with white bread and tortillas and a side of cowboy beans. Other sides have joined in: Cole slaw, potato salad, and banana pudding are now staples. Regional differences are still observable in some places, but a barbecue consensus seems to be emerging across Texas. In most places, you can even get sauce.

Read more about Texas barbecue and get some good recipes from Robb Walsh's *Legends of Texas Barbecue Cook Book*.

workers in the region. Men poured into the small towns around the new oil strikes. These boomtowns had to include cheap places to sleep and eat, saloons, and bordellos. An oil field man reported having to pay a dollar for a chair to sleep in—and another dollar for a second chair to rest his feet on. Some men didn't have the two dollars for chairs and shared the rent on a cot. Each man took his turn sleeping on the communally owned bed. Others simply slept outside as close to the wellheads as they could, so the flared off gas would keep them warm.

Oil field living conditions and lack of basic amenities led to epidemics of malaria, typhoid fever, and dysentery. At one time, oil was three cents a barrel and drinking water in the field was five cents a cup. Few doctors hung out in the rampaging oil towns, and most people had to treat themselves with home remedies—usually large doses of castor oil. The sulfurous smell of gas hung over these towns night and day. The hellish atmosphere was fueled by the gigantic fires that would frequently consume wells and the small shacks that surrounded them. The oil fields engulfed small towns, and fire and health hazards increased—until the fields went dry and the oil rigs moved on.

The oil field bonanza moved north and west. Electra (near Wichita Falls), Burkburnett, Breckenridge, Ranger, and other sites went through the oil boom and bust cycle. In 1918 the town of Breckenridge went from 800 residents to around 30,000 people. About 200 derricks were built within the town. People—usually single men—would rush into an area with a new strike, putting incredible pressures on public services. Unpaved streets and inadequate sanitation were the norm. An experienced oil field worker, Bing Maddox, spoke of the typical boomtown in his description of Borger, Texas: "It was made up of corrugated sheet iron buildings, tents, one-by-twelve hunter shacks, people living in their automobiles…some of them even digging holes back under the caprock and living in caves and half-dugouts."

Fortunes were made and lost in days—sometimes minutes. The story goes that one night in a bar near Spindletop a contractor named Howard R. Hughes bought the plans for an improved bit from Granville A. Humason. Hughes paid $150 for the idea. He then set up the Hughes Tool Company with his partner Walter B. Sharp. The

Humason bit was 10 times faster than other bits used at that time and could penetrate rock. When Hughes died in 1924, his company was worth $2 million and was to become the bedrock for his son's fortune. Eventually, Howard Hughes, Jr., would become the wealthiest—and most eccentric—person in the United States.

In 1896 the oil fields of Texas produced about 1,000 barrels; in 1902 production reached 21,000,000 barrels. Oil spearheaded the industrialization of the state. Not only oil companies but also related industries, like machine shops, grew up around the discoveries. Eventually, new professions, such as petroleum engineer and oil and gas lawyer, would also spring up. Spindletop was the force that propelled Texas into the industrialized age.

Must-See Sites

Forestry
The Texas Forestry Museum in Lufkin preserves many machines and artifacts of the logging period. Lufkin is nestled in the leftovers and replantings of the old forests. The town is just east of the Davy Crockett National Forest and west of Angelina National Forest.

Spindletop Boomtown
The Spindletop-Gladys City Boomtown Museum is on the campus of Lamar University in Beaumont. The museum recreates the boomtown of Gladys City that sprang up on the outskirts of the oilfield. The recreations have wooden oil derricks—but they only shoot water, not oil—a saloon, photographers shop, and other period buildings. Call (409) 835-0823 or go to www.spindletop.org.

TURN-OF-THE-CENTURY TEXAS

At the beginning of the 20th century, cities were growing, even though most Texans still lived in the countryside. In 1870, only two cities had populations of more than 10,000 people—Galveston with 13,818 and San Antonio with 12,256. In 1900, however, 11 urban areas had more than 10,000 people: San Antonio was the largest city followed by Houston, Galveston, Dallas, and Fort Worth. San Antonio and Galveston had always been major cities. Houston, Dallas, and Fort Worth used their transportation advantages to challenge the older towns.

NORTH TEXAS CITIES

Large Texas cities had always been in south Texas, especially on the coast. The sleepy north Texas burg of Dallas moved into predominance with the arrival of the Texas and Pacific Railroad and a cotton compress. Before the railroad came, north Texas cotton destined for the mills of the eastern United States had to go through the port of Galveston, a long arduous trip over land by ox wagon. In 1873 the railroad arrived in Dallas and the compress came in the next year, when 5,700 bales were sent east and north. Without the compress, which reduced bales of cotton to about half the size they were when they left the cotton gin, railroads would not have been able to ship the fiber.

Building on its railroad connections, Dallas diversified from a cotton shipping point to become a manufacturer of clothing and other light items. Eventually the movers of the city parlayed their ability to finance manufacturing into expertise on banking and insurance.

Fort Worth, too, grew because of the railroads. The town had begun as a western army post and was made the county seat in 1856. Even so, it remained a small town until the Texas and Pacific came through. Fort Worthians were so excited that they volunteered to lay track for the company. Rather than challenging Dallas for the cotton trade, Fort

Worth turned west and built stockyards to lure cattle owners. The city fathers even encouraged the construction of a meat-packing center, but it went bust in a depression during the 1890s. Meat packing was an industry of the future for turn-of-the-century Fort Worth.

In 1889, the Texas Spring Palace was built in Fort Worth to display Texas products and attract immigration and capital to the state. It was successful but burned down in its second year. City fathers eventually came up with the Fort Worth Fat Stock Show as a replacement. Courtesy Center for American History, UT-Austin.

While transportation was the backbone of both these cities, people who lived in Dallas, Fort Worth, and other Texas towns found getting around to be a chore. Long-distance train travel was usually safe and comfortable, but short-distance hauls within or between cities were difficult. A journey of 20 miles could take all day. Few people had automobiles yet—the first cars appeared in Texas around 1900. By 1905 Houston had 80 cars and had already had its first automobile fatality. In 1907 the state adopted its first speed limit—18 miles an hour.

Electric trains, called interurbans, filled the need for short distance transportation for some people. The first was built between Denison and Sherman in 1900, and Dallas and Fort Worth were connected in 1902. These four north Texas towns were soon connected to Denton, Waxahachie, Waco, Corsicana, and other settlements. Lines also opened in south Texas and west Texas. At their height the interurbans had 519 miles of track, but cheap cars and smooth highways eventually killed them.

The third of the new cities was Houston, and it too capitalized on its transportation advantages to pull itself into the top tier. Houston's rise, however, was connected to the decline of Galveston as the state's major port. Nature hastened that decline.

THE GALVESTON STORM

Since the days of Jean Lafitte, Galveston had been the major Texas port, and often the only one. By 1896 the U.S. Army Corps of Engineers had dredged a deep water port in the bay. The future of Galveston seemed assured—it would be the leading Gulf Coast city in Texas and maybe the entire South. Then came September 8, 1900.

A major hurricane had brewed up in the Caribbean and was headed toward Galveston. Isaac M. Cline, a climatologist in Galveston, could tell from the swells hitting the beach that something big was coming. On September 8, he urged everyone living on the gulf side of the island to head for higher ground. Unfortunately, not much of Galveston was higher—the highest point on the island was 8.7 feet above sea level. Those who left the island while they had the chance were the lucky ones. By the time the storm broke during the night, escape was impossible; the only link to the mainland had been destroyed. An estimated 6,000 people (including Cline's wife) died on the island; about 5,000 died on the mainland. The infrastructure of the city was destroyed. Wreckage covered the coast. Looters were shot on the spot. The 1900 hurricane is still considered the worst natural disaster ever to hit the United States.

Galveston had to bury the dead and rebuild. When investors did not snap up its municipal bonds, the citizens of the island purchased them. With this money they built a granite seawall, raised the level of the town by pumping sand up from the ocean bottom, and built an all-weather causeway to connect the island to the mainland. Believing that they needed a city government that could react quickly to danger,

Sights that Would Break the Heart of an Iron Man

Survivors of the great Galveston storm wrote to their loved ones elsewhere about their terrifying experiences. Charles W. Law was a traveling salesman from Georgia who had the bad luck to be staying in the Tremont Hotel on September 8, 1900. Many refuges sought shelter in the building. Law describes his ordeal to his wife in a letter dated September 12:

As the roof of our hotel had blown off and the bricks and stones were being blown off the building like they were little feathers, the hotel was in total darkness and there were several thousand people in the hotel that came in off the streets for protection….We were all huddled up in the hall ways, as we could not go into the rooms as the windows were blown through and the plastering in the rooms were all blown down. I went to my own room at 6 o'clock that eve and both my windows and ceiling [fell] in on me just as I opened the door….

On Sunday morning after the storm was all over I went out into the streets and the most horrible sights that you can ever imagine. I gazed upon dead bodies lying here and there. The houses all blown into pieces; women men and children all walking the streets in a weak condition with bleeding heads and bodies and feet all torn to pieces with glass where they had been treading through the debris of falling building[s]. And when I got to the gulf and bay coast I saw hundreds of houses all destroyed with dead bodies all lying in the ruins, little babies in their mothers arms….

I went from the shores to the interior of the City and every step you would take you could see dead bodies of all kinds: horses, mules, cats, dogs, chickens, and even snakes….

On Monday they took the bodies up and carried them out to sea and buried them there and Tuesday they could not take them up fast enough so they cremated them wherever they run up on them and when I left there today I saw them still at work with hundreds of hands cremating the bodies. None of the bodies the last two days were identified. They could not allow them to do so as the air was most foul. Most horrible! Most horrible!

On leaving there today on the sail vessel we saw more bodies than we could count out in the waters. The waters in some places were black with bodies and when we got way over across the bay we found the shore full of debris piled up on the dead bodies….I have seen sights that would break the heart of an iron man….

—*Through a Night of Horrors: Voices from the 1900 Galveston Storm*, ed. Casey Edward Greene and Shelly Henley Kelly

In response to the 1900 hurricane, Galveston constructed a seawall that lessened the effects of later storms and vecame a site of receation for subsequent generations. Jack Lewis, courtesy TxDOT

the people of Galveston instituted the first commission form of municipal government. Each city commissioner had complete power over a municipal department: police and fire, water and sewage, finance, streets, and public improvements. At first the governor appointed the mayor and all commissioners, but the state supreme court required that the officials be elected. Other Texas cities adopted the commission plan, including Houston in 1905 and Dallas, Fort Worth, and El Paso in 1907. By 1920 some 70 cities across the country had adopted Galveston's new plan for smooth government. Later in the decade, the commission form of government lost popularity to the city manager form.

Galveston may have been a leader in fashioning new forms of government, but rebuilding put the city behind at a strategic time in the forming of the Texas economy. While Galveston was reconstructing its houses and businesses, the oil boom passed it by. Other cities like Port Arthur reaped profits from the new industry. None took better advantage of Galveston's hard times than its neighbor Houston.

Senator Joe Bailey and the Waters-Pierce Oil Company

Joseph Weldon Bailey was born in Mississippi just before the Civil War ended. He moved to Gainesville, Texas, when he was 22, but never shook his vivid memories of Reconstruction. Bailey was tall and strong and wore his hair in a long Buffalo Bill style. A Dallas newspaperman described Bailey as "of heroic build, smooth face, long hair and longer coat, all at variance with prevailing styles, he struck me as a political masher, a sort of statesmanlike dude stuck on his intellectual shape." His gift for oratory, rather than his looks, helped him win election to the U.S. House of Representatives.

While Bailey considered himself a progressive, his record is a strange mix. He opposed both Woodrow Wilson's nomination for the presidency and Prohibition. In those days state legislatures, not the voters, picked U.S. Senators. Bailey had been a candidate for the U.S. Senate in 1900; at the same time he had approached the governor, state attorney general, and secretary of state on the behalf of the Waters-Pierce Oil Company.

Texans' strong anti-trust sentiments had banished Waters-Pierce because of its ties to the Standard Oil trust. Bailey convinced his listeners that the company had severed ties with Standard Oil and should be allowed back in the state. In reality a majority of the stock was registered in the name of one person—Henry Clay Pierce, the president—but Standard Oil actually held them. Bailey also swore that he had received no retainers from the company, but did not reveal that he had borrowed $5,000 from Pierce. When Bailey's reelection came up in 1906, the state senate investigated his ethics and exonerated him, but the house of representatives was more divided. Bailey received his second senatorial term, but in the hothouse climate of Texas turn-of-the-century politics whether one was for or against Bailey became an important political indicator.

Found guilty of violating Texas anti-trust laws, Waters-Pierce paid more than $1,718,000 in fines in 1909. To show their contempt for the proceedings, however, the company officers delivered the money to the state in cash. They carried it up the capitol steps in wheelbarrows. In 1913 Bailey retired from the senate.

An interesting view of Senator Bailey comes from Ely Green, who was born in Tennessee in 1893. His mother was an African American domestic and his father was one of the brothers in the family for which she worked. In 1912 Green moved to Waxahachie and eventually became a driver for one Judge Dunlap. He described a speech Bailey gave in Waxahachie:

We went to Dallas to bring Senator Baily [sic] to Waxahachie. Judge met him at the Dallas Club. Judge and his cronies and Senator made so many night caps for the road we were late getting back to Waxahachie. They didnt [sic] have time to eat supper. We had to rush to the Chautauqua grounds. I had listened to Judge and Senator talk. Senator told judge that he had a talk for the people that all he had to do was hold a cotton sack. All the farmers would walk into it. They had a big laugh over the plan.

When we got to the grounds every farmer of Ellis County was here, at least three thousand men. Senator said to Judge: I think I will speak out here. It is a clear night. I drove into the grounds. Senator stood in the back of the car as the top was down. This is his speech, as short as it was, that put every white man in the cotton sack Senator was holding.

He shouted out: I came here to bring you red bloody Texans and Sons of the Alamo and this great Lone Star State Texas. I want you to be posted so we wont [sic] be fooled by the long haired men and short haired women of Kansas. When they put over the Sufergettes [sic] it was the last freedom we had. Now they are coming to us with what they call a union. All it means is next five years the Negro will be going to recitation with our white children. Before letting that happen I would be willing to reinact [sic] the old Texas Law, property in man. Wouldnt [sic] you?

The crowd went wild, saying: No union in Texas. This blocked the union from Texas. It was for the white layman who worked in the cotton mills and to encourage industralization [sic] and wage scale for the white people. Just the prejudice word Negro shut the union out. Here I was thinking the Negro was not the only fool in the South.

—Ely: Too Black, Too White, ed. Elizabeth N. and Arthur Ben Chitty.

CITY ON THE BAYOU

Business leaders of Houston had long wanted to supplant Galveston as the leading port in the state. With Galveston devastated, the city fathers of Houston dusted off plans to dredge a deep-water ship channel out of Buffalo Bayou. There was a problem, however. Houston had always been known as a city with chronic "bowel complaint." Buffalo Bayou was the city's major source of drinking water, but it was also its sewer. Everyone knew that the "bowel complaint" was connected to the municipal drinking supply. The Corps of Engineers refused to work on deep-water channels in the bayou until Houston cleared up its water supply problem.

Alexander Potter, an engineer, developed a filtering system of rock, gravel, sand, and coke. Sewage was pumped through this filter and a reasonable facsimile of clean water came out the other end and drained into the bayou. To inaugurate the system, Potter showed his faith in the filter by publicly drinking a glass of the cleansed water.

By 1908 a ship channel 18.5 feet deep had been dredged out of the bayou, and a turning basin was built on the site of the old town of Harrisburg. With the help of federal money, the channel was deepened to 30 feet and extended to 50 miles by 1914. A town 50 miles from the coastline was now set to become the major port in Texas and the leader in shipping oil products. Galveston faded as a port and emerged as a tourist attraction.

TEXAS PROGRESSIVES AND JIM CROW

For the United States in general, the rise of an urban middle class at the turn of the century signaled a period of progressive reform. Progressivism was influential in Texas, but its effects were bound up in a one-party political system with a rigid racial code. Progressives throughout the country were concerned about the effects of uneducated and poor people on the political system. They seldom worried about using social control methods to achieve their goals. In Texas progressivism ignored the problems of minorities and poor whites while at the same time showing a strong suspicion of their abilities. Texas progressives came from old Hogg supporters, prohibitionists, women's clubs, former members of the Farmers Alliance and the Populist party, businessmen, and the State Federation of Labor.

With such a disparate group, the only reform all could agree on was improving election laws. Each group saw electoral change as advancing its interests. In 1903 the Terrell Election Law, named for state Senator A.W. Terrell, set up a uniform system of primaries to replace the chaos of nomination procedures that had led to frequent charges of fraud.

Part of the election reform package was a poll tax, which required people to pay in order to vote. (A major opponent of the new tax was the Texas Brewers Association, which apparently believed that more poor people than well-off opposed Prohibition.) Many progressives saw poor people of all races as inherently unstable voters and so did not object to the poll tax, which was probably aimed not only at African Americans but also at poor whites. The tax did indeed cut

The Gonzales County Courthouse is one of the remaining twelve designed by James Reily Gordon, whose designs epitomized the Texas courthouse of the early twentieth century. Courtesy TxDOT

into election turnouts: In the 1890s about 100,000 African American men voted, but in 1906 only 5,000 did.

At the same time, the executive committee of the Democratic party recommended that only whites be allowed to vote in Democratic primaries and most county commissions went along with the suggestion. (In 1927 the U.S. Supreme Court held that all-white primaries violated the 14th Amendment, and in the next year the Texas legislature declared that political parties were private organizations and as such could decide on their own who could vote in their primaries. This law stayed on the books until the 1940s.) At all levels, African Americans were being squeezed out of public life. Rural African American Texans, especially, stopped voting for decades and built parallel institutions outside of white control. With no check from African American votes, legislators now instituted the segregationists laws referred to as Jim Crow laws.

In 1910 the legislature required railroad stations to have separate waiting rooms for the races. African American porters had to have separate compartments on trains, so they could not sleep in unoccupied Pullmans. In the same year, the legislature called for repeal of the 15th Amendment

Sweet Home Colored School - Guadalupe Co 7/21/17

School desks made by the students. The seat lifts up. The iron was obtained from the old wagon tires of the community

The interior of the Sweet Home Colored School in Guadalupe County in 1917. According to the commentary on this photograph, the students made all of the furniture themselves. They used wagon wheels donated by the community for any metal parts. Courtesy Center for American History, UT-Austin.

(which gave freed slaves the right to vote) and revision of the 14th (which granted citizenship).

Streetcars, water fountains, and public restrooms were the next to be segregated, and in 1916 the Dallas city council required that neighborhoods be racially separate. When the U.S. Supreme Court ruled this ordinance unconstitutional, the state legislature allowed cities to rewrite their zoning regulations to create segregated areas. With residential quarters delineated by race, city services could be restricted or denied in African American neighborhoods, which now went without paved roads and often such basic services as water and sewage.

WETS VS. DRYS: THE RISE OF FERGUSONISM

In one-party Texas, the major political dividing lines for many people were wet vs. dry and Klan vs. anti-Klan. In 1887 a cursory attempt had been made to add an anti-alcohol amendment to the state constitution. The pro-liquor "wet" forces had beaten back statewide prohibition, but counties, cities, and precincts had the power to ban the sale of alcohol within their boundaries. Localities could vote on prohibition every two years, and some precincts regularly cycled back and forth between wet and dry status.

Many people who considered themselves progressives were dry, but not all. Other groups were more cohesive about the issue, including the Evangelical Christians, especially the Baptists and Methodists, who supported banning alcohol, while Hispanics, African Americans, and Texans of German, Czech, and other European descent opposed it. Prohibition was more popular in north Texas than in south Texas. Some conservatives argued that a government that could ban alcohol could also take away other liberties and maybe even threaten segregation.

In 1908 the drys again failed to pass a prohibition amendment and they turned their attention to the 1910 gubernatorial election. They allowed their strength to be divided between two dry candidates, and Oscar B. Colquitt, a wet, was elected. Another prohibition amendment failed in 1911, and Colquitt was elected to a second term in 1912. The margins were getting closer, however, and the drys marshalled their forces, seeing victory on the horizon. In the 1914 primary, they united behind one candidate, Thomas H. Ball, a Houston corporation attorney who had defended railroads. A spiritless campaigner, Ball lacked stump-speaking charisma. The Houstonian's absence of magnetism was unfortunate, because Ball was about to run up against one of the most spell-binding speakers in Texas history—James E. Ferguson, "Farmer Jim."

Ferguson was from Bell County but had rousted about as a field hand and day laborer in the west. He later returned to central Texas, where he farmed during the day and studied law at night. He entered law practice and started a bank in Temple. With this background, Ferguson could be all things to all men: In the city he was a banker and businessman; in the countryside he was a farmer who wore overalls. He kept a gourd and a wooden dipper by him when he was stumping in rural areas, where his political base was strongest. Taking a swig from his gourd and hitching up his overalls, he could look as rustic as any man in the crowd. He purposely spoke in bad grammar and told folksy stories that appealed to his rural spectators.

Ferguson also had a strong emotional issue for his rustic audiences: fairness for the tenant farmer. Among his campaign proposals was a law that would curb the landlord's take of the tenant's crops when the tenant supplied everything except the land. Limiting the law to those who supplied their own tools and seeds meant it would not apply to most non-white tenant farmers.

Ferguson profited from his opponent's ineptness and apparent hypocrisy. Ball claimed to be a dry but he was a member of the Houston Club, which was most definitely a wet organization. When Ferguson pointed out this inconsistency, Ball claimed he was a member of the club only for its library. Ferguson delighted in telling the voters of Texas that in 1913, the Houston Club had spent $112 for books and magazines and $10,483 for alcohol (there was also the expenditure of $361 for cards and poker chips). In desperation Ball asked Woodrow Wilson and members of his administration to endorse him. After some hesitation, President Wilson and some of his cabinet members announced that they supported Ball. Ferguson immediately denounced federal interference in a state primary.

Although Ferguson was a political wet, personally he was an abstainer who never touched alcohol. He vowed that he would remove the issue from the political ring by vetoing any bill about liquor no matter which side it took.

Ferguson beat Ball by 45,504 votes in the Democratic primary. Texas was still a one-party state and winning the Democratic primary was the same as winning the election. In his first term, Ferguson got a farm tenancy bill passed, but it was later declared unconstitutional by the U.S. Supreme Court. In addition, he publicly denounced the Ku Klux Klan and faced down Senator Joe Bailey. During his first term, state aid for rural schools became policy and colleges were allowed to build programs. One of his lasting contributions was the establishment of the Texas Forest Service, but Ferguson apparently had little understanding of the agency's goals: When W. Goodrich "Hackberry" Jones approached his fellow Temple native for $10,000 to start the service, Ferguson responded, "Why for $500 I can get you a good man to cut all the trees you want."

Like so many colorful politicians, Ferguson had a vainglorious streak that lead to his downfall. His core supporters re-elected him in 1916, but by then his administration was crumbling. Ferguson had been putting state money into "pet banks" in which he had a financial interest, and he had received questionable loans from banks and an unknown party, later identified as the Texas Brewers' Association. He might have weathered the financial controversy if he had not alienated a significant part of the population—the University of Texas and all of its alumni.

Ferguson opposed a candidate for president of the university, but the Board of Regents appointed Robert E. Vinson anyway. Furthermore, they refused to do the governor's bidding and fire faculty members who had supported Thomas Ball. In retaliation Ferguson vetoed almost all of the university's appropriation. With that one act, he created an anti-Ferguson coalition of alumni, prohibitionists, and advocates of votes for women (Ferguson was opposed to female suffrage). In July 1917 the speaker of the house called a special legislative session to consider impeaching the governor even though the state constitution did not give the speaker this power. Governor Ferguson, however, made the special session legal by issuing a call himself. In August the Texas House of Representatives passed 21 articles of impeachment. By a vote of 25 to 3, the Texas Senate convicted him on 10 articles. Only three of the articles related to the university; the others involved misuse of state funds and the personal loans. Farmer Jim was removed from office and barred from holding any Texas offices ever again. He may have been down, but he was not yet out.

Lieutenant Governor William P. Hobby, a prohibitionist, stepped into the office immediately. Hobby appointed a new Board of Regents for the University of Texas and signed the appropriation bill for the institution. Things seemed to be quieting down, but the squabble over the governor had distracted Texans from major world events—some on their own doorstep.

THE MEXICAN REVOLUTION AND WORLD WAR I

In 1910 discontent with the 35-year administration of Mexican President Porfirio Díaz broke out south of the Rio Grande. In 1908 a son of one of the richest families in the country, Francisco I. Madero, published a book called *The Presidential Succession in 1910*, which sparked an anti-

The First Hamburger?

Lots of places, including Athens, Texas, claim that the hamburger was invented in some greasy spoon within the city limits. When you look at the competing claims, a pattern emerges and you can see that the hamburger was not so much invented as perfected. A town in Wisconsin claims that the first hamburger was sold there in 1885, but that was a flattened meatball stuck between two pieces of bread.

The next tale comes from New Haven, Connecticut, and involves meat scraps fried up and served between bread at Louis' Lunch in 1890. Still not a real hamburger. In 1894 sailors who had been to Hamburg, Germany, told New York cooks about a really good German sandwich. It consisted of a patty of ground beef sausage fried in butter and served, with a fried egg on top, between two pieces of lightly buttered bread. Still not a hamburger but perhaps the source of the name.

So, the idea of some kind of cooked beef between slices of bread was floating around when Fletch Davis (also called Old Dave or Uncle Fletch) of Athens, Texas, brought the concept to its perfect expression. Sometime before 1904, he started browning a piece of ground up beef on the grill in his café on the downtown square. The story goes that he put the meat on toast and added sliced raw onion and mustard. He served it with a cucumber pickle on the side. Now that's a hamburger.

Friends and family took up contributions and sent him to the St. Louis World's Fair in 1904. He set up a concession stand and the rest is history. Some people add to this tale and say that on his way to St. Louis, Uncle Fletch stopped in Paris, Texas, where someone taught him to make these really great fried potatoes to go with his sandwich. They add that people misunderstood which Paris he was talking about and called them French-fried potatoes. That has to be a legend.

The town of Athens has occasionally sponsored Uncle Fletcher's Hamburger Cook-off and American Music Festival. Check with the chamber of commerce, (903) 675-5181 or www.athenscc.org, to see if it is on when you are passing through east Texas.

reelection movement. Díaz arrested Madero. His family obtained Madero's release, but he jumped bail and fled to the United States the day after the Chamber of Deputies declared Díaz president.

Mexico now split into warring bands. Emiliano Zapata led guerrilla forces in the south, especially in the state of Morelos. In the northern state of Chihuahua, the former rustler Pancho Villa gathered his forces to oppose the central government. In May 1911 the decisive Battle of

Cuidad Juárez sent President Díaz into exile in France. Madero became president, but his period in power was short. In February 1913 fighting broke out in Mexico City, Madero was arrested by forces loyal to Díaz, and on February 22, Madero was assassinated. The sinister General Victoriana Huerta, in league with the nephew of Porfirio Díaz, became president.

Now Pancho Villa and his ragtag army in the north of Mexico began a campaign against Huerta's forces. By 1915 Villa was convinced that the United States would support his candidacy for president. Instead, the republic to the north backed Venustiano Carranza. Villa was irate and never forgave the United States or its citizens.

In Texas itself the border region was a tinderbox. In 1915 flame was added to the fuel. Police in the Lower Rio Grande Valley picked up a Mexican national and found a document on him. Eventually called the Plan de San Diego (a town in Duval County), the paper outlined a purported plot for Hispanics, African Americans, Native Americans, and other minority groups in Texas to rise up and kill all white males older than 16. After the bloodbath, an independent republic would be created out of the land Mexico lost to the United States.

The Plan de San Diego may have been a forgery or a pipe dream, but it did lead to a bloodbath—not of whites, however. Governor Ferguson sent Texas Rangers to the border area and eventually called out the National Guard. These forces plus local policemen and civilian vigilantes indiscriminately killed and terrorized Hispanics. The Texas Rangers were so deeply incriminated in atrocities that the state legislature eventually decreased the number of ranger companies and upgraded personnel standards. Border violence continued.

In March 1916, Villa and his forces attacked the camp of the 13th U.S. Cavalry near Columbus, New Mexico. As they retreated from the camp, the Villistas pillaged the small New Mexican town. When the raid was over, 14 U.S. soldiers and 10 civilians were dead.

President Woodrow Wilson stationed militia along the border and ordered the commander of Fort Bliss, Brigadier General John J. Pershing, to capture Villa. On March 16, 1916, a U.S. punitive expedition crossed the Rio Grande into

German and other European immigrants settled in San Antonio and prospered. This porch can be found today in the King William Street Historical District; the street was originally named Kaiser Wilhelm Strasse after Wilhelm I, King of Prussia. Anti-German sentiment during WWI led to a name change. Bob Parvin, courtesy TxDOT

Chihuahua. The expedition was notable for several things: It was the last cavalry expedition of the U.S. Army and the first U.S. use of aerial reconnaissance. Lieutenant Benjamin Foulois had already assembled the First Aero Squadron of nine planes. Their pursuit of Villa was unsuccessful, but the reconnaissance did prepare them for World War I.

In addition the campaign gave Lieutenant George S. Patton his first taste of warfare. Already Patton was perfecting the weird military statement. In May 1916 Patton and 10 soldiers from the 6th Infantry killed three Villa underlings; Patton returned to headquarters with the three bodies tied to the top of car hoods.

The formal U.S. forces were at a disadvantage trying to find Villa in the vast canyons and high mountains of the Sierra Madre. In January 1917 the expeditionary force left Mexico and regrouped at Fort Bliss. General Pershing declared that the exercise had been a good learning experience for his troops.

On April 6, 1917, the troops put that experience to the test when the United States declared war on Germany and General Pershing and his troops shipped out to France. Almost 200,000 Texans—including 31,000 African Americans—entered the military during World War I. Texas women also served—449 were military nurses. Texas was also a major site for basic training of soldiers from other parts of the country. Kelly Field in San Antonio and other bases and training facilities made the state a leader in flight instruction.

The war also allowed some people to release nativistic emotions. The legislature made it a crime to criticize the war effort, the flag, soldier's uniforms, or the U.S. government. African American soldiers stationed in Texas were frequently the brunt of discrimination. The all-black Third Battalion of the 24th Infantry rioted in Houston. German Texans were also suspect. A legislative committee recommended that libraries withdraw all books that portrayed German culture positively. Governor Hobby vetoed the appropriation for the German Department at the University of Texas, and Kaiser Wilhelm Strasse in San Antonio was renamed King William Street.

Concern for the morals of soldiers stationed in Texas led the legislature to prohibit the sale of alcohol within 10 miles of military camps. In May 1919 Texas voters approved prohibition for the entire state but denied women the right to vote in all elections.

As Texans turned to peace in the 1920s, the state was becoming more urban—one-third of Texans lived in cities, but many of the problems of the past remained. Race relations were becoming more inflammatory, with riots in Port Arthur, Longview, and Houston and lynchings throughout the state. The Ku Klux Klan was awakening and championing such issues as prohibition and moral conformity. Texans prepared for the modern world, but brought with them many of the attitudes of the past.

URBAN BEGINNINGS

The governor's race of 1920 featured the spotless Pat Neff of Waco against the sullied former senator, Joe Bailey. Neff could truthfully say that his lips had never touched tobacco, alcohol, coffee, or tea; Bailey questioned the manhood of anyone who had never shot a gun or smoked. Neff responded that three inflated egos had been produced in the world, "One was Napoleon and Senator Bailey the other two." Neff was indefatigable as a campaigner. Some days he gave seven speeches. He traveled by Ford, airplane, and mule and showed up in 37 counties that had never seen a gubernatorial candidate before. He beat Bailey handily.

Pat Neff took office in a mixed atmosphere of moral rigidity and license. Prohibition made alcohol illegal—and illicitly attractive. While some Texans tried to enforce the new morality on themselves and, especially, their neighbors, others took every opportunity to flout the law.

THE FREE STATE OF GALVESTON

Galveston always had a free and easy attitude toward enforcing the law. Partly this outlook was the result of geography. Deserted night beaches invited Lafitte's pirates to land their booty and slave smugglers to drop their human contraband. During Prohibition, liquor from Canada and the Caribbean was smuggled into the bay and shipped out across the Heartland.

Two parties controlled the illegal liquor trade in Galveston. "Johnny Jack" Nounes headed the downtown gang, and Dutch Voight ran the beach gang. Competition between the two gangs often led to gunfights on the main streets of the town—gunfights that rivaled anything from the Old West or gangland Chicago. Eventually, Voight took on two new protégés, Rose (really Rosario) and Sam Maceo. A series of arrests and deaths put the Maceos in charge of

Galveston's underworld, including not only alcohol but also prostitution and especially gambling. When Prohibition ended, control of gambling gave the Maceos an illicit income to fall back on.

In 1926 the Maceo brothers bought what would become the most famous gambling establishment in the state. Originally a Chinese restaurant, the Balinese Room became, under the Maceos, the hub of sin city. Dancing, drinking, and games of chance were the attractions, but the Balinese Room had several added features. First, the entrance was a long covered walkway over the water. A guard sat at the entrance and could notify the Maceos whenever law enforcement was in the area. The major part of the club was about 200 feet out over the water. When word came from the guard, all gambling equipment and alcohol could be dumped from trap doors into the water below. Legend has it that on one occasion, as the Texas Rangers barged into the main room, the band struck up "The Eyes of Texas" and the stage manager announced, "Ladies and Gentlemen, we give you, in person, the Texas Rangers!"

Galveston remained the free and open sin city of Texas until the 1950s.

The Mexia Raid

Not all Texas towns took to vice with the easy attitude of Galveston. In 1921 the desperate, respectable citizens of Mexia appealed to Governor Neff for help. The discovery of oil in this small town about 70 miles southeast of Dallas pushed the population from some 2,500 to 30,000 in a few months. Not all of these new citizens were upstanding. Hidden stills in the woods surrounding Mexia turned out homemade liquor, and almost 20 gambling dens opened in the town.

Undercover Texas Rangers commanded by a new captain named Frank Hamer moseyed into Mexia and reported that the gambling was run out of a building called the Winter Garden. Armed guards protected the turnoff from the main road to the Winter Garden and hid behind lattice screens inside the establishment. Most of these guards were local law officers who had gone over to the other, more lucrative side.

On January 7, 1922, Hamer led a combined force of

Texas Rangers and National Guard, guns blazing, into the Winter Garden. They captured most of the ringleaders, along with 660 quarts of whiskey, gambling devices, weapons, and drugs. Hamer complained to Neff that the local judges warned suspects whenever the Ranger captain applied for a search warrant. On January 12, Neff put the town under martial law and, unimpeded by the legal niceties, Hamer arrested more than 600 people, broke up 27 stills, seized 9,000 additional quarts of liquor, recovered 50 stolen cars, and broke up a national drug ring. Hamer turned the Winter Garden into a prison camp for those he arrested. Neff held that after he declared martial law, 3,000 people left Mexia.

Martial law lasted for 47 days and extended into two counties. Brigadier General Jacob Wolters of the Texas National Guard drew up a plan for establishing law and order in the area and local citizens adopted it. Meeting "somewhere in Mexia," the Mexia Ku Klux Klan, Number 47, endorsed Wolters's plan. The Klan members told the world, "We hereby serve notice on the lawless element of our population because of the withdrawal of the state constabulary force, we will not countenance any of the acts of lawlessness and violence that was so prevalent in our midst sixty days ago." Warning that "our numbers are legion," the Klan added, "If your acts are such as merit court action we will see that you are carried to court. If the courts cannot handle your case or will not do so, we will handle it ourselves in our own way."

The Ku Klux Klan and Lynching

The Ku Klux Klan came back to life in the Deep South in 1915. It returned to Texas in 1920. In September of that year, the KKK recruited at the United Confederate Veterans annual reunion. To join, you had to be a white Protestant born in the United States with $10 to spend on the initiation fees. The reborn Klan emphasized its support of good order and morality, as well as the importance of "True Americanism." While violence against African Americans was central to the Klan and Protestant ministers frequently supported the organization as the only way to fight "the Catholic menace," the new KKK also combated bootleggers, gamblers, and "loose women."

This coercive probity appealed to many middle-class Texans. The Klan policy of "vocational klanishness" also called on members to trade only with other KKK members. Small businessmen frequently joined the organization to attract new customers. The KKK sought out judges, sheriffs, district and county attorneys, and other members of the establishment for membership. In northeastern Collin County, for instance, Klan members approached the sheriff about joining. He refused, telling them that his oath as a sheriff would conflict with the KKK oath. The Klansmen assured him that, if they contemplated any illegal actions, his brother Klansmen would safeguard his conscience and not tell him about it.

In Dallas the police commissioner, police chief, most police officers, sheriff, and deputy sheriff were believed to be members. The situation was the same in Austin where a minor gambler was whipped, tarred and feathered, and dumped in an alley behind East Fifth Street. The city detective and deputy sheriff involved with the case, as well as the chief of police and police commissioner, were all Klan members. The grand jury found that "Jeans [the gambler] was operated on by the plain clothes men of the order, and when he returned to Austin his case was investigated by the uniformed crew who wore the badges of constituted law enforcement officers and whose membership in the Klan is to be presumed by their refusal to testify because 'it might tend to incriminate them,' when asked if they had joined the order."

While the KKK called attention to its moral agenda, violence against racial and religious groups remained a key part of its activities. In 1921 alone, the Texas Klan was known to have carried out at least 80 attacks on Catholics, Jews, Hispanics, and immigrants. African Americans bore the brunt of the brutality. African American individuals throughout the state were threatened, beaten, mutilated, and killed. The Klan also menaced African American businesses, such as newspapers in Houston and Dallas.

Some white-owned newspapers and leading citizens, such as Maury Maverick of San Antonio, denounced the KKK; Governor Neff did not. In Galveston Rabbi Henry Cohen and Father James Kirwin together appealed to the city leaders for help in ending Klan violence. A few local judges and police got indictments of Klan members, and in some towns parades were prevented. In 1922 the Klan retaliated by entering its supporters in local political races. KKK sympathizers and members won throughout north and east Texas that year. The Klan candidate Earl B. Mayfield defeated former governor Jim Ferguson in the Democratic primary for U.S. senator. When Mayfield became senator, the Klan reached its pinnacle of political power in Texas.

The Klan was not the only force for racial intimidation in the state. In the early part of the 20th century, Texas ranked third in the country in number of lynchings. Between 1882 and 1930, 492 lynchings occurred in Texas. Most of the victims were African American, and most of the killings happened in east Texas, in the areas where slavery and plantation life had been the strongest and where the African American population was still concentrated. The "Waco Horror" mutilation and burning of a 17-year-old illiterate African American farmhand in 1916 focused national attention on the use of vigilante murder to intimidate African Americans. The National Association for the Advancement of Colored People issued a special report on this lynching and sent it to all members of the U.S. Congress, 750 newspapers, and its own membership.

In June 1919 a white mob in the east Texas town of Longview lynched Lemuel Walters for a supposed relationship with a white woman from Kilgore. Some sources say that Walters was a dentist and had been to college with the white woman. In the July 10 issue of the *Defender*, a national African American newspaper based in Chicago, an article about the lynching said that Walters and the unnamed woman were in love and would have married if interracial marriages had been permitted.

The local correspondent for the *Defender* was Samuel L. Jones, a schoolteacher. On the day the article appeared, a gang of white men attacked Jones. The next day whites stormed Jones's house only to be surprised by gunshots. The white men rang the fire alarm and others joined them. They ransacked the hardware store and returned to Jones's house with more guns and ammunition. The house, however, was empty. So the white gang burned it, the homes of other prominent African Americans, and an African American dance hall.

Frank Hamer Hunts Bonnie and Clyde

In 1934 the United States was in its worst crime wave yet. Depression-era newspaper readers, however, tended to make celebrities of the most colorful of the modern outlaws. Chief among them were the murderous lovers Clyde Barrow and Bonnie Parker.

Clyde Barrow was born in Teleco on March 24, 1909, one of eight children of an illiterate field hand. He never got past fifth grade. Bonnie, however, had been an honor student and finished high school in her home town of Rowena, where she had been born on October 1, 1910 into a middle-class family. When she met Clyde Barrow, however, she fell in love and into a life of crime. In 1930, she smuggled a gun to Clyde in jail and he escaped, only to be caught a few days later and sent to the state prison at Huntsville.

He was in prison for two years while his family tried to get a pardon from the governor. They succeeded, but not before Clyde had another prisoner cut two of his toes off so he would not have to work in the fields. Freed from prison, Clyde joined up with Bonnie and their rampages soon fueled the national press.

In April 1933 the police of Joplin, Missouri, surprised the Barrow gang (now including Clyde's brother Buck and Buck's wife Blanche) in a rented stone bungalow. The gang escaped with Clyde at the wheel of their speeding car. Searching the bungalow, a newspaperman found a roll of film that showed Bonnie packing a pistol and smoking a cigar, Clyde standing in front of his car fondling guns, and Bonnie pretending to menace Clyde with a sawed-off shotgun. These pictures made front pages across the country and the legend of Bonnie and Clyde took off.

In 1934 Bonnie and Clyde sprang several prisoners from the Eastham State Farm near Huntsville, an escape that left one guard dead. The head of the prison system, Lee Simmons, decided he would finish off the Barrow gang by hiring the most experienced law officer he could find, former Texas Ranger captain Frank Hamer.

On July 4, 1934, Hamer described his hunt for the outlaws to historian Walter Prescott Webb: "On February 10, I took the trail and followed it for exactly 102 days. Like Clyde Barrow I used a Ford V8 and like Clyde I lived in the car most of the time.... Barrow played a circle from Dallas to Joplin, Missouri, to Louisiana, and back to Dallas. Occasionally he varied the beat, but he always seemed to return.... The thing to be decided was whether to set the trap in Texas, Missouri, or Louisiana." Barrow had killed police officers in Texas and Missouri but not in Louisiana, so Hamer concluded that Clyde would head where he was not wanted for murder.

Hamer also described how he studied Barrow's thinking patterns: "When I began to understand Clyde Barrow's mind, I felt that I was making progress. I learned that Barrow never holed up at one place; he was always on the go; and he traveled farther in one day than any fugitive that I have ever followed. He thought nothing of driving a thousand miles at a stretch. Barrow was also the master of side roads, which made his movements irregular. Around Dallas, Joplin, and in Louisiana, he seemed to know them all." Hamer finally picked up the team's trail near Texarkana. They bought whiskey in Logansport and gasoline in Keechi, underwear and an automatic shotgun in Shreveport, made camp near Wichita Falls, and left behind some bills for clothes they had bought in Dallas. From these Hamer drew up a description of what Bonnie might be wearing and alerted police. The trail, as Hamer described it, "always led back to Louisiana, where I located their hideout on February 17." Hamer continued:

> On several occasions I went alone to this secret place….There was always plenty of sign in the camp; stubs of Bonnie's Camels—Clyde smoked Bull Durham—lettuce leaves for their white rabbit, pieces of sandwiches, and a button off Clyde's coat. I found where they had made their bed.
>
> The end would have come two or three weeks earlier had not some local and federal officers made a drag on Ruston, Louisiana, and when Clyde heard of it, he quit the country and I had to wait for him to return.

During this time Bonnie and Clyde killed three more police officers, two in Texas and one in Oklahoma. They also kidnapped the police chief of Commerce, Oklahoma. Hamer was on their heels:

> All criminals who work in groups must have some way of communicating with one another when they get separated. I learned that Clyde had his post office on a side road about eight miles from Plain Dealing, Louisiana. It was under a board which lay on the ground near a large stump of a pine tree. The point selected was on a knoll from which Bonnie in the car could command a view of the road while Clyde went into the forest for his mail.
>
> By the night of May 22, we had good reason to believe that Clyde would visit this mail box within a short time. About midnight we drove out to Gibsland, secreted our cars in the pines and made arrangements to furnish him more news than he had ever received at one time.

Hamer wanted to take the couple alive. He believed they could be surprised while they were both looking in the direction of the mail drop, so he set up watch:

> With everything ready, we had nothing to do but wait about seven hours, without breakfast or coffee…. As daylight came a few cars passed, and occasionally a logger's truck…. It was probably about 9:10 when we heard a humming through the pines that was different from that made by the other motors. A car was coming from the north at a terrific speed, singing like a sewing machine. We heard it when it must have been three miles away.

As Hamer had predicted, both Bonnie and Clyde were distracted at the mail drop, and he and his men were able to take them by surprise. He said, "At the command, 'Stick 'em up!' both turned, but instead of obeying the order as we had hoped, they clutched the weapons they either held in their hands or in their laps." Clyde carried a 12-guage shotgun and Bonnie a sawed-off shotgun. Hamer opened fire and his first shots hit both of his targets. Clyde's foot released the clutch. The car rolled into a ditch and officers riddled the car with bullets.

When Hamer opened the car's door, Clyde Barrow's body fell out of the car and Bonnie lay slumped in the passenger seat. Inside the car the police found three Browning automatic rifles, two sawed-off shotguns, one double action Colt revolver, nine Colt automatic pistols, and thousands of rounds of ammunition.

Public fascination with the couple only increased after their death. Crowds descended on Arcadia, Louisiana, and ripped blood-stained cloth and fittings from Clyde's Ford. At last, the door of the funeral parlor was ripped from its hinges by crowds trying to get a glimpse of the infamous criminals.

Frank Hamer's version of this and other law enforcement crises can be found in H. Gordon Frost and John H. Jenkins, *I'm Frank Hamer: The Life of a Texas Peace Officer*.

That same day the sheriff asked Governor William P. Hobby for help. The governor declared martial law. The National Guard and the Texas Rangers moved into the town and confiscated all private firearms. The rangers arrested 17 whites for attempted murder and 21 African Americans on various charges. The whites were each released on $1,000 bond; the African Americans were sent to Austin for protection. No one was ever tried. Martial law was lifted in less than a week and all firearms were returned to their owners. Fear of racial violence did not lessen.

THE RETURN OF FERGUSONISM

The 1924 gubernatorial election focused on the Klan, which supported Judge Felix D. Robertson of Dallas. Unable to run himself, the anti-Klan Jim Ferguson decided on a surrogate—his wife. Despite her life as the upper middle-class wife of a banker and lawyer, Miriam A. Ferguson campaigned in a farm woman's sun bonnet and tried to pass herself off as a rube, just as her husband had. Her husband's appeal helped her carry Texas's rural areas. Her campaign slogans were "Two governors for the price of one" and "Me for Ma—and I ain't got a dern thing against Pa." Robertson campaigned on a pro-dry platform painting both Fergusons as opponents of prohibition, which they were.

In the first primary, Robertson won by about 50,000, but he did not get a majority. In the Democratic runoff, Ma Ferguson (her nickname came from her initials) won by about 100,000 votes. Some progressives who could not stomach the Fergusons and considered prohibition more important than defeating the KKK supported Robinson and in the general election bolted for the Republican candidate. Ma won again, keeping her husband's rural supporters and adding urban voters who might have ordinarily gone for the Klan candidate. On January 25, 1925, Ma became the first female governor of Texas and the second in the country.

Ma Ferguson's victory was not exactly a triumph for feminism; she was quite clearly a substitute for her husband, who pitched his desk right beside hers in the governor's office. (In fact, both Fergusons opposed votes for women.) Together they attacked two of their traditional enemies— the University of Texas by reducing its budget and the Klan by signing a law banning the public wearing of masked regalia. During Ma's two years in office, the Fergusons pardoned around 3,600 prisoners from prison. Ma reasoned that most of them had violated only the anti-liquor laws and the state did not need to be feeding them when they could be home taking care of their families.

Her pardon policy gained Mrs. Ferguson the enmity of a former ally—Dan Moody, the newly elected attorney general. Moody had also campaigned against the Klan and had polled more votes than Ma. The Taylor-born lawyer had made his reputation by prosecuting and convicting a prominent Klansman who had viciously beaten a local. Moody then turned around and convicted a Baptist preacher of perjury for supplying the Klansman with an alibi. Among those Ma pardoned was the Klansman Moody had prosecuted.

Moody, a straight arrow if ever there was one, got 225,000 more votes than Ma in the 1926 race for governor. He immediately set about reforming the prison system, the highway department (a scene of much patronage under the Fergusons), and the system for auditing state funds. For the

first time since the Civil War, the national Democratic party held its convention in a southern city—Houston. Al Smith, the Roman Catholic and wet governor of New York, was nominated. Try as hard as he could, Moody could not swing the state for the Democrats in the national election. Texas went for Herbert Hoover but also re-elected Dan Moody.

Too bad for Moody. His second term corresponded with the beginning of the Great Depression. Neither he nor the next governor, Ross Sterling—former president of Humble Oil Company—could come up with workable state plans for dealing with the unemployed, farm failures, and ruined banks. State revenue fell and Sterling ended his term with a deficit despite vetoing $3 million in appropriations including funding for summer schools.

Abandoned home near Texline in the farthest reaches of the Panhandle.
Randy Green, courtesy TxDOT

Ma Ferguson opposed Sterling for the Democratic nomination. When the first primary rolled around, 132 counties reported a total of 40,000 more people voting than had paid poll taxes. Most of these irregularities came from east Texas—a Ferguson stronghold. In the runoff Sterling lost by a little less than 4,000 votes and again votes outnumbered poll taxes. Sterling tried to call a special session of the legislature to investigate vote fraud but failed. He also failed to convince the Texas Supreme Court that Ma's nomination was fraudulent. The Fergusons were once again in the Governor's Mansion, and Ma had to face the effects of the Great Depression.

The Great Depression

Without state help, cities and towns were facing the economic crisis on their own. Some sponsored public jobs for the unemployed, offered free gardening areas, and opened soup kitchens. West Texas cities sponsored rabbit hunts and gave the meat to the needy. The fishing industry of Aransas Pass donated tons of fish to the poor of Dallas. In some cities African Americans and Hispanics were denied aid to ensure that whites would have enough resources. Several cities stationed armed officers at train stations to keep out transients. Women were often fired from their jobs so men could be hired. Beaumont and Houston cut off their street lights, and some cities paid their employees in scrip.

In Texas and other southern plains states, the national economic collapse was trumped by a serious climatic and agricultural disaster: the Dust Bowl. Even in the 1880s, cattlemen had overgrazed the area, but modern conditions made the situation even worse. In the 1920s farmers could afford new gasoline tractors, and speculators saw the plains as a place for quick money from fast-growing crops. In their search for wealth, speculators and some farmers ignored both the cumulative knowledge of previous settlers and scientific data. Plowed-up land was left bare and native grasslands destroyed. The plains had none of its traditional protection when wind, drought, and high temperatures bore down on the area.

Droughts come about every 20 years to the plains, with strong winds an everyday occurrence, but the dust storms of the 1930s and accompanying soil erosion were unprecedented. In 1932 the region experienced 14 dust storms, and gradually the number of major dust storms increased. In 1933 the region had 38; 1934, 22; 1935, 40. Then things really got bad—in 1936, 68 storms blew over the region. The worst year followed with 72 storms in 1937. A leveling out occurred in the next year with 61 storms. Then conditions moderated with 30 in 1939 and 17 in 1940 and 1941 each.

These storms were blizzard-like. Giant walls of dirt rose 7,000 to 8,000 feet, blotting out the sky. Sometimes their terrifying effects were accompanied by thunder and lightning; other storms were eerily silent. People swept dirt up from inside their houses into bushel baskets. Animals often suffocated on dust.

Fort Worth during the Depression

John Graves is best known for his classic meditation on the Brazos River, *Good-by to a River*. The passage below comes from an essay he contributed to Bertha McKee Dobie's edited volume, *Growing Up in Texas: Recollections of Childhood*:

Inhabited by a hundred and fifty thousand souls or so [Fort Worth] was not big as we understand urban bigness now…people knew other people much better than we do now. There was a sort of small-town feel to life—natural enough, for most of our parents had been born in little places and had brought small-town ways, including an interest in other folks, to the prairie metropolis with them.

Some families had vegetable gardens out next to the alley, and on summer evenings there were talk and domino games on the lawns, and in most neighborhoods someone kept a few chickens, so that roosters crowed in the dawn as they crowed for men through the thousands of years since they were brought up out of Asia. Horses clipclopped along the streets in the mornings pulling wagons loaded with ice or milk or vegetables compatible enough with the automobile traffic of the day. People tended to know who you were— you were the "Graves boy," or less favorably "that Graves boy"—and if you exhibited your human imperfection within a radius of half a mile from home, you were likely to be held accountable for it.

Suburbs, as far as I recall, were not yet known as suburbs nor had they begun to smother one another. Mainly there was just a single ring of residential areas around "downtown," the central city where practically all fathers went to stores and offices in the mornings, driving or taking the streetcar that clicked and sang its way down Camp Bowie Boulevard—the motormen seemed always to chew Tinsley or Brown Mule and spat sedately from time to time through an admirable brass hole in the floor….

Outside the ring of suburbs around the central city, there was open country. When I was nine the Depression blew in and more less froze things that way. Toward the rim of development the houses thinned and the vacant lots increased in number, full of Johnson grass and prairie flowers and mesquites and jackrabbits, and horned toads and other splendors. And beyond this you reached a place where there were no houses at all. Much of it was still owned by men who had been going to develop it—unfenced and untilled and ungrazed, with maybe a few paved streets and storm sewers built in the days of hope but the rest as the roving Comanches had known it. It was wasteland, symbolic of hard times, but it was also a fine place to wander and hunt and play.

In April 1933 a Dust Bowl storm prepares to engulf an unidentified Panhandle settlement. Courtesy Center for American History, UT-Austin.

The Dust Bowl probably ended because of natural forces, but humans had contributed to its beginnings and they made an effort to end it. In 1935 the state legislature established soil conservation districts with the authority to force farmers to use techniques that halted erosion. In the same year the U.S. Department of Agriculture coordinated such efforts as tree planting, the creation of ridges to block wind, and the distribution of seed to re-establish ground cover. Perhaps most helpful to the land was the exodus of 34 percent of the farmers from the area.

Texas had enthusiastically embraced Herbert Hoover for president, but then turned on him. Armadillos were renamed Hoover hogs because they could be easily captured and butchered, and tent settlements of hobos on city outskirts were called Hoovervilles. The election of 1932 pitted the beleaguered president against Franklin D. Roosevelt of New York heading the Democratic ticket and John Nance Garner of Uvalde, Texas, for vice president. Texans returned to the Democratic party and gave the national ticket 89 percent of the state's vote. A bevy of powerful men also represented the state in the U.S. Congress. Garner's protégé, Sam Rayburn of Bonham, was the chair of the Interstate and Foreign Commerce Committee. Already people were saying he would soon be

Speaker of the House. Other Texans chaired the House appropriations, judiciary, and agriculture committees; in the Senate Texans were in charge of the military affairs and public buildings committees. Perhaps the most influential New Deal Texan was unelected—Jesse H. Jones, head of the Reconstruction Finance Corporation. The Houston banker was in charge of dispersing $10 billion to banks, railroads, public works projects, and other organizations. Texans in Washington consistently supported emergency unemployment funds and other federal projects, and much of the money found its way to Texas.

Back home in Texas, Ma Ferguson geared up for her second administration. She repeatedly suggested that the legislature might pass sales or income taxes, but only a two-cent tax on each barrel of oil made it through. She could reduce the deficit only by making cuts. Then the federal government made money available to governors to disperse among counties. Ma set up the Texas Relief Commission, which assumed oversight of local relief efforts, and put funds into pet banks. The Ferguson tactics again raised corruption accusations and both houses of the state legislature called for investigations.

Ma decided not to run for another term, and Attorney General Jimmie Allred succeeded her. Allred continued to bring New Deal money to Texas, but now he focused on putting the unemployed to work. He emphasized the Civilian Conservation Corp, Work Projects Administration, National Youth Administration, and similar projects. The NYA offered summer work for high school and college students throughout the state; its administrator was the 27-year-old Lyndon Baines Johnson. The NYA employed 10,000 to 18,000 students a month, and Johnson saw to it that African Americans had a chance at the jobs.

During her second administration, Ma Ferguson had fired every Texas Ranger who had not already resigned when her election was assured. Ma appointed 32 new rangers and then appointed more than 2,000 "special rangers." Through these special appointments, the rangers became a source of patronage and corruption. Governor Allred's lasting contribution was the Texas Department of Public Safety, which brought the rangers and the highway patrol under one jurisdiction and made professionalism a realizable goal.

The rangers were again becoming an item of national interest. In 1935 Texas historian Walter Prescott Webb published *The Texas Rangers*, a celebration of the rangers' exploits. Popular writers mined not only the rangers, but cattle drives and ranching lore to fill their pulp novels. And a new medium, the B movie, turned out westerns set, at least nominally, in Texas. Popular entertainment turned Texas identity from the South to the West. And at home Texans still had their own home-grown amusements to keep them engaged. Chief among them was local politics.

Politics as Entertainment

Allred was a true New Deal governor, but many other influential Texans were beginning to have doubts about the direction of national politics. Conservative and New Deal Democrats jousted for control of the party. But their squabbles soon took backstage to a phenomenon that would outshine them all.

In 1925 a Kansas flour salesman had been transferred to the Fort Worth office of the Burrus Mill and Elevator Company. W. Lee O'Daniel knew he could sell flour using music and new media, such as radio and statewide tours. An unemployed singer named Bob Wills approached O'Daniel for sponsorship, and the salesman agreed. The Light-Crust Doughboys were born—and so was Texas Swing. At some point, so the story goes, Wills suggested to O'Daniel that he should do the promotions and the salesman accepted. The radio show's opening lines—"Pass the biscuits, Pappy"—became attached to O'Daniel with audiences calling him "Pappy."

O'Daniel soon peppered his pitches with homespun philosophy, his own poetry, and advice for good living. The response showed him that he could use the radio to contact people throughout the state. He urged his audience to send in postcards asking him to run for governor. If he got enough postcards, he said, he would be a candidate. Thousands of Depression-plagued Texans shelled out a penny each for postcards to send to Pappy and urge him to run. He said that he received 54,499 postcards and that only four opposed his candidacy.

O'Daniel criss-crossed the state giving free concerts that often reached the intensity of a revival meeting. He passed collection plates shaped like barrels with the slogan "flour not pork." Soon Pappy Lee O'Daniel was able to out-Ferguson Farmer Jim himself.

The center of O'Daniel's campaign was a promise to deliver a $30-a-month pension to every Texan 65 or older. His only other campaign statements were the Golden Rule, the Ten Commandments, and the slogan "less Johnson grass [a weed] and politicians and more smokestacks and businessmen." He won the primary without a runoff. Pappy had never paid the poll tax and so could not vote, but he managed to convince 473,000 Texans to vote for him in the general election—his Republican opponent got only 11,000. His inauguration party in the University of Texas Memorial Stadium, with 100 bands and barbecued buffalo the new governor himself butchered, attracted around 100,000.

The legislature had no respect for the flour salesman, but his pension scheme was so popular they dared not vote against it. Instead, they passed a small pension but refused to pass any of the revenue bills that would have funded it. Seeking revenge against the hostile legislators, the governor used his line veto to kill state hospital construction, funds for the department of public safety, and other important items. Despite his lack of accomplishments, Pappy was re-elected in 1940; he was the first Texas governor to poll a million votes.

Then in April of 1941, long-time U.S. Senator Morris Sheppard died. The governor had to appoint a replacement to hold the office until a special election could be called. Pappy wanted the position himself, so he had to appoint someone who would not challenge him in the called election. On San Jacinto Day, O'Daniel announced that he was appointing Andrew Jackson Houston, the only surviving child of Sam Houston. The 87-year-old took office in June, attended one committee meeting, and promptly died. He had served for three weeks.

Many O'Daniel enemies wanted him to be elected to the Senate just to get him out of the state. Chief among these was Coke Stevenson, the lieutenant governor who would become governor if O'Daniel moved on. Even Jim Ferguson wanted to see O'Daniel elected to national office so he could not make more appointments to state boards.

O'Daniel won by a little over 1,000 votes; his major opponent was U.S. congressman Lyndon B. Johnson, who always felt that O'Daniel's election was fraudulent.

Pappy Lee O'Daniel's act did not travel well. In the nation's capital his demagogic bumpkin act failed to attract any support from other legislators. As legend has it, during his seven years in the senate, none of the bills he proposed ever got more than four votes. He served out Sheppard's term and then was elected to one full term of his own. In 1948 he realized that his tactics would no longer work in post-war Texas and retired from political life.

O'Daniel's message looked and sounded as if he were harking back to better, simpler times, but he expertly used modern techniques. He followed the Ferguson model of portraying himself as a slightly goofy hick, but he was a shrewd businessman who could smooth-talk the poor, elderly, and forgotten into believing that he would speak for them. Despite his veneer of country simplicity, O'Daniel was a harbinger of the consultant who understood the value of the new radio medium and of public appearances. O'Daniel always gave voters some entertainment for their time. His kind would certainly be seen again.

WORLD WAR II

While O'Daniel had no power at the national level, other Texans did. And the collection of national decision makers from the state ensured that Texas would play an important part in the next national drama, World War II. During the war, about one out of every ten military personnel trained in Texas. Texas had 15 army posts, and about 40 air bases took advantage of the state's generally clear skies and infant airline industry. Even prisoner-of-war camps sprang up with more than 30 holding German, Italian, and Japanese prisoners. On Texas farms, the prisoners worked picking fruit and cotton, harvesting rice, and threshing grain.

Outside the state, Texans played an important part in the war. Chester A. Nimitz did not let being a native of land-locked Fredericksburg interfere with his navy career; he became the admiral of the Pacific Fleet. The allied supreme commander in Europe, Dwight D. Eisenhower, was born in Denison, and Oveta Culp Hobby of the influential Houston family was in charge of the Women's Army Corps. Congressman Lyndon B. Johnson was the first congress-person to join the military; he left his seat in the House of

Representatives the day after Pearl Harbor and became a lieutenant commander in the Naval Air Force, only to return later to the House by order of President Roosevelt.

By the end of the war, 36 Texans, five of whom were Hispanic, had won the Congressional Medal of Honor. Two Texans were the most decorated in their services: Lieutenant Audie Murphy of the army and Commander Samuel Dealey of the navy. Medal of Honor recipient Sergeant José M. López of Brownsville killed more enemy soldiers than any other U.S. combatant in the war.

Family and admirers continue to lobby for the Medal of Honor to go to African American Doris Miller of Waco who received the Navy Cross for shooting down four Japanese airplanes at Pearl Harbor. When Miller seized the guns and began shooting, he was a cook and he was still a cook two years later when he was killed in action. Miller's position was similar to that of others in the military. Of the 257,798 African American Texans in the services during World War II, one-third were in segregated units. Others found themselves locked into service positions rather than serving in combat. Texas training camps mirrored the society that surrounded them, with "little Harlem" sections offering African Americans fewer amenities. In a camp near Mineral Wells, African American troops started their own service club since they were prohibited from using the base club. Race riots broke out in El Paso, Beaumont, and other places. At the end of the war, African Americans who had fought for the United States began to force Jim Crow laws and practices to change.

The war changed other aspects of Texas as well. Military spending fed the state economy, but federal payrolls to soldiers, sailors, and civilian employees were only one part of the recovery. Private businesses grew to fill military needs and many became the sources for future development. The Gulf Coast mushroomed with oil refineries and other petrochemical enterprises. Oil fields pumped at full capacity again. In 1939 value added by manufacturing in Texas was at $453,105,423; by 1944 it had reached $1,900,000,000. Manufacturing joined agriculture and oil as a major contributor to the Texas economy.

Texas agriculture was changing too, with farms gearing up to produce enough food for the military and civilian populations. Few workers were available for harvesting, however. While an occasional prisoner of war was some help, farmers wanted a more dependable way to harvest crops, and the solution lay in two disparate directions.

As part of this solution, more than 220,000 farm workers came to the United States between 1942 and 1947 under the federal Bracero Program that guaranteed the imported workers some rights, such as a minimum wage. The Mexican government, however, protested that its citizens had no legal protections in Texas and were treated poorly. In 1943 Governor Coke Stevenson convinced the legislature to pass the Caucasian Race Resolution, which held that in Texas no Caucasians would be discriminated against and implicitly classed Hispanics as whites. Stevenson also set up the Good Neighbor Commission of Texas to encourage better understanding and cooperation between the state and Mexico.

Some farmers solved their labor problems in a different way—mechanization and consolidation. In 1945 the farm census showed a 33 percent increase in the value of farm machinery and a decrease in the number of farms. The size of farms increased, as did the value, while tenancy and sharecropping began to fall away.

Governor Stevenson saw no reason why Texas with plenty of oil and cattle, should share in national war rationing. Texans needed their cars just to take care of the necessities of life. The three gallons a week allowed for private automobiles, he argued, were not adequate in a state of vast distances and little public transportation. But federal officials noted that lots of automobiles were parked outside of football stadiums during game times. A final compromise on gas rationing issued higher priority cards to farm families. The prioritizing was a local decision, however, and in many localities African Americans and Hispanics were not issued ration cards for meat, sugar, and other items on the reasoning that minorities did not usually eat these foods and could not afford them anyway. But the times for such blatant inequalities were fast drawing to a close.

Must-See Sites

Mother Neff State Park
Former Governor Pat Neff started the Texas parks system, not only by signing a law to make the parks official, but also by donating land for the first state park. His mother died in 1921, and the governor created Mother Neff State Park out of family land. In 1934, more land was deeded from the family and other private owners. Today the park has 250 acres for hiking, camping, and fishing. The park is south of Waco in Coryell County.

The Balinese Room
Still standing at 21st St. and Seawall Boulevard, Galveston's infamous Balinese Room has been empty for some time. The Art Deco interior is said to be in good shape and plans have been made to renovate it with a restaurant in the old gaming room.

The War Museum in Admiral Nimitz's Hometown
The National Museum of the Pacific War is in Admiral Chester A. Nimitz's birthplace of Fredericksburg. The former Nimitz Steamboat Hotel, his family's business, is now the museum. Features of the seven-acre site include the Japanese Garden of Peace, donated by Japan, and the History Walk of the Pacific War. Call (830) 997-4379.

POST-WAR TRANSITIONS

The end of the war finished Texas as a rural state. Having seen the world, former soldiers and sailors took advantage of the G.I. Bill and flocked to colleges and universities. They then moved to Houston, Dallas, and other cities to work in the state's new industries or to start up businesses of their own. Some smaller towns grew too. In the 1950s, oil strikes in west Texas, for example, caused enormous population growth in Odessa and Midland; newcomers included the family of George W. H. Bush, formerly of Connecticut.

BEGINNING OF MODERN TEXAS POLITICS

The war years hardened a split in the Texas Democratic party that had been developing for years. In 1936 a minority of Texas Democrats had opposed Franklin D. Roosevelt. As the New Deal unfolded, its changes rankled many conservatives in the state. In 1940 Roosevelt further increased their pique by deciding to run for a third term, thereby denying Vice President John Nance Garner the chance. Then in 1944 their disgruntlement with the federal government increased when the supreme court held, in *Smith vs. Allwright,* that the Texas Democrats' whites-only primary was unconstitutional. The conservatives, calling themselves the Texas Regulars, tried, but failed, to block the nomination of the Roosevelt-Truman ticket. Despite the split within the party, Governor Stevenson won reelection handily.

In 1946 Coke Stevenson did not seek reelection, so when the presidential election rolled around in 1948, the governor was Beauford Jester. Stevenson ran for U.S. senator against Congressman Lyndon B. Johnson. Despite Jester's call that all stay within the party, the Texas Regulars bolted and helped form the Dixiecrats, whose nominee was South Carolina governor Strom Thurmond. Nationally, many left-of-center Democrats supported Henry Wallace who objected to Truman's containment policy against the Soviet Union. Despite the splintering of his party, Truman won the election and even carried Texas by 750,700 votes to Thomas Dewey's 282,240. The Dixiecrats got 106,909 votes, primarily in east Texas, and carried the city of Houston.

The race for U.S. Senate generated more heat in Texas than the presidential contest did. Ma Ferguson endorsed Johnson and, thus, raised the number of votes he received in east Texas. Still, Stevenson led in the first primary, 477,077 to 405,617. In the second, however, Johnson won by very few votes. Some say 87, some 150. Stevenson contested the vote, but the Democratic Election Committee declared Johnson the winner. Shouting matches and fistfights broke out at the state convention, but the Democrats upheld the findings of the election committee. Stevenson tried to get a restraining order to keep Johnson's name off the general ballot but failed. Lyndon Johnson went to the U.S. Senate, but many continued to be suspicious of the way he had won his seat.

Even though the urban portions of the state were growing, the legislature still reflected a rural bias. Governor Jester tried to convince the predominately rural legislators to consider some of the state's pressing concerns. While Jester was a pretty conservative fellow, he knew the government had to address new state needs. He managed to get through an anti-lynching bill, public school re-organization, prison reform, the farm-to-market road system and other highway improvements, and further reforms. The legislature, however, got its revenge by failing to assess the taxes needed to put the changes into action. Governor Jester called a special session, but before it could convene he died.

THE 1950S: THE SHIVERS YEARS

With Jester's death, the lieutenant governor, Allan Shivers, became governor. Shivers was young, 41, and had made a reputation as a pro-labor legislator, but his years in office pushed him toward business interests. His established relationships with legislators helped him obtain the tax increases needed to meet the new expenditures: "If we are going to appropriate in the spring, we must tax in the winter," he warned.

Shivers was probably one of the most powerful governors in Texas history. He was also very much a conservative

Governor Allan Shivers and Miss Ima Hogg contemplate a portrait of her father, James S. Hogg. Courtesy Center for American History, UT-Austin.

Democrat. He had always adamantly opposed racial integration. In 1952 he consolidated his hold on the state executive committee of the party and purged liberals from the committee. The Truman administration's civil rights policies and the war in Korea were not popular in Texas. The final blow for conservative Texas Democrats, however, was the national government's tidelands policies.

The tidelands area lies under the ocean but close to land. Because of its time as a republic, Texas claimed control of land a little more than 10 miles into the Gulf of Mexico. The Texas tidelands were thought to be rich in oil. Twice President Truman vetoed bills recognizing states' rights to these lands. The U. S. Supreme Court also held in two cases that the federal government had "paramount" claims to these lands. U.S. Attorney General Tom Clark, a Texan, refused to grant any federal leases of tidelands.

When the 1952 presidential election rolled around, Democratic nominee Adlai Stevenson did not endorse Texas's tidelands claims. Governor Shivers decided to bolt the party, but publicly he was noncommittal. Texas Republicans were also divided going into the national convention; some strongly supported Ohio Senator Robert A. Taft and saw his opponent, former general Dwight D. Eisenhower, as a liberal Democrat in a general's uniform.

The "Shiverscrats" controlled the vote in Texas at all levels, especially after the two wings of the Republican party re-united. Eisenhower carried the state by more than 100,000 votes. In May 1953 the new president signed a quit claim bill giving control of the tidelands to the states and extending the disputed areas to "historic limits." For Texas and Florida, states that had been ruled by Spain, these limits reached 10 and a half miles. But more than four years later the U.S. Supreme Court ruled that Texas and Florida had to limit their tidelands claims to the U.S. standard of three miles.

Despite Eisenhower's assent to the tidelands issue, conservative Texas Democrats were still uncomfortable with the Republican party. Governor Shivers himself stated that Eisenhower's victory was a personal triumph not a party win. When the president sent troops to preserve integration at Little Rock's Central High in nearby Arkansas, many conservative Texas Democrats lost faith in him.

Other changes kept Republicans from consolidating their hold on Texas. In the midterm elections of 1954, the Republicans lost control of Congress. Two Texans now controlled the national legislature. Sam Rayburn of Bonham was speaker of the house and Lyndon B. Johnson was majority leader of the senate. Eisenhower realized that if he tried to build a strong Republican party in Texas, he would antagonize these two powerful men and risk losing his own legislative goals. For the moment, the Texas Republican party remained weak.

INTEGRATION AND SCANDALS: DECLINE OF THE SHIVERSCRATS

In 1954 the U.S. Supreme Court held in *Brown vs. Board of Education* that public school systems must be desegregated. Governor Shivers and Texas Attorney General John Ben Shepperd announced they would follow a policy of interposition, using state power to stop federally mandated integration. In July 1956 they saw to it that the Democratic primary included referenda calling for interposition, making racially mixed marriages illegal, and ending compulsory attendance at integrated schools. These measures passed by a margin of four to one. Such initiatives would eventually be thwarted by rising African American and Hispanic voting power.

The last years of the Shivers administration were beset by scandals. In the 1950s state regulation of insurance companies was so lax that more insurance companies operated from Texas than in all other states put together—1,875 in 1954 alone. Wildcat companies would enter the Texas market, sell policies, and disappear. Investigators found that members of the oversight board had accepted gifts from a company that then went bankrupt. The head of that company, Ben Jack Cage, was indicted for bribery, but he escaped prosecution by fleeing to Brazil, which had no extradition treaty with the United States at that time. The next governor, Price Daniels, appointed an entirely new insurance board.

The State Land Commission was another source of scandal for the Shivers administration. The board had been created in 1950 to oversee the veterans' land program. A veteran could choose some land and the state would buy it for resale at a low interest rate. The land commissioner, Bascom Giles, bypassed many legislative checks on the board by hand-picking his own appraisers, colluding with corrupt real estate dealers, and directly approving all purchases of large tracts. Indicted, Giles pled guilty to fraud and was sentenced to six years. Eventually, more than 300 indictments were issued. Since Governor Shivers and Attorney General Shepperd served on the land board, the public assumed they should have had some knowledge of these transactions. The governor's approval rating fell from 64 to 22 percent.

With the legal death of the all-white primary and the return of African American veterans, African American Texans began to change the racial landscape of state politics. More African Americans started voting after the war; by 1958 more than a third of the potential African American voters were registered (by contrast, half of eligible whites were registered). In 1950 the U.S. Supreme Court ordered the University of Texas School of Law to admit Heman M. Sweatt, an African American. By 1958 two-thirds of the colleges and universities in Texas were integrated, at least in theory.

The great 1950s drought was especially hard on farmers and ranchers. In 1954, these cattlemen were arrayed along the top and sides of a stock tank in McMullen County in south Texas. In normal times the earthen dam would enclose water for domestic live stock and wild animals. It is completely dry. Courtesy Institute of Texan Cultures at UT-SA.

While not subject to the extreme legal discrimination faced by African Americans, Hispanics worked to claim the civil rights they had frequently been denied in Texas. Since 1929 the League of United Latin American Citizens (LULAC) had been fighting discrimination in wages, jobs, and political life. In 1948 a court ruled that Hispanic students could not be segregated in public education; three years later exclusion from juries was declared illegal. During the 1950s Hispanics became more politically active, and in 1956 San Antonio voters sent Henry B. Gonzales to the state senate. Eventually he was elected to the U.S. House of Representatives.

Frustrated by roadblocks to obtaining benefits from the Veterans Administration, some Hispanic veterans formed the G.I. Forum. Dr. Hector P. Garcia, a physician and veteran, led the group, which mainly concerned itself with veterans' affairs, until 1948, when it tangled with the funeral directors of Three Rivers, Texas. The morticians refused to arrange for services for Private Félix Z. Longoria, who had been killed in action in the Philippines. Senator Lyndon Johnson, the governor, and many other powerful people in Texas and Washington became embroiled in this affair. In the end, Longoria was buried in the National Cemetery in Arlington, Virginia, and the G.I.

Forum broadened its role to include securing civil rights for the Hispanic population of the state.

DROUGHT

After World War II many changes buffeted Texas agriculture, but the most drastic blow to farmers and ranchers was the "super drought" of the 1950s. For a biblical seven years, rainfall was significantly below average. More intense and prolonged than the Dust Bowl drought in Texas, the 1950-1956 drought left ranch land bare and water for animals and crops nonexistent. Some say it was the worst drought in 700 years. By 1956, 244 of the 254 counties were official drought disaster areas. Even the mesquite trees of west Texas began to die.

The drought began in 1949 in the Lower Rio Grande Valley, but soon every part of the state was drying up. By the end of 1952, Lake Dallas, a water source for both Dallas and Fort Worth, contained only 11 percent of its capacity. Dallas experimented with piping water from Lake Texoma, but the water was so salty it destroyed car radiators and was dangerous for people with health problems to drink. The city then opened stations where people could buy cartons of water for 50 cents—more than a gallon of gas. The towns of Llano and Royce City completely ran out of water and had to ship it in on trucks.

Rivers, lakes, springs, and creeks dried up, some completely. New Braunfels's Comal Springs, the largest spring in the southwest, went dry for five months in 1956. Without the feed from that spring, the flow of the Guadalupe River dwindled so rapidly that salt water from the Gulf rushed into the mouth of the river.

Grain yields dropped by 20 percent and ranchers ran out of feed for their cattle. Those who still had cactus growing on their land used butane torches to burn the spines off the prickly pears and fed them to the cattle. Farmers tried to deal with the lack of rainfall by digging wells deeper into ground water for irrigation, thereby increasing water problems for the future. Ranch debt went above $3 billion. People left rural counties in desperation. Vacated farm and ranch lands meant that consolidation of large holdings could move that much more quickly.

The story goes that in 1950, a Junction family bought their

Manned Space Center

In 1961 President John F. Kennedy set as a national priority landing a man on the moon by the end of the decade. The National Aeronautics and Space Administration (NASA), created in 1958 by President Dwight D. Eisenhower, now had new functions. To reach this new goal it needed a place to train astronauts and to serve as an administrative center. Within a few months, NASA administrators announced that the new facility would be constructed in Clear Lake, Harris County, Texas, about 25 miles from downtown Houston. Rice University donated a thousand-acre tract of land to the facility.

Local politicians in places that had also been considered for the site expressed doubts about Houston's suitability and wondered aloud how influential Vice President Johnson had been in the selection. No one in Congress seemed prepared to investigate this charge and construction began within the year. A little more than 10 years later, in August 1973, the space center was named the Lyndon B. Johnson Space Center, but before then it had many milestones to set.

In September 1963 the Houston Manned Spacecraft Center opened and by the fall of 1966 had more than 5,000 employees. The Mission Control Center became the brains and heart of all subsequent U.S. manned space flights. After projects Mercury and Gemini had perfected such basic techniques as docking and landing, the space center turned to Project Apollo, a series of manned flights designed to culminate in landing on the moon.

On July 16, 1969, within the schedule set by President Kennedy, *Apollo 11* headed for the moon with astronauts Neil Armstrong, Edwin "Buzz" Aldrin, and Michael Collins aboard. Four days later Armstrong became the first man to walk on the moon. Apollo landings continued, including the almost-disastrous *Apollo 13*—in which the astronauts were forced to return in a lunar module and landed with 15 minutes of power left.

In 1972 President Richard Nixon approved the first shuttle project and nine years later the shuttle *Columbia* flew into space. The shuttle program weathered the explosion of the *Challenger* in 1986, and in 1988 the United State, Japan, Canada and nine European countries formally agreed to an international space station program. After the fall of the Soviet Union, Russia also joined.

Over the years the space center has attracted development to the area, and housing, shopping centers, and other projects have sprung up on the coastal prairie. The high tech life of the NASA community attracted thousands of immigrants. In 1992 a visitor center designed by Walt Disney Imagineering opened at the space facility. Today the visitor center includes interactive exhibits, an IMAX theater, and more.

You can tour the visitor center on your own or take a tram tour of the Johnson Space Center itself. Call (281)244-2105 or check out the web site at www.spacecenter.org. After your tour of the space center, try the boardwalk in Kemah along the Kemah-Seabrook channel with its waterfront restaurants. Look up www.kemahboardwalk.com.

daughter a new raincoat for her tenth birthday. She never got to wear it. Neither did her sister who was five years younger. By the time the rains came, both girls had outgrown the coat, which had fallen apart hanging in the closet.

The rains did finally come. In the spring of 1957 Dallas reported its second wettest May in recorded history. Three inches of rain fell on Kingsville in an hour. By June the counties of Cooke and Grayson had to apply for flood relief. The drought was over for the time being. Some forecasters predict that similar droughts could occur every 50 to 100 years. The great drought of the 1950s did force water onto the political agenda, with more money set aside for reservoirs. For a while, west Texans pushed the slightly crackpot Texas Water Plan that called for transferring water from the Mississippi River to the plains. Voters rejected the idea. More realistic planning was needed.

The Johnson Years

In the postwar years, Lyndon B. Johnson materialized as a major force in Texas political life. Shivers had left the governorship an embittered man, having failed either to build up the Texas Republican party or to influence the course of the national Democratic party. Johnson would accomplish the latter.

In 1959 Johnson persuaded the state to move the primary date so he could run both for renomination to the senate and as a candidate for the presidency. Johnson had to walk a very tight line between the conservative opinions of his state delegation and the more liberal ideas of the national party. He tried to convince the national delegates that Texas was a western state rather than part of the Old South, but most of his support in the party was from the southern tier of the country.

When John F. Kennedy won the nomination, he stunned his supporters by offering the vice presidency to Johnson. The senator in his turn stunned his supporters by accepting—despite John Nance Garner's advice that the vice presidency wasn't worth a "pitcher of warm spit." Johnson did hedge his bets by ensuring that his name was on the ballot twice—as nominee for the vice presidency and as a candidate for reelection to the senate. Shivers organized Democrats for Nixon, but the Kennedy-Johnson ticket led in Texas by a narrow margin.

While the Republicans lost the presidential race, 1960 can be seen as the turning point in building a strong Republican party in Texas. In the general election, a little-known economics professor at Midwestern State University in Wichita Falls, John Tower, had made a strong race against Johnson for the senate seat. In the special election, Tower ran against a conservative Democrat. Many liberal Democrats voted for Tower on the theory that his election would produce a two-party state with Democrats for the center-left and Republicans for the center-right. Tower then became the first Texas Republican to be elected to the U.S. Senate since Reconstruction. His election signaled the beginning of the rebuilding of the Republican party in Texas, and perhaps in the South.

Johnson did find the vice presidency a dispiriting position, but his influence over Texas Democratic politics was boosted when his former aide John Connally won the governorship in 1962. The Republican nominee still did very well; Jack Cox, who had left the Democratic party, garnered 45.6 percent of the votes cast in the gubernatorial race. In addition, the Republicans added legislators to its list of elected Texans. The Republicans looked forward to

challenging a divided Democratic party in 1964.

And the Democrats were seriously at odds with each other. Governor Connally did not get along with the more liberal Senator Ralph Yarborough, and various factions in the Texas Democratic party fell in behind one man or the other. The state party was being torn apart by bickering between the two camps. President Kennedy decided that he needed to go to Texas to mediate.

In his search for Democratic unity, Kennedy went to Dallas on November 22, 1963. As his motorcade wove through the downtown streets, someone shot and killed the president and severely wounded Governor Connally, who was riding in the presidential limousine. Later in the same day, former Marine Lee Harvey Oswald, who had worked in the Texas School Book Depository that overlooked the motorcade route, was arrested for the murder.

In unanticipated ways Kennedy's death did unite the Texas Democratic party and also temporarily set back the Republican resurgence. Now president, Johnson could use his prestige to iron out disputes in his home state's party. Governor Connolly's wounds also lent him an air of martyrdom and made him unbeatable.

When President Johnson ran for reelection in 1964, he was endorsed by all extremes of the Texas Democratic party—everyone from former Governor Shivers and Oveta Culp Hobby, who had served in the Eisenhower cabinet, to Senator Yarborough. Not only did Johnson carry the state by 700,000 votes, the Republicans retained only one seat in the state legislature and lost the seats they had held in the U.S. Congress. George H.W. Bush, now of Houston, lost in his bid to unseat Senator Yarborough.

In 1968 neither Johnson nor Connolly ran for reelection. Johnson bowed to the unpopularity of the Vietnam War, took himself out of consideration, and returned to his Hill Country ranch. As for Connolly, he seemed to have lost his taste for office. Johnson's vice president, Hubert Humphrey, was not popular in Texas, but Johnson, Connolly, and Yarborough all campaigned for him. This show of unity carried Texas for Humphrey, but by less than 40,000 votes. Nationally, Humphrey lost to former Vice President Richard M. Nixon. The national delegation of Texas Republicans now consisted of Senator Tower and three U. S. congressmen, including George H. W. Bush. Two state senators and eight members of the Texas house were Republicans.

A confounding factor in the 1968 presidential race was Alabama Governor George Wallace, who ran as an independent. Wallace picked up the electoral votes of five southern states, but in Texas he only got 584,000 votes out of the three million cast. Maybe Texas was indeed losing its identification with the South.

National forces were also forcing political changes on Texas. In 1964 the U.S. Supreme Court had ruled that state legislatures had to be reapportioned regularly so that each legislator represented roughly the same number of people. Until this one-man, one-vote principle became active in Texas, small towns and rural areas had dominated both houses of the state legislature. These areas were bastions of conservative Democrats, people who had always voted Democratic but were gradually losing touch with the national party. African Americans, Hispanics, liberal Democrats, and Republicans lost out in this arrangement.

In 1964 the 24th Amendment outlawed the poll tax in federal elections, but Texas continued to use it until the U.S.

Supreme Court held that the poll tax in any election was a violation of the 14th Amendment. The legislature replaced the poll tax with a system that required yearly registration during four months ending in January—as far from election day as could be managed. Within a few years, the Supreme Court found this system also unconstitutional.

Minority voters brought lawsuits based on the federal Voting Rights Act and contested more offices. In 1966 Barbara Jordan of Houston became the first African American in the state senate since Reconstruction, and Curtis Graves and J.E. Lockridge were elected to the house. In 1970, 42 African Americans and 723 Hispanics held local office in Texas. The grip of conservative white male Democrats on Texas politics seemed to be weakening.

Sharpstown

When the votes were counted in the 1968 state election, one man emerged as the person to watch: Ben Barnes polled more than 2 million votes for lieutenant governor, more than any Texan had ever gotten. Conservative Democrats seemed to have formulated an approach to keeping power. They would use their clout among better-off white voters to win in the primaries and then entice minorities and union members back to the party in the general election. This strategy led to the primary defeat of Ralph Yarborough in 1970 by the more conservative Lloyd Bentsen, a Houston millionaire. Bentsen then went on to win over the Republican candidate George H. W. Bush. A two-party state still seemed a long way off.

Political observers assumed that the handsome and engaging Ben Barnes would be governor as soon as the inarticulate Preston Smith had served his two terms. Barnes and Speaker of the House Gus Mutscher controlled the legislative process and could thwart any of Governor Smith's initiatives. The Barnes-Mutscher duo seemed destined to rule Texas into the foreseeable future.

In 1969 a banking bill designed to protect state-chartered banks from federal oversight moved through the legislature. Frank Sharp had helped the legislators write the bill, which he stood to benefit from since he controlled the Sharpstown State Bank. Speaker Mutscher had worked closely with Sharp on the bill, and Governor Smith, the chair of the state

The Branch Davidians: Waco Siege

On April 19, 1993, a 51-day siege came to an end in an inferno that destroyed a huge wooden building outside of Waco. More than 10 years later, the standoff and its aftermath remain controversial among groups such as gun rights, religious freedom, and anti-child abuse advocates. Getting to know the facts about the Branch Davidians and their fate is difficult.

The Branch Davidians broke off from the Seventh-Day Adventists in the 1930s after a man named Victor Houteff announced that he was a messenger from God. He and 11 others settled in at what they named Mount Carmel Center near Waco. Houteff died in the 1950s, and his wife took over the congregation, which believed that soon God would clear Jews and Arabs from Palestine and the Davidians would take over that land. Mrs. Houteff could not hold the group together and the renegade Adventists splintered even further. Some version of the group always remained at Mount Carmel, living a communal life and practicing organic gardening. Most of Waco saw them as odd but harmless religious eccentrics in a region where religious eccentricity was not unknown.

Then in 1983 Houston-born David Koresh revealed that he was the new messenger, if not Christ reborn. In 1989 Koresh announced that he was the rightful husband of any woman in the compound, including those already married to someone else. In the winter of 1990 Koresh unleashed more extreme behavior, requiring that believers watch violent war movies and increasing his sexual demands. Disillusioned Davidians left Mount Carmel and spoke out about sexual improprieties, child abuse, and the illegal gun stockpiling they had seen at the compound.

The tale of illegal weapons attracted the interest of the Bureau of Alcohol, Tobacco and Firearms (ATF), and almost 100 ATF and FBI agents moved in to arrest Koresh on February 28, 1993. A 45-minute shoot-out resulted in the deaths of four agents and five Davidians. The federal agents settled in for a siege.

On April 16, the federal forces used tanks to clear debris from around the compound. Three days later, just before 6:00 a.m., the agents called the compound and told the Davidians that they would be gassed if they did not surrender. At 6:04 an armored vehicle smashed through the front wall of the compound, and other vehicles battered the wooden building all morning. At 10 minutes after noon, fire and smoke shot from the compound. Within 30 minutes the structure was totally destroyed. Inside the compound 76 people, including 21 children and David Koresh, died.

In 1999 the FBI acknowledged that it had used pyrotechnic tear gas rounds in the final assault. In 2000 a federal prosecutor pled guilty to failing to give relevant materials to the special counsel investigating the siege and he received two years of probation.

Waco does not advertise the Mount Carmel site as a place to visit. The compound is about 10 miles east of town. A wooden chapel has been built on the site.

Democratic Executive Committee, and many legislators participated in a complicated money-making scheme Sharp thought up. Sharp offered the politicians unsecured loans from his bank and they used this money to buy stock in Sharp's National Bankers Life Insurance Company. Then, they would turn around and offer the stock to a Jesuit organization. Sharp was the Jesuits' financial advisor and his advice always involved paying the politicians more than the market share for their stock.

The bottom fell out of the system when Smith vetoed the banking bill. He later explained that he did not understand it. The Jesuits lost their investments, and the federal Securities and Exchange Commission began to investigate.

Mutscher, however, worked quickly and appointed a legislative investigatory committee made up of his cronies. The committee exonerated everyone involved in the scheme. Outraged liberals, Republicans, and others disaffected with the speaker's grip on the legislative process came together and spoke out against the report, calling themselves the Dirty Thirty. Mutscher then drew up a redistricting plan that did away with every member of the Dirty Thirty. The redistricting plan was overturned, and Mutscher and two others were indicted and convicted of bribery and conspiracy.

Even Texas voters, who tend to believe that a little scandal is to be expected in politics, demanded some changes. Reform was in the air as the 1972 election began. Mutscher ran for reelection despite being convicted. He lost. Governor Smith also lost, placing fourth in the primary. Barnes, who had not been implicated in the scandal, placed third. Apparently, the voters were in a hang-'em all mood. The Democratic gubernatorial contest ended as a toss up between a millionaire rancher and a member of the Dirty Thirty. Of course the rancher, Dolph Briscoe, won, but the Dirty Thirty candidate, Frances "Sissy" Farenthold, was a change from the usual. Farenthold campaigned for gun-control laws, corporate taxes, and increased spending for education. Her supporters thought they could ride the reform wave into office and build a center-left Democratic party as a player in a two-party system.

Again the conservative Democrats managed to hold onto power—partly because many left-of-center Texas voters did not see Dolph Briscoe as a threat. In general, he had good relations with Hispanic Texans and union members.

The unions did not contribute to Farenthold's campaign, and she ran a severely underfunded contest. In 1974 the two faced off again, but Briscoe triumphed for a second time. The conservative Democrats thought they had found the winning combination: a moderately conservative candidate who could get along with key minority voters and not antagonize union members. With this combination they felt they could continue to push back the rising Republican threat without giving in to the liberal wing.

POLITICAL SURPRISES

In 1978 Governor Briscoe announced that he would seek a third term. Third terms were not unusual for Texas governors, but Briscoe's would be unprecedented since the term had increased to four years in 1974. Major opposition came from John Hill, the attorney general and a moderate liberal. With strong backing from teachers, Hill defeated Briscoe in the primary. In the Republican primary, William Clements, a wealthy Dallas oilman and political newcomer, defeated Ray Hutchinson, an experienced party leader, in a well-financed campaign. Clements then went on to defeat John Hill in the general election.

Bill Clements became the first Republican governor of Texas since, well, Reconstruction. Two-party politics appeared to have come to Texas at last.

Clements was a contrast to the reticent Briscoe. Outspoken to the point of brashness, Clements eventually alienated many of the independents who had voted for him in 1978. He also faced the problems of anyone elected as an outsider—he couldn't get his programs passed. When time came for his re-election in 1982, Clements seemed to think that his identification with President Ronald Reagan and now Vice President George H.W. Bush would carry him to victory. Again, the electorate shocked observers, this time electing Democrat Mark White, the attorney general, to the office.

Victory came at a bad time for White, however. The national recession had become a full-fledged depression in Texas. Oil prices declined and the industry, still the bedrock of the state's economy, was in deep trouble. In addition, White had promised to improve teachers' salaries and education in general. To reach this goal, he appointed a select committee with Dallas millionaire Ross Perot at its head.

Enron: Biggest Bankruptcy Yet

In 1985 Houston Natural Gas merged with a Nebraska-based company, a merger that resulted in the first nationwide natural gas pipeline system. The new company's name was Enron, and the chairman and chief executive officer became Kenneth Lay, who had been the CEO of Houston Natural Gas.

Within three years, the company had opened a British office to take advantage of the privatization of English power. A new strategy emerged—go after unregulated markets while continuing to build on the regulated pipeline business. In 1989 Enron opened its Gas Bank to help natural gas buyers lock in fixed prices for long-term supplies. Enron's first trading in electricity came in 1994.

In 1996 Jeffrey Skilling was elected president and chief operating officer. In the late 1990s the company branched out into areas other than energy. It bought a water company in Britain and started a broadband services unit and a commodity-trading internet site.

The year 2000 was the company's peak. Annual revenues were listed at $100 billion, more than double what they had been the year before. Riding this crest, the company bought the naming rights and helped with construction costs of Enron Field in downtown Houston. At this point Enron was the sixth largest energy company in the world, based on market capitalization. But things were not as they seemed.

Between 1996 and 1999 Enron reported to its shareholders that it had made a profit of $2.3 billion. During the same period, the company told the Internal Revenue Service that it had lost $3 billion. It had used a series of complex schemes, with nicknames like Renegade and Apache, to hide income. Executive pay was tied to stock price and the Enron administration was desperate to keep stocks—and pay—going up. In 1998 the compensation of the top 200 executives was $193 million. By 2000 their combined pay was $1.4 billion.

Events began to move fast in 2001. Skilling became CEO and Lay stayed on as chair of the board. In March a deal with Blockbuster to provide movies over the internet fell through and in the next month Enron disclosed that the bankrupt Pacific Gas and Electric of California owed it $570 million. During the summer, Skilling abruptly resigned and Lay again became CEO. Wall Street insiders asked the company for more details on its finances. In October, after Enron issued its third quarter report, the Securities and Exchange Commission started a formal investigation into investment partnerships that appeared to be covers for losses. Enron then had to issue new earnings statements covering 1997 through the first three quarters of 2001. Its stock dropped 89 percent from the beginning of the year.

Eventually, Enron let go most of its employees, began bankruptcy proceedings, and held "the largest garage sale in Houston history." Everything that could be sold, including the company's signature giant E that had adorned the front of the building, went. From the pinnacle of a new business concept, Enron had fallen to the bottom of bankruptcy.

The resulting legislation included several items that offended major groups. Certainly annoying to football-loving Texans was the "no pass-no play" rule that required participants in extracurricular pursuits to pass all of their academic subjects. Teachers found that many of the new requirements took up extra bureaucratic time and kept them away from the classroom. Most importantly, many of the reforms advocated by Perot's committee called for more income for the state, income that would probably require new taxes. In 1986 Governor White lost to former Governor Clements. In the same election, the seat of retiring Senator Tower was held for the Republicans by Phil Gramm, a former Democrat.

The 1988 presidential election featured two Texans running for top national positions. Vice President George H. W. Bush was the Republicans' nominee for president and Senator Lloyd Bentsen took advantage of the Lyndon Johnson Law and ran for both U.S. Senate and the vice presidency on the Democratic ticket. Bush won in his home state by 56 percent and in the nation by similar percentages. Bentsen was reelected, however, with the most votes cast in the state, 60 percent. George H.W. Bush became the second Texan to be president—or the third if you want to count Dwight D. Eisenhower.

In 1990 observers predicted an easy gubernatorial win for the Republicans. A particularly vicious three-way primary fight among Attorney General Jim Mattox, former Governor Mark White, and State Treasurer Ann Richards had scarred the Democrats. The runoff between Richards and Mattox was even more vitriolic, with White refusing to take sides. The nastiness of the primary left many Democrats exhausted and sick of politics. In the Republican primary, west Texas rancher Clayton Williams spent millions of his own money portraying himself as a good old boy who would return Texas to its glorious past. He easily won the Republican nomination with no runoff.

Again the results surprised Texans, but mainly because of Williams' incompetence as a campaigner. He admitted that he had not paid any income tax in 1986, and his comments made it obvious that he did not understand that a constitutional amendment was on the ballot. He told an off-color joke in public and then refused to shake Richards's hand after a debate. Poor manners were the last straw for many Texans and Richards became the first female Texas governor since Ma Ferguson and the first ever to be elected on her own terms.

Republicans had hoped to capture the governor's and other top offices and the legislature, but they were disappointed. Senator Gramm held onto his U.S. Senate seat by a hefty margin, and Kay Bailey Hutchinson captured Richards's old position as state treasurer while Rick Perry became agriculture commissioner. The Democrats, however, had triumphs besides Richards's election. Bob Bullock became lieutenant governor, Dan Morales of San Antonio became the first Hispanic attorney general, and control of the legislature remained in Democratic hands.

Governor Richards gained a national reputation. Her witty speeches seemed to win friends for the state and her personal popularity was high. With the election of Bill Clinton to the presidency over the incumbent President George H.W. Bush, the Democrats in Texas seemed posed to recoup. Then in a 1993 contest to fill the senatorial seat vacated by Lloyd Bentsen, President Clinton's new secretary of the Treasury, Republican Kay Bailey Hutchinson, took 65 percent of the vote. Governor Richards, however, seemed more popular than ever.

Her personal popularity was not enough, however, to carry her through the 1994 campaign. George W. Bush, the son of the former president, successfully challenged her. Republicans held the Texas governor's office and the two U.S. Senate seats. Other statewide positions, like attorney general and lieutenant governor, remained Democratic, as did control of the legislature. Governor Bush was reelected in 1998 and then announced that he would be a candidate for president in 2000.

The governor captured the White House by the narrowest of margins—four votes in the electoral college. But his popularity in Texas enabled the Republicans to sweep the state in 2002. The governor and all other statewide office holders were Republicans and the Democrats lost control of the state legislature. Had Texas exchanged one-party control by Democrats for Republican control? Did the turn mean that Texas truly was a southern state prepared to follow the rest of the Deep South into the Republican fold? Only the future would tell.

Dallas at night shows how far Texas has come from its rural beginnings. Richard Reynolds, courtesy TxDOT

Must-See Sites

Eisenhower's Birthplace
In his large family, Dwight D. Eisenhower was the only child born in Texas; the family lived on the corner of Lamar Avenue and Day Street in Denison on 14 October 1890. To visit the Eisenhower Birthplace State Historical Park call (903) 465-8908.

The Kennedy Assassination
In Dallas, the Sixth Floor Museum commemorating November 22, 1963, is in the old School Book Depository at 411 Elm Street. The spot thought to be Oswald's perch is preserved as it was in that November—except the window is kept closed. The museum documents Kennedy's presidency as well as the assassination. Call (214) 747-6660.

Lyndon B. Johnson

Two parks—one national and one state—and a national presidential library are devoted to the various phases of Lyndon B. Johnson's life. In Johnson City, the Lyndon B. Johnson National Historical Park includes the home of the 36th president from the age of five until he left home and the headquarters of his grandfather's trail-drive business. In the nearby town of Stonewall, another historical park features a dogtrot cabin and a living-history farm. In Austin, Johnson's presidential years are the focus of the Lyndon Baines Johnson Library and Museum. For the national park, call (830) 868-7128. For the state park, call (830) 644-2252. For the presidential library, on the University of Texas campus, call (512) 916-5136.

George H.W. Bush

The George Bush Presidential Library and Museum is in College Station. Call (979) 260-9552 or go to www.bushlibrary.tamu.edu.

Sources

The main source for this book is the always valuable six-volume *New Handbook of Texas*, especially its on-line version: www.tsha.utexas.edu/handbook. Other online sources include www.texasbeyondhistory.net, www.texasescapes.com and the online resources of Texas state agencies, municipalities, counties, museums, and other institutions. Packed with facts about the state's past and present, the *Texas Almanac* is published by the *Dallas Morning News* and comes out every two years. Many sources have already been mentioned in the text, but others need to be listed here.

Several general histories of Texas were useful:

Calvert, Robert A., and Arnoldo De León. *The History of Texas*. 2nd ed. Wheeling, Ill.: Harlan Davidson, 1990.

Fehrenbach, T. R. *Lone Star: A History of Texas and the Texans*. Updated ed. [Cambridge, MA, and New York] Da Capo Press, 2000.

Frantz, Joe B. *Texas: A History*. New York: Norton, 1984.

Haley, James L. *Texas: From Spindletop Through World War II*. New York: St. Martin's Press, 1993.

Richardson, Rupert N., Adrian Anderson, and Ernest Wallace. *Texas: The Lone Star State*. 7th ed. Upper Saddle River, NJ: Prentice Hall, 1997.

Specialized books that have contributed in their areas include the following:

Barr, Alwyn. *Black Texans: A History of African-Americans in Texas, 1528-1995*. 2nd ed. Norman: University of Oklahoma, 1996.

Bomar, George W. *Texas Weather*. Austin: University of Texas Press, 1995.

Brear, Holly Beachley. *Inherit the Alamo: Myth and Ritual at an American Shrine*. Austin: University of Texas Press, 1995.

Brown, Norman D. *Hood, Bonnet, and Little Brown Jug: Texas Politics, 1921-1928*. College Station: Texas A&M University Press, 1984.

Campbell, Randolph. *An Empire for Slavery: The Peculiar Institution in Texas*. Baton Rouge: Louisiana State University Press, 1989.

Carlson, Paul H., ed. *The Cowboy Way: An Exploration of History and Culture*. Lubbock: Texas Tech University Press, 2000.

Caro, Robert A. *The Years of Lyndon B. Johnson: Master of the Senate*. New York City: Knopf, 2002.

Carroll, Mark M. *Homesteads Ungovernable: Families, Sex, Race, and the Law in Frontier Texas, 1823-1860.* Austin: University of Texas, 2001.

Cotner, Robert C., et al. *Texas Cities and the Great Depression.* Austin: Texas Memorial Museum, 1973.

Crouch, Barry A. *The Freedmen's Bureau and Black Texans.* Austin: University of Texas Press, 1992.

Crutchfield, James A. *It Happened in Texas.* Helena, MT: Two Dot, 1996.

Doughty, Robin W. *Wildlife and Man in Texas: Environmental Change and Conservation.* College Station: Texas A&M University Press, 1983.

Flores, Dan. *Horizontal Yellow: Nature and History in the Near Southwest.* Albuquerque: University of New Mexico Press, 1999.

Francaviglia, Richard V. *The Cast Iron Forest: A Natural and Cultural History of the North American Cross Timbers.* Austin: University of Texas Press, 1998.

Foley, Neil. *The White Scourge: Mexicans, Blacks, and Poor Whites in Texas Cotton Culture.* Berkeley: University of California Press, 1997.

Hodge, Larry, and Ed Syers. *Backroads of Texas.* 4th ed. Lanham, MD: Lone Star Books, 2000.

Jamison, Cheryl Alters, and Bill Jamison. *Texas Home Cooking.* Boston: Harvard Common Press, 1993.

Jones, Jacqueline. *The Dispossessed: America's Underclass from the Civil War to the Present.* New York: Basic Books, 1992.

Jordan, Theresa. *Cowgirls: Women of the American West.* Lincoln: University of Nebraska Press, 1992.

Katz, William Loren. *The Black West.* 3rd ed. Seattle: Open Hand, 1987.

Lack, Paul D. *The Texas Revolutionary Experience: A Political and Social History, 1835-1836.* College Station: Texas A&M University Press.

McQueen, Clyde. *Black Churches in Texas: A Guide to Historic Congregations.* College Station: Texas A&M University Press, 2000.

Meinig, D. W. *Imperial Texas: An Interpretive Essay in Cultural Geography.* Austin: University of Texas Press, 1993.

Montejano, David. *Anglos and Mexicans in the Making of Texas, 1836-1986.* Austin: University Of Texas Press, 1987.

Myres, Sandra L. *Westering Women and the Frontier Experience, 1800-1915.* Albuquerque: University of New Mexico Press, 1999.

Pool, William C. *A Historical Atlas of Texas.* Austin: Encino, 1975.

Rathjen, Frederick W. *The Texas Panhandle Frontier.* Lubbock: Texas Tech University Press, 1973.

Reichstein, Andreas V. *Rise of the Lone Star: The Making of Texas.*

Trans. Jeanne R. Wilson. College Station: Texas A&M University Press, 1989.

Rhinehart, Marilyn D. *A Way of Work and a Way of Life: Coal Mining in Thurber, Texas, 1888-1926*. College Station: Texas A&M University Press, 1992.

Sitton, Thad, and James H. Conrad. *Nameless Towns: Texas Sawmill Communities, 1880-1942*. Austin: University of Texas Press, 1998.

Stephens, Ray, and William M. Holmes. *Historical Atlas of Texas*. Norman: University of Oklahoma Press, 1989.

Swanson, Eric R. *Geo-Texas: A Guide to the Earth Sciences*. College Station: Texas A&M University Press, 1995.

Texas A&M University Cartographics Laboratory. *The Roads of Texas*. Fredericksburg, TX: Shearer, 1995.

Texas Monthly. *Texas Traveler: The Ultimate Guide to the Lonestar State*. Austin: Texas Monthly, 2001.

Truett, Joe C. *Circling Back: Chronicles of a Texas River Valley*. Iowa City: University of Iowa, 1996.

Tyler, Ron C. *The Big Bend: A History of the Last Texas Frontier*. College Station: Texas A&M University Press, 1996.

Tyler, Ron, and Lawrence R. Murphy, eds. *The Slave Narratives of Texas*. Austin: State House Press, 1997.

Veselka, Robert E. *The Courthouse Square in Texas*. Austin: University of Texas Press, 2000.

Williams, J.W. *The Big Ranch Country*. Lubbock: Texas Tech University Press,1999.

Wooster, Ralph A. *Civil War Texas: A History and a Guide*. Austin: Texas State Historical Association, 1999.

Wooster, Ralph A., ed. *Lone Star Blue and Gray: Essays on Texas in the Civil War*. Austin: Texas State Historical Association.

San Antonio Riverwalk. © Joy Bull

Chronolgy of Major Events

1854	Kansas-Nebraska Act allows state-based decisions about slavery
1859	Juan Cortina attacks Brownsville
1860	Abraham Lincoln elected president of the United States
1861	January 28: Texas secession convention votes to leave the Union
	February: Colonel "Rip" Ford takes the mouth of the Rio Grande
	Summer: Colonel John Baylor secures southern New Mexico
1862	March: Union forces drive Texans out of New Mexico
	October: Union forces take Galveston
1863	January 1: General John B. Magruder retakes Galveston
	November: Union troops take Brownsville
1865	April: Lee Surrenders at Appomattox; Civil War ends; Lincoln assassinated
	May: Colonel Rip Ford fights Battle of Palmito Ranch, the last land battle of the war
	June 17: Andrew Jackson Hamilton appointed provisional governor
	June 19: Texas slaves learn they are free
1867	U.S. Congress imposes radical Reconstruction; General Philip Sheridan appoints Elisha M. Pease interim governor; Joseph G. McCoy develops Abilene, Kansas, as transport point for cattle; Chisholm Trail becomes popular route for cattle drives
1869	March 30: Texas officially restored to the Union
1871	Battle of Salt Creek leads to U.S. Army offensive against Native Americans of the plains
1873	Texas and Pacific Railroad reaches Dallas
1874	Battle of Palo Duro Canyon destroys Comanche horse herd; Texas Rangers called in to defuse Sutton-Taylor feud in DeWitt County; barbed wire imported into Texas
1875	Last Comanche groups surrender at Fort Bliss in Oklahoma; Farmers' Alliance starts in Lampasas County
1876	Texas drafts new constitution; Texas and Pacific Railroad reaches Fort Worth; Charles Goodnight establishes JA Ranch in Palo Duro Canyon
1877	Salt War in El Paso area heightens tensions between whites and Hispanics; Compromise of 1877 ends Reconstruction
1879	Legislature sells 3 million acres of public land to Illinois company to fund construction of new capitol; land eventually becomes XIT Ranch
1883	Fence cutting breaks out throughout western Texas;

1883	Cowboy strike begins and ends; University of Texas opens
1885	Severe winter kills off cattle herds
1886	Knights of Labor call the Great Southwest Strike against railroads
1888	Capitol building completed
1890	Fort Worth Stockyards open; James S. Hogg elected governor
1891	Texas Railroad Commission established to oversee railroad rates
1895	Constable John Selman kills John Wesley Hardin
1900	Great hurricane devastates Galveston; greatest loss of life in a natural disaster in U.S. history
1901	Spindletop gusher comes in; John Henry Kirby organizes the Kirby Lumber Company, the first multimillion dollar company in Texas
1910	Mexican revolution against regime of Porfiro Díaz begins
1913	Sam Rayburn elected to U.S. House of Representatives
1914	50-mile Houston Ship Channel opens
1915	James E. "Pa" Ferguson elected governor; William J. Simmons revives Ku Klux Klan in Georgia
1916	March 9: Pancho Villa attacks Columbus, New Mexico; General John J. Pershing enters Mexico to chase down Villa
1917	Legislature draws up charges against Governor Ferguson, who resigns; United States enters World War I; Houston riot results in court martials for soldiers from all African American Third Battalion of the 24th U.S. Infantry
1918	Legislature extends right to vote in primaries to women and ratifies the 18th Amendment, which instituted Prohibition
1922	Ku Klux Klan reaches zenith of influence with election of Earle B. Mayfield to U.S. Senate
1924	Mirian A. "Ma" Ferguson defeats Klan candidate to become first woman governor in Texas
1926	Crusading reformer Dan Moody defeats Ma Ferguson for governor
1929	Stock market crashes; Depression begins; LULAC founded
1930	Oil discovered near Kilgore; east Texas oil field opens
1932	Unemployment reaches 400,000 in Texas
1935	U.S. Congress creates Big Bend National Park
1936	Texas Centennial Exposition opens in Dallas to mark 100 years of Texas
1941	United States enters World War II
1947	Texas City explosion kills 500

1948	Lyndon B. Johnson wins seat in U.S. Senate by 87 votes
1949	Heman Sweatt enters the University of Texas Law School
1953	U.S. Congress holds that tidelands—and their oil—belong to Texas
1954	*Brown vs. Board of Education* ends legally segregated schools
1960	Lyndon B. Johnson elected John F. Kennedy's vice president
1963	John F. Kennedy assassinated and Johnson becomes president of the United States
1964	NASA headquarters opens in Houston
1966	Rio Grande farm workers strike and march on Austin
1967	Barbara Jordan becomes first African-American woman in Texas Senate
1972	Sharpstown scandal results in indictment of Speaker of the House and others and rejuvenates reform
1979	William Clements takes office as first Republican governor since Reconstruction
1981	Oil prices peak
1984	Educational Reform Act, spearheaded by Ross Perot, passes
1985	Oil prices plunge; state economy busts
1988	George H.W. Bush elected president of the United States
1991	Ann Richards becomes first female governor of Texas since Ma Ferguson
1994	George W. Bush elected governor
1998	George W. Bush reelected governor
2000	George W. Bush elected president
2002	Governor Perry reelected. Republicans sweep all statewide offices and gain control of both houses of the state legislature.
2003	First Republican-controlled legislature convenes and introudces a redistricting plan; 50+ House Democrats decamp to Oklahoma; Special session called to address redistricting; 11 Senate Democrats leave for New Mexico; a third special session passes the new redistricting act.
2004	Redistricting makes its way through the courts; Enron indictments begin; George W. Bush reelected president.

TEXAS MOVIES

Although this list contains some great movies, it is not strictly a best movies list. Rather the films on this list give some insight into the history, myth, or present culture of Texas or into what others think about the state. It is worth noting that the first Oscar for best picture went to *Wings*, shot in San Antonio in 1927.

The Alamo (1960) John Wayne, dir. John Wayne, Richard Widmark, Lawrence Harvey. Familiar story of the doomed defense told in flag-waving spectacular. A version starring Billy Bob Thornton was released in 2004.

Alamo Bay (1985) Louis Malle, dir. Amy Madigan, Ed Harris, Ho Nguyen. A Texas shrimper faces economic and population changes in his town and business.

Blood Simple (1984) Joel Coen, dir. John Getz, Frances McDormand, Dan Hedaya. Texas bar owner hires private eye to take care of his cheating wife; things turn grisly and confusing. The first Coen brothers movie.

Bonnie and Clyde (1967) Arthur Penn, dir. Warren Beatty, Faye Dunaway. The ultimate crime couple shoots their way across Texas and adjoining states.

Brewster McCloud (1971). Robert Altman, dir. Bud Cort, Sally Kellerman, Shelley Duvall. A young man lives in the basement of the Astrodome, where an angel tries to teach him to fly.

Come Back to the Five and Dime, Jimmy Dean, Jimmy Dean (1982) Robert Altman, dir. Sandy Dennis, Cher, Karen Black. The James Dean Fan Club of (fictional) west Texas town McCarthy has its 25-year reunion with resulting truths and deceptions.

Dancer, Texas (1998) Tim McCanlies, dir. Breckin Meyer, Peter Facinelli. High school seniors in tiny Big Bend town face the future.

Fandango (1985) Kevin Reynolds, dir. Judd Nelson, Kevin Costner. Recent college graduates facing the draft and Vietnam take a road trip through west Texas.

Frailty (2002) Bill Paxton, dir. Bill Paxton, Matthew McConaughey, Powers Booth. Psychological thriller told in flashbacks of an east Texas family's scary divine mission.

Giant (1956) George Stevens, dir. Rock Hudson, Elizabeth Taylor, and the last appearance of James Dean. Based on a novel by Edna Ferber, this movie pits ranch money against oil and changing times; great supporting cast

Hands on a Hard Body (1998) S.R. Bindler, dir. Documentary shows modern Texans willing to submit themselves to torture for the chance at a new pickup.

Happy, Texas (1999) Mark Illsley, dir. Steve Zahn, Jeremy Northern, William Macy. Two escaped convicts end up in small Texas town where they are mistaken for gay beauty pageant advisors.

Hud (1963) Martin Ritt, dir. Paul Newman, Patricia Neal. Hands-down the best movie ever made about Texas. Based on the Larry McMurtry book, *Horseman, Pass By,* it captures the changes modern materialist culture forces on ranching life.

The Last Picture Show (1971) Peter Bogdanovich, dir. Timothy Bottoms, Cybil Shepherd, Jeff Bridges, Ben Johnson, Cloris Leachman, Ellen Burstyn, Eileen Brennan, Randy Quaid. The quintessential small-town-dying story, based on another McMurty novel.

Lone Star (1996) John Sayles, dir. Chris Cooper and Elizabeth Peña. Race and the law become explosive on the Texas-Mexico border when the story of an old crime is uncovered.

North Dallas 40 (1970) Ted Kotchoff, dir. Nick Nolte, Mac Davis, Dabney Coleman. Cynical football managers manipulate players in a team that resembles the Dallas Cowboys.

Old Yeller (1957) Robert Stevenson, dir. Dorothy McGuire, Fess Parker, Chuck Connors. Based on the Fred Gipson novel, this three-Kleenex boy-and-his-dog movie is set in Mason, Texas.

Paris, Texas (1984) Wim Wenders, dir. Harry Dean Stanton, Nastasja Kinski, Dean Stockwell. Based on Sam Shepard's story, this road movie features an amnesiac trying to reassemble the pieces of his life.

Places in the Heart (1984) Robert Benton, dir. Sally Field, John Malkovich, Danny Glover. A depression-era widow saves the farm by harvesting her cotton crop with the help of an illiterate African American and a blind man.

Raggedy Man (1981) Jack Fisk, dir. Sissy Spacek, Eric Roberts, Sam Shepard. Written by William Wittliff, this World War II period piece has a violent ending out of place with the rest of the story.

Red River (1948) Howard Hawks, dir. John Wayne, Montgomery Clift, Walter Brennan. A cattle rancher and his son work out their conflicts on a trail drive north.

The Searchers (1956) John Ford, dir. John Wayne, Ward Bond, Vera Miles, Natalie Wood. The morally ambiguous Ethan Edwards searches for the Comanches who destroyed his brother's home and kidnapped his nieces; this movie gave the world the idea that Texas looks like southern Utah.

Slacker (1990) Richard Linklater, dir. Follows the lives of some real Austinites as they veer aimlessly around town.

The Southerner (1945) Jean Renoir, dir. Zachary Scott. Based on George Sessions Perry's story of a tenant farmer in central Texas.

Sugarland Express (1974) Steven Spielberg, dir. Goldie Hawn, Ben Johnson. Cops chase couple across Texas after woman busts her husband out of prison so they can rescue their baby from an adoption agency.

Tender Mercies (1973) Bruce Beresford, dir. Robert Duvall. In a Horton Foote script, a country music singer's career falters because of drink and a failed marriage.

Terms of Endearment (1983) James Brooks, dir. Shirley MacLaine, Debra Winger, Jack Nicholson. Another McMurtry novel turned into a movie, this one focuses on unusual and often tear-jerking family dynamics in modern Houston.

The Thin Blue Line (1988) Errol Morris, dir. Documentary about an innocent man convicted of killing a Dallas police officer; wonderfully icy score by Philip Glass.

Trip to Bountiful (1985). Peter Masterson, dir. Geraldine Page, John Heard. In the 1940s, an elderly woman leaves the depressing home of her son and daughter-in-law to make a nostalgic visit to her past. Written by Horton Foote.

Urban Cowboy (1980) James Bridges, dir. John Travolta, Debra Winger. The real star is the mechanical bull ridden by the major characters at the Houston honky-tonk Gilley's.

Viva Max (1969) Jerry Paris, dir. Peter Ustinov. A deranged Mexican army officer retakes the Alamo; written by newscaster Jim Lehrer with comedic cameo appearances by Jonathon Winters and others.

Texas Music

The story goes that "gringo," the Mexican slang for white, arose during the Mexican War. Supposedly, U.S. soldiers sang as they moved from place to place and one song they particularly liked was "Green Grow the Rushes." According to this tale, Mexicans identified the song with the U.S. Army and took to calling the soldiers "gringos," because the first lines of the song sounded like that to their ears.

That's the story and who knows if it is true. But it does indicate the centrality of music to Texas identity. Coyotes may have been the first Texas singers, but Native Americans made the first human music in Texas. While it is difficult to know how this music sounded eons ago, hints can be derived from present-day Native American chants. A cassette of Caddo tribal dances, originally recorded in 1955, is available from Indian House of Taos, New Mexico. Smithsonian Folkways also has recordings of Apache music (recorded in 1968) and Comanche flute playing. Smithsonian also recorded an overview of Native American music of the southwest in 1957.

Music must have been integral to the religious life of the Spanish missions. Some idea of that experience can be approximated by listening to *Mexican Baroque* (Das Alte Werk, 1994) by the a cappella group Chanticleer. Although the frontier choirs were untrained compared to Chanticleer, they probably had access to at least some of this music. Manuscripts of 18th-century masses have been discovered in Los Angeles missions; it seems reasonable that Texas worshippers could have heard something similar.

Spanish, French, and Anglo settlers brought their own songs and dances that helped them work and pass their free time. *The Stars and the Lily*, a 1977 recording from Smithsonian Folkways, shows French influence in colonial times. Another Smithsonian Folkways recording, *Simple Gifts* by George and Gerry Armstrong, features Anglo-American folksongs that may have been brought to Texas by settlers from the eastern states. *Ethnic Music of French Louisiana, the Spanish Southwest, and the Bahamas* covers a lot of territory, but gives some idea of music in early Texas. It was recorded by John and Ruby Lomax in the 1930s and 1940s and is available from the U.S. Library of Congress. The Lomax recording *Cowboy Songs and Other Frontier Ballads* is a classic, but it is now out of print. You can hear the second Lomax generation in Legacy records' *Cowboy Songs of the Old West*, sung by Alan Lomax and Ed McCurdy.

In the 19th century, the religious musical tradition continued in small churches and great cathedrals. Roman Catholic Bishop Jean Marie Odin introduced the first Texas organ to his congregation in Galveston. Both blacks and whites sang gospel songs and spirituals in their congregations and at home. The white frontier tradition of Sacred Harp singing is still practiced today. Each year in College Station the last weekend in February features an all-day singing for Sacred Harp singers of all experience levels. With their minor chords and harmonies, these songs sound strange to most modern ears; the words too stand out for their emphasis on suffering. You can get some feeling of the flavor from the Sacred Harp tradition from the 1998 *Sacred Harp Singing* by Rounder Records.

While English, Scotch, Welsh, and Irish folk tunes took over as mainstream secular music, some other ethnic groups preserved their musical ways both at home and in other settings. Hispanics made up small orchestras and bands to play in public and private. Dances on plazas and in homes became a part of Hispanic life in Texas. The Germans put together singing groups and practiced in beer gardens. Hispanic and European music cross-fertilized. The Germans and Czechs were thought to have introduced the button accordion to Hispanic musicians; all three ethnic groups were playing the instrument in the 1870s. Adolf Hofner was a Czech bandleader of the 1930s who performed until the 1990s; his music combined Cajun, Tex-Mex, and western swing—all with Czech lyrics. Arhoolie has a Hofner CD called *South Texas Swing*.

Guitars, accordions, and violins became the staples of Hispanic music. The polka beat, probably picked up from the Germans and Czechs, was incorporated into what is now called conjunto music. Conjunto is made up of a small group of musicians (*conjunto* means "ensemble") and is the music of working people of northern Mexico. Narciso Martínez and Pedro Ayala are regarded as the founding fathers of conjunto. Martinez first recorded in the 1930s. Arhoolie has recordings of both Martínez, *Father of Texas-Mexican Conjunto*, and Ayala, *El Monarca del Acordeon*. The first Hispanic singing star was Lydia Mendoza of San Antonio. She is supposed to have learned her hit "Mal Hombre" from a gum wrapper. You can find it on another Arhoolie recording, *Mal Hombre and Other Original Hits From the 1930s*.

At some point the bass was added to the conjunto ensemble; this innovation was thought to be the work of San Antonio's Santiago "Flaco" Jiménez, Sr. By the 1940s some conjunto bands, such as the one led by Beto Villa, were incorporating the Big Band sound. In the 1950s Isidro López of Bishop incorporated conjunto, mariachi, and rock and roll into a style he called Texachi.

In the 1980s a fusion of rural and urban sounds came to be known as Tejano music. Latin sounds have crossed over into mainstream popular music and many Hispanics artists have large followings: Among them Little Joe y su Familia, *20 de Coleccion* from Sony; "Flaco" Jiménez, Jr., *Un Mojado sin Licencia* from Arhoolie; and the late star from Corpus Christi, Selena, *Exitos y Recuerdos* from EMI-Capitol.

The blues are another important ethnic strain in Texas music. Polyrhythmic, with call and response patterns and slurred notes called "blue notes," the blues originated in work songs and "field hollers" that went wherever slavery was in the United States. If you want a taste of how these work songs might have sounded, listen to *Texas Prison Recordings, 1933-1934*; John and Alan Lomax made this field recording, which is now available from Rounder.

After the Civil War, blues singing became more individual, with one person singing a line, repeating it, and then rhyming with it. One of the earliest known blues singers was Henry Thomas, who was born in Gladewater in 1875. His *Texas Worried Blues* is available from Yazoo Records. Blues great Robert Johnson even has a connection with Texas; he made a series of recordings in the Gunther Hotel in San Antonio. Other major figures in Texas blues include Huddie Ledbetter, "Leadbelly," Blind Lemon Jefferson, T-Bone Walker, Sam Lightnin' Hopkins, and Mance Lipscomb. Recordings of all of these men are readily available.

A center for Texas blues playing in the 1920s and 1930s was the Dallas area called Deep Ellum. Alan Govenar, through his Dallas organization Documentary Arts, has a one-CD compilation featuring the many styles of music that flourished in this area; it is called *Deep Ellum Blues*. Go to www.docarts.com.

The bridge between blues and country music is Jimmy Rodgers, "the singing brakeman." A native of Mississippi, Rodgers probably heard early bluesmen in that state. He moved to Texas and lived in Kerrville and San Antonio, seeking a drier climate for his tuberculosis. His contribution to country music was the "blue yodel." He recorded a series of songs called "Blue Yodel 1," "Blue Yodel 2," all the way to "Blue Yodel 12." One became famous as "T for Texas." Many Rodgers recordings are still available.

The king of country music in 1930s Texas was Bob Wills, with his distinctive blend of several styles that became known as western swing. One of Wills's band singers was Milton Brown, who went on to start his own band, Milton Brown and His Musical Brownies. The Origin Jazz Library has released a one CD pressing of Brown (the only other available recording is a five-CD set). Bob Wills's music is readily available today—probably because of the work of Asleep at the Wheel, a group that has done much to reawaken interest in western swing.

After World War II large western swing bands became economically impossible. A new kind of country music was playing in honky tonks and anywhere else people danced. Ernest Tubb began as a Jimmie Rodgers imitator and was helped along in his career by Rodgers's widow. Others in this genre were Lefty Frizell and Ray Price. The honky tonk sound eventually morphed into the outlaw country sound of Willie Nelson and Waylon Jennings.

Texas gave at least three founding parents to rock and roll: Buddy Holly of Lubbock, Roy Orbison of Wink, and Janis Joplin of Port Arthur. (Each of these towns now has a museum or other memorial to commemorate their home town rockers.) The 13th Floor Elevators of Austin are often listed as the first psychedelic band. Stevie Ray Vaughan and his brother Jimmie made the connection of blues and rock obvious.

A list of all musicians working in Texas today would go on for pages. Several sources can give you an overview. The Center for Texas Music History at Texas State University, San Marcos, for example, has a multi-volume compilation of contemporary Texas music called *Travellin' Texas CDs*. Go to http://www.txstate.edu/ctmh.

In 1980 Lubbock unveiled this statue by Grant Speed of native rock pioneer Buddy Holly, which became the central point for a west Texas musician walk of fame. Richard Pierce, TxDOT

TEXAS WRITERS

Cabeza de Vaca wrote the first book about Texas, but lots more have followed him. Many of these works can only interest specialists today, but some are still worth a glimpse, and some deserve more than that.

NONFICTION

Other works in Spanish followed Cabeza de Vaca's, but the first English-language book devoted to the state was Mary Austin Holley's *Texas* (1833), enlarged into *History of Texas* in 1836. She was Stephen F. Austin's cousin and planned to settle in Texas but never did. Her diary and family letters have been published. Some of her letters included pencil sketches of Houston and other sites.

After the Civil War, Texas writings tended to focus on cowboys and rangers: *Six Years with the Texas Rangers, 1875-1881* (1921) by James Buchanan Gillet is an engaging read, as is Charles Siringo's *A Texas Cowboy or Fifteen Years on the Hurricane Deck of a Spanish Pony* (1912). One work that gives some idea of city life during and after the Civil War is Amelia E. Barr's *All the Days of My Life: An Autobiography* (1888). Mrs. Barr wrote about 50 forgettable novels to support her family after her husband died; her autobiography, her best work, has a large section detailing life in Austin.

The Texas Folklore Society was founded in 1909, and from this source came many of the best explorations of Texas past and present. The foremost writer connected with the group was J. Frank Dobie. His output was voluminous and many of his works remain in print: *A Vaquero of the Brush Country* (1929), *Apache Gold and Yaqui Silver* (1939), *The Longhorns* (1941), and *The Mustangs* (1952) are just a few. Other prominent folklorists of the period included John A. Lomax who collected cowboy songs into *Cowboy Songs and Other Frontier Ballads* (1910) and Dorothy Scarborough, who published *On the Trail of Negro Folk Songs* (1925) and *A Song Catcher in the Southern Mountains* (1937, posthumous). Mody C. Boatright, who was connected with the folklore society after World War II, wrote many books about the oil industry including *Folklore of the Oil Industry,* (1963) and *Tales from the Derrick Floor* (1970, with William A. Owens).

William A. Owens mined his own life and produced an autobiographical trilogy about growing up in and leaving east Texas life: *This Stubborn Soil* (1966), *A Season of Weathering* (1973), and *Tell Me A Story, Sing Me a Song* (1983). Another account of growing up in east Texas, from a different perspective, is C.C. White's *No Quittin' Sense* (1969). White was an African American who became a preacher and folklorist. J. Mason Brewer was the first African American member of both the Texas Folklore Society and the Texas Institute of Letters. His many books include *The Word on the Brazos* (1953), *Aunt Dicy Tales* (1956), and *Dog Ghosts and Other Texas Negro Folk Tales* (1958).

Two of Dobie's friends, Walter Prescott Webb and Roy Bedicheck, explored different areas of Texas life. Webb was a historian whose romanticized *The Texas Rangers* (1935) shaped present attitudes toward the law enforcement group. In *The Great Plains* (1931) he studied the effects of aridity on the economy and life of the west. Bedicheck was more interested in Texas creatures, and his *Adventures of a Texas Naturalist* (1948) explored the natural world. Bedichek's letters, however, are his real legacy; they were collected by William A. Owens and Lyman Grant in 1985.

The inheritor of Bedicheck's mantle is John Graves. *Goodbye to a River* (1960) describes a canoe trip down the Brazos before a series of dams were completed; it is considered one of the gems of Texas writing. Graves continued this vein of writing in *Hard Scrabble* (1974) and *From a Limestone Ledge* (1980). Several writers contend for the Graves mantle. Stephen Harrigan, perhaps best known as a novelist, has two collections of nature essays, *A Natural State* (1988) and *Comanche Midnight* (1995). Rick Bass contributed *The Deer Pasture* (1985) and *Oil Notes* (1989), and has written an introduction to a new edition of *Goodbye to a River*. Dan L. Flores made a name for himself with *Caprock Canyonlands* (1990) and continued with *Horizontal Yellow* (1999), a strange mix of history, nature writing, and memoir.

In many ways the anti-Webb is Americo Paredes's *With a Pistol in His Hand: A Border Ballad and Its Hero* (1958), a portrayal of the many border songs that describe a ranger posse pursuit of Gregorio Cortez Lira, who had shot a sheriff. In this telling the rangers are not the romantic heroes of Webb's book. (In 1990 Paredes wrote a novel called *George Washington Gómez*, which includes a parody of Dobie in the rambling racist K. Hank Harvey.)

The letters of Waco native C. Wright Mills had been gathered by his daughters. Chapter 1, "Growing up in Texas, 1916-1939" has some interesting insights into his home state by the ultimate sociologist. The letters were published by the University of California Press in 2000. Growing up in west Texas has been described by A.C. Greene, *A Personal Country* (1979), Larry L. King, *The Old Man and Lesser Mortals* (1974), and Allan R. Bosworth, *New Country* (1962).

A book almost impossible to classify is John Howard Griffin's *Black like Me* (1961). Griffin, a white man, underwent treatments to darken his skin. He then traveled through the pre-civil-rights-movement South and recorded his experiences as a faux African

American. Controversial and stunning in its time, the book was
influential in the looming discussions of race.

We cannot turn to fiction without a look at a subgenre of
nonfiction that seems to fascinate Texans: the true-crime book,
especially when it deals with the scheming rich. Two of the
archetypes of this field are Thomas Thompson's *Blood and Money*
(1976), about a Houston murder case, and Gary Cartwright's *Blood
Will Tell* (1979). The latter covers the trial of Fort Worth
millionaire Cullen Davis, who was charged with killing his
stepdaughter and his wife's lover. With the help of "Racehorse"
Haynes, a truly flamboyant Houston defense lawyer, Davis was
acquitted. The genre reached spine-chilling effects with John
Bloom and Jim Atkinson's *Evidence of Love* (1985), in which two
middle-class church ladies have a confrontation from which only
one emerges. Novelist Beverly Lowry explored the death of her
own son and the death sentence of murderer Karla Faye Tucker in
Crossed Over: A Murder, A Memoir (1992).

FICTION AND POETRY

Most Texas fiction and poetry written before the 20th century is
unreadable by today's standards. Racial and religious animosities
and heavily romanticized patriotism are so prevalent in most
publications that they are difficult if not offensive to read. One
early work that still holds up is Mollie E. Moore Davis's *The Wire
Cutters* (1899), set in the fence wars of the 1880s. Cowboy poems
and oral tradition were an important part of late 19th century
Texas literature. Perhaps the most famous example of the genre
was Lawrence Chittenden's "The Cowboys' Christmas Ball,"
published in *Ranch Verses* (1893). The poem celebrates an 1885
dance held in Anson and reenacted there each year.

Cowboy material continued to be popular in the early 20th
century. Andy Adams wrote *The Log of a Cowboy* (1903) as a novel,
but it depicts the realities of cowboy life by describing a drive from
south Texas to Montana. It includes campfire scenes with the
cowboys telling tall tales to each other. O. Henry's tales set in Texas
can most easily be found in his *Heart of the West* (1907).

East Texas was the focus of Depression-era novels dealing with
agrarian unrest and poverty. In *The White Scourge* (1940) Edward
Everett Davis called cotton fields a "great open air slum." The
most durable of the agrarian novels is George Sessions Perry's *Hold
Autumn in Your Hand* (1941), the first Texas book to win a National
Book Award. Director Jean Renoir made it into a film in 1945.
Fred Gipson also dealt with agrarian themes in *Hound Dog Man*
(1949), *The Home Place* (1950), and the ever-popular juvenile novel
Old Yeller (1956).

For many years the most well-known and acclaimed Texas

Texas State University San Marcos, preserves Katherine Anne Porter's childhood home in Kyle. The home is now a writer's center.
J. Griffis Smith, courtesy TxDOT

writer has been Katherine Anne Porter. *Pale Horse, Pale Rider* (1939) and *The Leaning Tower and Other Stories* (1944) have long been considered the pinnacle of Texas literary writing. Others who write literary novels in a southern voice include William Goyen and William Humphrey. Goyen's experiment in modernist writing, *The House of Breath* (1950) shows the onslaught of modern life on a small community. In *Home from the Hill* (1958), *The Ordways* (1964), and *Farther off from Heaven* (1975), Humphrey also explores the timelessness and changes of east Texas.

Texas has also been home to writers of the hard-boiled school. Edward E. Anderson's *Thieves Like Us* (1937) has been filmed twice and Jim Thompson's *The Grifters* (1964) has also made it to Hollywood. Thompson was born in Oklahoma but lived in Texas off and on; his tales focus on the small towns of Texas, Oklahoma, and Nebraska. *The Transgressors* (1961) deals with an oil-field killing. Edwin M. Lanham also produced such hard-boiled works as *The Paste-Pot Man* (1967) and *Speak Not Evil* (1964). Before turning to detective fiction, Lanham wrote mainstream novels. His *Thunder in the Earth* (1941) about an oil man and his fortune was praised for its realistic portrayal of oil field life.

Other genre writers include Elmer Kelton, who has concentrated on westerns in such works as *The Day the Cowboys Quit* (1971) and *The Time it Never Rained* (1973). Joe R. Lansdale has produced recurring wise-cracking characters in a series that includes *Mucho Mojo* (1994) and *Bad Chili*. Others writing crime fiction today include David L. Lindsey, Bill Crider, Kinky Freidman, and Mary Willis Walker.

Of Texans writing mainstream novels today, Larry McMurtry must be the most widely read and filmed. His first book *Horseman, Pass By* appeared in 1961 and was filmed as *Hud*. During the 1960s he also produced *Leaving Cheyenne* (1963) and *The Last Picture Show* (1966) and finished the decade with a collection of essays, *In a Narrow Grave* (1968). He then turned his attention to modern urban Texas in his Houston trilogy: *Moving On* (1970), *All My Friends Are Going to Be Strangers* (1972), and *Terms of Endearment* (1975). In 1985 he produced *Lonesome Dove* and followed it with a sequel, *Streets of Laredo* (1993) and a prequel, *Dead Man's Walk* (1995).

Another modern writer mining the western is Cormac McCarthy who has produced novels of extreme violence and elegant language: *Blood Meridian* (1985), *All the Pretty Horses* (1992), and *The Crossing* (1994). McCarthy was born in Tennessee, but now lives in El Paso. People tend to forget that John Rechy, a writer mainly identified with Los Angeles and with gay-themed novels, is also from El Paso. Some of his early work is set in the area: *City of Night* (1964) and *Marilyn's Daughter* (1988).

In the sweepstakes for best modern Texan writer, however, a major contender has to be Billy Lee Brammer; *The Gay Place* (1961) was his only work. The work, which is actually a trilogy published in one 500-page book, draws on Brammer's experience as an aide to Lyndon B. Johnson in its presentation of a powerful Texas politician.

Among those writing fiction today are Laura Furman, *Drinking with the Cook* (2001); Dan Jenkins, *The Money-Whipped Steer-Job Three-Jack Give-up Artist* (2001); Shelby Hearon, *Ella in Bloom* (2001); Sarah Bird, *The Yakota Officers Club* (2001); Beverly Lowry, *Come Back Lolly Ray* (1977); Stephen Harrigan, *The Gates of the Alamo* (2000); Dagoberto Gilb, *Woodcuts of Women: Stories* (2000); Sandra Cisneros, *The House on Mango Street* (1994); Dao Strom, *Grass Roof, Tin Roof* (2003); and Oscar Casares, *Brownsville Stories* (2003). Rolando Hinojosa sets his work in the Valley; in fact the English title of one is *The Valley* (1983). His Klail City Death Trip series began in 1973 and continues. Hinojosa writes in both Spanish and English and a mixture thereof.

Vassar Miller was probably the outstanding Texas poet for most of the 1960s and 1970s. Her work was collected in *If I Had Wheels of Love* (1991). Albert Goldbarth was a University of Texas professor for a while and produced *Different Fleshes* (1979), a novel in poetry that mixes 19th century Texas with 1920s Paris. Other poets of modern Texas include David Oliphant, R.G. Vliet, Naomi Shihab Nye, Thomas Whitbread, Paul Woodruff, Walter McDonald, Rosemary Catacalos, Lorenzo Thomas, and Tino Villanuevo.

SPECIAL EVENTS

Times of events can change; be sure to find out if an event is still scheduled before you plan to include it in your trip.

FAIRS AND FESTIVALS

January
Texas Citrus Fiesta (Mission)

February
Charro Days (Brownsville)
Mardi Gras (Galveston, Jefferson, Port Arthur)
Sahawe Indian Winter Ceremonials (Uvalde)
South Texas Ranching Heritage Festival (Kingsville)
Texas Independence Day Music Festival (Dallas)

March
Borderfest (Hidalgo)
Cowboy Poetry Gathering (Alpine)
Goliad County Fair and Rodeo
Texas Independence Day (Washington, Luckenbach)
Texas Storytelling Festival (Denton)
Texas Tropics Nature Festival (McAllen)

April
Antique Tractor Show (Henderson)
Bluebonnet Festival (Burnet)
Buccaneer Days and Rodeo (Corpus Christi)
Cotton Gin Festival (Burton)
Don Juan de Oñate Thanksgiving Festival (San Elizano)
Easter Fires Pageant (Fredericksburg)
East Texas Gusher Days (Gladewater)
Fiesta (San Antonio)
General Sam Houston Folk Festival (Huntsville)
Spamarama (Austin)
Strawberry Festival (Poteet)

May
Cinco de Mayo (Del Rio, Grand Prairie, San Antonio, San Marcos)
Historic Home Tours (Galveston)
International Tribal Pow-Wow (Fredericksburg)
Maifest (Brenham)
Stagecoach Days (Marshall)
Texas Star Party (Fort Davis)
Texas State Arts and Crafts Fair (Kerrville)

Rodeo traces its roots to the conquistadores, cattle drives, the open range, and today's business-based professional sports. © Norm Jones

June
Alabama-Coushatta Annual Powwow (Livingston)
Cowboy Roundup USA (Amarillo)
Texas Folklife Festival (San Antonio)
Watermelon Thump (Luling)

July
Viva! El Paso (starts in June and goes into August)
Fourth of July (Addison, Arlington, Granbury, Greenville, Lubbock, Wimberley)
Texas Cowboy Reunion (Stamford)

August
Blanco County Fair and Rodeo
Cantaloupe Festival (Pecos)
Gillespie County Fair (Fredericksburg)
North Texas State Fair (Denton)

September
Championship American Indian Pow Wow (Grand Prairie)
Diez y Seis de Septiembre Celebration (Del Rio, Lubbock, San Antonio)
Four States Fair and Rodeo (Texarkana)
Grapefest (Grapevine)
Hummingbird Festival (Rockport)
Permian Basin Fair and Exposition (Odessa)
Pioneer Days (Fort Worth)
Seminole Days (Brackettville)

State Fair of Texas (Dallas)
Texas-Oklahoma Fair (Wichita Falls)
Texas State Forest Festival (Lufkin)
Tri-State Fair (Amarillo)
Washington County Fair (Brenham)

October
Butterfly Flutterby (Grapevine)
Chamizal Festival (El Paso)
Fair on the Square (Huntsville)
Fannin County Fair (Bonham)
Fiesta de Amistad (Del Rio)
Gonzales "Come and Take it" Days
Grayson County Fair (Sherman)
Guadalupe County Fair and Rodeo (Seguin)
Kerr County Fair (Kerrville)
Oktoberfest (Fredericksburg)
Wurstfest (New Braunfels)

November
Dickens on Main (Boerne)
Enchanted Forest (Granbury)
Heritage Syrup Festival (Henderson)
Nine Flags Festival (Nacogdoches)
Pioneer Village Fall Festival (Gonzales)
Rio Grande Valley Birding Festival (Harlingen) November

December
Christmas at Old Fort Concho (San Angelo)
Dickens on the Strand (Galveston)
Frontier Christmas (Fort Davis)
Weihnachten im Fredericksburg

COOKOFFS

February
Gumbo Cookoff (Orange)

March
General Granbury's Birthday and Bean Cookoff (Granbury)

April
Mills County Goat Barbecue Cookoff (Goldthwaite)
Prairie Dog Chili Cookoff and Pickled Quail Egg Eating Contest
    (Grand Prairie)
Wild Hog World Championship Barbecue Cookoff (Crowell)

May
Viva! Cinco de Mayo (San Marcos), menudo cookoff

June
Alley Oop Cookoff (Iraan)
Mex-Tex Cookoff (Midland)
Shrimporee (Aransas Pass)

July
Black-Eyed Pea Jamboree (Athens)
Spring Ho Barbecue Cookoff (Lampasas)

August
National Championship Barbecue Cookoff (Meridian)
Taylor International Barbecue Cookoff

September
National Cowboy Symposium and Celebration and
    Championship Chuckwagon Cookoff (Lubbock)
Republic of Texas Chilympiad (San Marcos)
Southern Hushpuppy Olympics (Lufkin)
World Championship Barbecue Goat Cookoff (Brady)
World Champion Hopkins County Stew Contest (Sulphur Springs)

October
Cowboy Captial of Texas Cookoff (Bandera)
Ladies State Championship Chili Cook-off (Luckenbach)
Rockport Seafair, Gumbo cookoff

November
Terlingua World Championship Chili Cookoff

Music
(For more information contact Texas Music Office, P.O. Box
13246, Austin, TX 78711)

January
Bell County Jamboree (Salado)
Janis Joplin Birthday Bash (Port Arthur)

February
South Texas Music Festival and Antique Car Show (Mercedes)
Wimberley Winter Jazz Festival

March
John A. Lomax Chisholm Trail Music Festival and Chuckwagon
    Cookoff (Meridian)

Nederland Heritage Festival
South by Southwest (Austin)
Star Select Opry (Mineola)
Texas Old Time Fiddlers Spring Fling (Bellville)
Texas Western Swing Fiddling Showcase (Belton)

April
Bob Wills Day (Turkey)
Denton Arts and Jazz Festival
Glen Rose Bluegrass Festival
Houston International Festival
Larry Joe Taylor's Texas Music Festival and Chili Cookoff (Stephenville)
Old Settlers Music Festival (Austin)
Texas Blues Festival (Tyler)
Texas Gospel Singing Convention (Stephenville)
XIT Bluegrass Festival (Littlefield)

May
Kerrville Folk Festival
National Polka Festival (Ennis)
Tejano Conjunto Festival (San Antonio)
Texas Crawfish and Music Festival (Spring)
Texas Natural and Western Swing Festival (San Marcos)

June
Roy Orbison Festival (Wink)
Texas State Bluegrass Festival (Brownwood)
West Texas Western Swing Music Festival (Snyder)
World Championship Fiddlers Festival (Crockett)

July
Bluegrass Festival (Overton)

August
International Festival Institute at Round Top (classical) lasts
    through May

September
Austin City Limits Music Festival
Buddy Holly Music Symposium and Tribute Concert (Lubbock)
Cactus Jazz and Blues Festival (San Angelo)
Nagcogdoches Red River Radio Americana Music Festival
North Texas New Music Festival (Dallas)

October
Fall Bluegrass Festival (Glen Rose)

Red Steagall Cowboy Gathering and Western Swing Festival
(Fort Worth)
Texas Jazz Festival (Corpus Christi)

Sports (including rodeos and stock shows)

January
Cotton Bowl Classic (Dallas)
Sandhills Stock Show and Rodeo
Southwestern Exposition and Livestock Show/Rodeo (Fort Worth)
Southwestern International Livestock Show and Rodeo (El Paso)

February
San Angelo Stock Show and Rodeo
San Antonio Stock Show and Rodeo
Somervell County PRCA Rodeo (Glen Rose)

March
Houston Livestock Show and Rodeo
Star of Texas Fair and Rodeo (Austin)

April
Big Bend Open Road Race (Fort Stockton to Sanderson)
George Paul Memorial Bull Riding (Del Rio)
Henderson County PRCA Stampede Rodeo (Athens)
Mesquite Championship Rodeo
Sunburn Grand Prix (Abilene)

May
EDS Byron Nelson Championship (Irving)
Western Heritage Classic (Abilene)

June
Cowboy Roundup (Amarillo)

July
Fourth of July Rodeo (Wimberley)
Gainesville Area Chamber of Commerce Rodeo
Kueckelhan Ranch Rodeo and Western Week (Bonham)
West of The Pecos Rodeo (Pecos)

August
Grand Prix of Dallas
Texas Ranch Roundup (Wichita Falls)

September
Valero Texas Open (San Antonio)
Wild West Century Bike Ride (Waco)

October
San Angelo Roping Fiesta
Women's National Finals Rodeo (Fort Worth)
WRCA World Championship Ranch Rodeo (Amarillo)

November
National Cutting Horse Futurity (Fort Worth)
Texas Senior Open (South Padre Island)

Houston Skyscrapers. © Martin McHughes

Contact Information

www.dot.state.tx.us   Web site of the Texas Department of Transportation with road conditions, wildflower sightings, and other information.

www.texasoutside.com   Camping, fishing, hiking, and other current information about out-of-doors Texas.

www.tpwd.state.tx.us   Texas Department of Parks and Wildlife site with complete coverage of parks, hunting, fishing, and other outdoor events.

www.traveltex.com   Official Texas tourism site, part of the Office of the Governor, Economic Development and Tourism.

www.tripadvisor.com/Tourism-g28964-Texas-Vacations.html. This site has links to reviews of most Texas destinations.

Just about every town and city in Texas has a chamber of commerce web site. Try doing a search for the place you are interested in visiting.

East Texas Azalea

FURTHER READING

Ajilvsgi, Geyata. *Wildflowers of Texas*. Fredericksburg: Shearer, 2003.

Andrews, Jean. *Texas Shells: A Field Guide*. Austin: University of Texas Press, 1981.

Aston, B. W., et al. *Along the Texas Forts Trail*. Denton: University of North Texas Press, 1997.

Awbrey, Betty Dooley. *Why Stop? A Guide to Texas Historical Roadside Markers*. Houston: Gulf, 1992.

Baker, T. Lindsay. *Building the Lone Star: An Illustrated Guide to Historic Sites*. College Station: Texas A&M University Press, 1986.

Buckner, Sharry. *Exploring Texas with Children*. Plano: Republic of Texas Press, 1999.

Campbell, Randolph B. *Gone to Texas: A History of the Lone Star State*. Oxford: Oxford University Press, 2004.

Capito, Diane. *San Antonio on Foot*. Lubbock: Texas Tech University Press, 1993.

Crow, Melinda. *Rockhounding Texas*. Guilford, CT: Falcon, 1998.

Cummings, Joe. *Moon Handbooks: Texas*. Emeryville, CA: Moon, 1998.

DeMers, John, and Rhonda K. Findley. *Food Lovers' Guide to Texas*. Guilford, CT: Falcon, 2003.

Drago, Gail, et al. *Texas Bed and Breakfast*. Houston: Gulf, 1999.

Evans, Jeff. *Insight Guide Texas*. London: Insight Guides, 2002.

Fanselow, Julie, et al. eds. *Lonely Planet Texas*. Oakland, CA: Lonely Planet Publications, 2002

Gehlbach, Frederick R. *Messages from the Wild: An Almanac of Suburban and Unnatural History*. Austin: University of Texas Press, 2002.

Gelo, Daniel J., and Wayne J. Pate. *Texas Indian Trails*. Plano: Republic of Texas Press, 2003.

Gordon, Alice. *Smithsonian Guides to Historic America: Texas and Arkansas River Valley*. New York: Stewart, Tabori and Chang, 1998.

Jameson, W.C. *The Guadalupe Mountains: Island in the Desert*. El Paso: Texas Western Press, 1994.

Kutac, Edward A. *Birders' Guide to Texas*. Houston: Gulf, 1998.

Little, Mildred J. *Camper's Guide to Texas Parks, Lakes, and Forests*. Houston: Gulf, 1990.

Loughmiler, Campbell, and Lynn Loughmiler. *Texas Wildflowers: A Field Guide*. Austin: University of Texas Press, 1984.

McAlister, Wayne H., and Martha K. McAlister. *Aransas: A Naturalist's Guide*. Austin: University of Texas Press, 1995.

Metz, Leon. *Roadside History of Texas*. Missoula, MT: Mountain Press, 1994.

Naylor, June. *Texas Off the Beaten Path*. Guilford, CT.: Globe Pequot, 2003.

Parent, Laurence. *Hiking Texas*. Guilford, CT: Falcon, 1996.

Peacock, Howard H. *Nature Lover's Guide to the Big Thicket*. College Station: Texas A&M University Press, 1994.

Peterson, Roger Tory. *Field Guide to the Birds of Texas and Adjacent States*. New York: Houghton Mifflin, 1998.

Spearing, Darwin. *Roadside Geology of Texas*. Missoula, MT: Mountain Press, 2003.

Vines, Robert A. *Trees of East Texas*. Austin: University of Texas Press, 1977.

Watson, Geraldine Ellis. *Reflections on the Neches*. Denton: University of North Texas, 2003.

Wauer, Roland H., and Mark A. Elwonger. *Birding Texas*. Guilford, CT: Falcon, 1998.

Wauer, Roland H. *Naturalist's Big Bend*. College Station: Texas A&M University Press, 2002.

Wauer, Roland H. *Naturally…South Texas: Nature Notes from the Coastal Bend*. Austin: University of Texas Press, 2001.

White, Mel. *Smithsonian Guides to Natural America; South Central States*. New York: Random House, 1996.

Wooley, Bryan, et al. *Final Destinations: A Travel Guide for Remarkable Cemeteries in Texas, New Mexico, Oklahoma, Arkansas, and Louisiana*. Denton: University of North Texas, 2000.

Zak, Bill. *Field Guide to Texas Critters*. Dallas: Taylor Publishing, 1988.

INDEX OF PLACE NAMES

Must-see sites are highlighted in bold throughout the index.